IMAGES
of America

WALPOLE

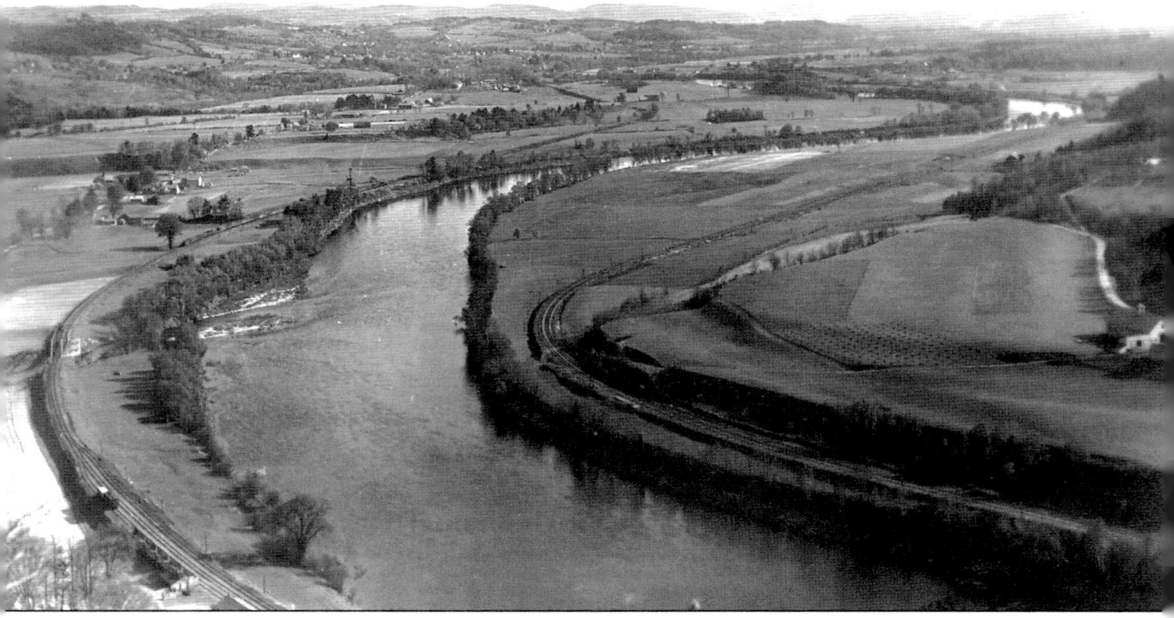

WALPOLE VALLEY VIEW. Walpole lies on New Hampshire's western boundary and the eastern banks of the Connecticut River near the Great Falls. The river slows beneath the falls, with broad sweeps to the west, then east, forming a broad valley floor, as shown in this 1927 photograph. New Hampshire and Vermont hills descend to the valley, a remnant of glacial Lake Hitchcock, formed after the last ice age. The river and its soils provided the economic basis for native and European settlements. (Courtesy of the Walpole Historical Society.)

On the cover: **THE ACADEMY BUILDING.** "Like a temple on a knoll," the old Walpole Academy building overlooks Main Street. It was designed and built in 1831 by Aaron Howland, who was greatly influenced by the Greek Revival style. The academy operated as a private school serving students from the surrounding area. In 1853, the town purchased the building for public education and maintained the high school there until 1950. Today it is the home of the Walpole Historical Society. (Courtesy of the Walpole Historical Society.)

IMAGES
of America

WALPOLE

Walpole Historical Society
Foreword by Ken Burns

ARCADIA
PUBLISHING

ISBN 978-0-7385-6549-1

Published by Arcadia Publishing
Charleston SC, Chicago IL, Portsmouth NH, San Francisco CA

Printed in the United States of America

Library of Congress Control Number: 2008941922

For all general information contact Arcadia Publishing at:
Telephone 843-853-2070
Fax 843-853-0044
E-mail sales@arcadiapublishing.com
For customer service and orders:
Toll-Free 1-888-313-2665

Visit us on the Internet at www.arcadiapublishing.com

This book is dedicated to the citizens of Walpole—
to those of the past, for the rich stories and images they have left for us;
to present residents, who create such a vibrant community;
and to future citizens, may they aspire to the same spirit and vitality.

Contents

FOREWORD

We are so blessed in this otherwise distracted culture of ours—and with the glorious English language we use each day—to have a word that transcends the mere description of where we live. *House* does not quite do it, but *home* does—at once simple and yet loaded with meaning, and for most of us that meaning connects at the highest levels of our being. Home is a place, to be sure, but also family, safety, history, love, and fellowship.

I am personally blessed to call Walpole my home, with all its attendant meanings. I can remember as if it were yesterday the day in 1974 I first laid sight on the town. I came in from the south that day along County Road from Keene, and it seemed impossibly far north, indeed the farthest north I had ever penetrated into New Hampshire. Walpole was that day like Brigadoon, a perfect place revealed only sparingly to the outside world, its beautiful houses, small business district, immaculate green, and slower pace a counterpoint to the busy world that consumed most of my attention. I had no idea that within five years I would make Walpole my permanent home, but those first glimpses stayed with me over the next few years, a vision of what a true home could be. I yearned to live there even when the siren call of the big city pulled me into its metropolitan shadows. But soon I could not resist Walpole's original invitation, and I moved "home" in August 1979. And in those intervening 30 years nothing has changed that powerful sense I get as I climb up from Route 12 into the village. Every time I come back I experience the place anew, as I did in 1974, and I know without a doubt that I am, and forever will be, home.

Ken Burns
Walpole, New Hampshire
October 31, 2008

ACKNOWLEDGMENTS

The Publications Committee book team of the Walpole Historical Society wishes to thank its board of directors and dedicated society librarian Virginia Putnam for their support in making this work possible. We also extend thanks to the Town of Walpole selectmen's office; Alan Rumrill and staff of the Historical Society of Cheshire County in Keene for their assistance and research in additional materials; David L. Deen and other members of the staff of the Connecticut River Watershed Council; Charles de Grandpre, counsel to the Walpole Foundation; Emily Zervas of the Rockingham Public Library, Bellows Falls, Vermont; Susan E. Dunham, clerk of Marlboro Probate Court, Brattleboro, Vermont; Annette Cappy, town clerk of Brattleboro, Vermont; Linda Pappas of the Fall Mountain Supervisory Union No. 60 Superintendent's Office; Jane Kelly of Hubbard Farms, LLC for research assistance; Pam T. Baucom of Florentine Films; and to the many members of the Walpole community who generously gave of their time and resources to assist this project.

To our editor at Arcadia Publishing, Erin Rocha, special thanks for her expertise, guidance, and patience in this production process; to her coworker Rebekah Collinsworth, a Fall Mountain High School graduate who initially inspired this project; and our deep appreciation to Leo Drouin, without whose technical assistance this book would not have been possible.

The source document for much of the material in this book is gleaned from the last history of Walpole, *History of Walpole, New Hampshire*, published jointly in 1963 by a citizen committee of the town of Walpole and the Walpole Historical Society. Appreciation to the team members of that publication, including Anita Houghton Aldrich, Howard Sartwell Andros, Martha McDanolds Frizzel, Donald Eldred Hubbard, Donald Hawkes Spitzli, and Mary Anna North Tatem for their dedication and contributions to Walpole.

Images in this book are those of the Walpole Historical Society, unless otherwise noted. Spelling in the book reflects its time period, for example, "Thomas Flint" appears as "Thomas Flynt."

Donna M. Drouin, Kerry D. Grenier, Barbara W. Hunter,
William S. Perron, and Tara Sad
Publications Committee book team
Walpole Historical Society

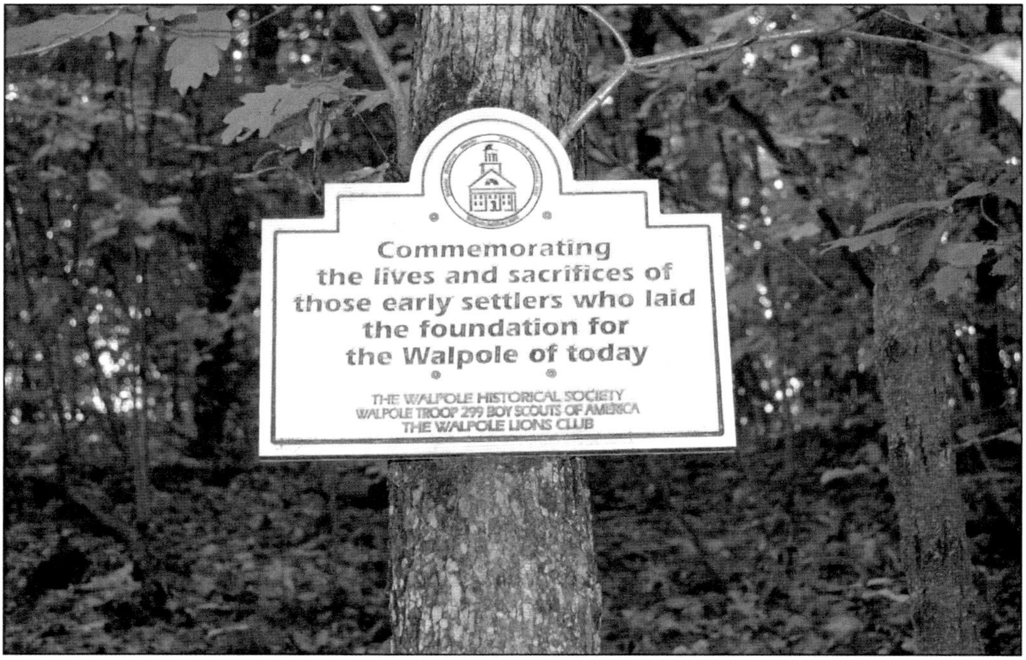

COMMEMORATING SETTLERS. The above memorial stands at the site of the Native American massacre of early Walpole, which occurred in 1755. To begin this history, it seems appropriate to repeat its message. Early settlers of Walpole endured hardship and adversity nearly unimaginable in 21st century America and met those challenges with strength, ingenuity, and good humor.

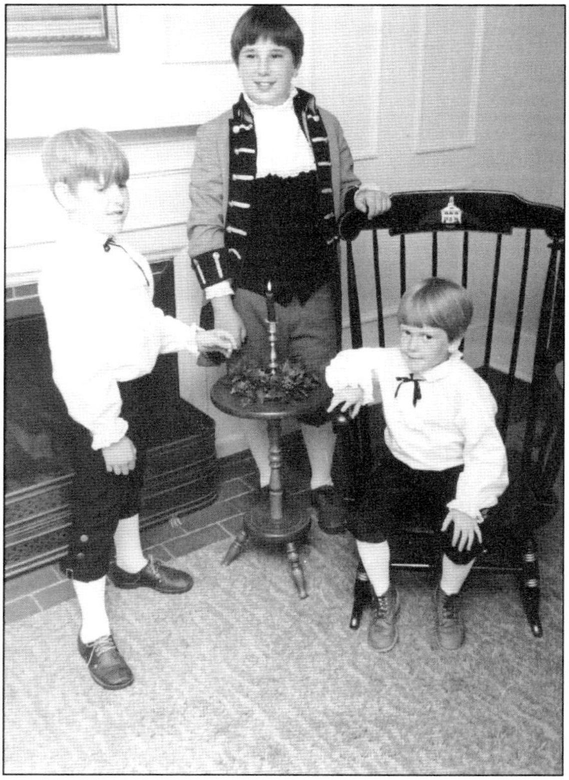

NATION'S BICENTENNIAL. Three brothers await their opportunity to help Walpole celebrate the nation's bicentennial in 1976. The team assembled from left to right are Scott, James, and Jay Daniels in period costume.

INTRODUCTION

On the eastern shore of the Connecticut River near the Great Falls lies the township of Walpole. Here the river plunges abruptly—one of the greatest drops on the entire 400-mile-long river's course. In the past, vast numbers of salmon and shad negotiated the Great Falls. Fish, water, and soils provided rich sustenance for seasonal migrations of the western Abenaki people up and down the river. Thus, the falls were named. Ancient, native sites, dating to the end of the last ice age, dot the area. Below the falls, the river sweeps to the west and then back toward the east, smoothing a broader floodplain and depositing rich alluvial soils. The forested hills of New Hampshire and Vermont descend to the valley. Streams falling from the hills to the river provided power for the early mills. There is evidence that the Abenaki grew corn in the area on their summer visits; permanent Abenaki settlements also existed in nearby Springfield, Vermont. The Connecticut River served as the earliest route for settlement and commerce for Native Americans and for the European settlers who arrived later.

It is a small wonder the early history of Walpole involved competition and conflict—between Abenaki and Europeans and between settler and colonial claims. Competition became fierce and deadly. Colonial Massachusetts, New Hampshire, New York, and, later, the Republic of Vermont argued territorial and individual claims. Ultimately, the river itself provided the western boundary for the state of New Hampshire and for Walpole.

This rich site of approximately 37 square miles provided the land and resources for a wealth of opportunities. Agriculture, forestry, industry, transportation, and other services have all thrived in this setting through the centuries. The first bridge across the Connecticut River was built here. Today there are more public access bridges in Walpole than in any other community on this American Heritage River—three for automobiles and two for the railroad.

From the days of the earliest turnpikes, Walpole was an important stop on the route from Boston to Burlington, Vermont, and Montreal. In the early 1800s, stage lines, taverns, and inns proliferated in the town, with Walpole soon known as a stop worth savoring. With the coming of the railroad in 1848, hotels and boardinghouses dotted Washington Square and Main Street in Walpole Village, including the Elmwood, the Walpole Inn, the Wentworth House, and later the Red Mill Inn.

The township contains three distinct villages—Drewsville, North Walpole, and Walpole Village—each with its own history and course of development.

Walpole Village was the first settlement around 1752, when Benjamin Bellows obtained a charter to the town from New Hampshire's Colonial governor, Benning Wentworth. Wentworth named Walpole in honor of Sir Robert Walpole, King George I's former prime minister.

However, the first white inhabitant of the town preceded Bellows, when John Kilburn established a homestead between what is today Cold River and the Connecticut River in 1749. "Large and fertile meadows at the mouth of Cold River, slightly covered with tall butternuts and ancient elms, presented an inviting prospect and easy harvest to the hand of cultivation," according to the Reverend Henry W. Bellows, writing in 1856. On August 17, 1755, Kilburn and his family held off a raid of nearly 200 Abenaki for the entire day in one of many conflicts in the Connecticut River valley to determine who would ultimately people this land.

Drewsville, on higher ground to the northeast, was the site of early industrial development, with mills springing up along the fast-moving falls of Cold River and Blanchard Brook. Agricultural and other industrial enterprises followed. By 1810, Thomas Collins Drew erected a brick hotel on the common. By 1835, power from Cold River ran cotton and woolen mills, while stores and artisans flourished. As D. Hamilton Hurd writes, "and the place did more business at that time than was done in Walpole Village."

Still later, North Walpole evolved at the Great Falls. With the coming of the Cheshire Railroad in 1848, waves of Irish, Polish, and Italian immigrants arrived in the area to aid in its construction. Mill development across the Connecticut River in Bellows Falls, Vermont, helped retain these new Americans, and North Walpole became a village in its own right. The cultural imprints of these later settlers endure today.

Walpole has had its share of natural calamities. Blizzards, floods, and hurricanes have impacted life in the mid-Connecticut River valley. Nonetheless, cultural richness has thrived in this location. Walpole has been a town of deep beliefs steeped in tradition. High among them is the value of education, with the town raising money in support of education as early as 1771. Walpole citizens have been artistic, courageous, inventive, and political, as well as hardworking and hard playing. Walpole men and women have engaged in and become victims of nearly every war in colonial and national history, exhibiting their strong and binding senses of patriotism, community, and camaraderie.

As Walpole, with its 3,600 residents, enters its fourth century, it continues to change with the times. Agriculture, its economic foundation, has evolved in technical and specialized ways. Enterprising services, from banking to tourism and cinematography to transportation, have provided a broad-based economic spectrum. Global information systems thrive in the rural environment.

Older than the nation, Walpole is a classic New England village resplendent with period homes, gardens, squares, and commons. Louisa May Alcott and James Michener were frequent visitors, using Walpole as a source of inspiration in their writings. Creative people from away and near, whether they be chocolatiers, film-makers, studio artists, musicians, or writers, have sought the rural beauty and solace of Walpole and have made it their respite or their home.

Walpole Historical Society
2009

One

Origins 1700–1760

What is today Walpole was inhabited by Native Americans at least as early as the last ice age, approximately 10,000 years ago. Most recent were the western Abenaki Indians, who lived in what would become New Hampshire, Vermont, northwestern Massachusetts, and southern Quebec. As European settlers migrated up the Connecticut River from the colonies of Massachusetts and Connecticut, the Native Americans fought to stop those incursions. By the time of Walpole's royal charter in 1752, the fight was already in progress and was exacerbated by wars between France and England in North America. To address this state of hostility, a chain of settler forts was established on the Connecticut River frontier—Walpole often referred to as No. 3. Several events, including killings and kidnappings of white settlers, had occurred in the 1740s at Upper Ashuelot (Keene), Lower Ashuelot (Swanzey), and Great Meadow in what is today Putney, Vermont.

Given that this region was largely uncharted and seen as uninhabited, land grants were being awarded to individuals by governors of New Hampshire, Massachusetts, and New York. The grants along the Connecticut River were especially problematic, as no boundaries had been established. Vermont did not exist. Enter Benjamin Bellows, who surveyed the controversial boundary between New Hampshire and Massachusetts and later the township of Westmoreland for the Colonial governor of New Hampshire. So impressed was Gov. Benning Wentworth with Bellows's work, he rewarded Bellows with his choice of three land grants. Bellows chose the land that became Walpole.

Other settlers had preceded Bellows in the town through earlier grants by the General Court of Massachusetts, as New Hampshire was not a separate entity until 1738. Whether by grant or transfer of such, John Kilburn and others were busy clearing and working the land by 1753, when Bellows and his family arrived to establish their homestead.

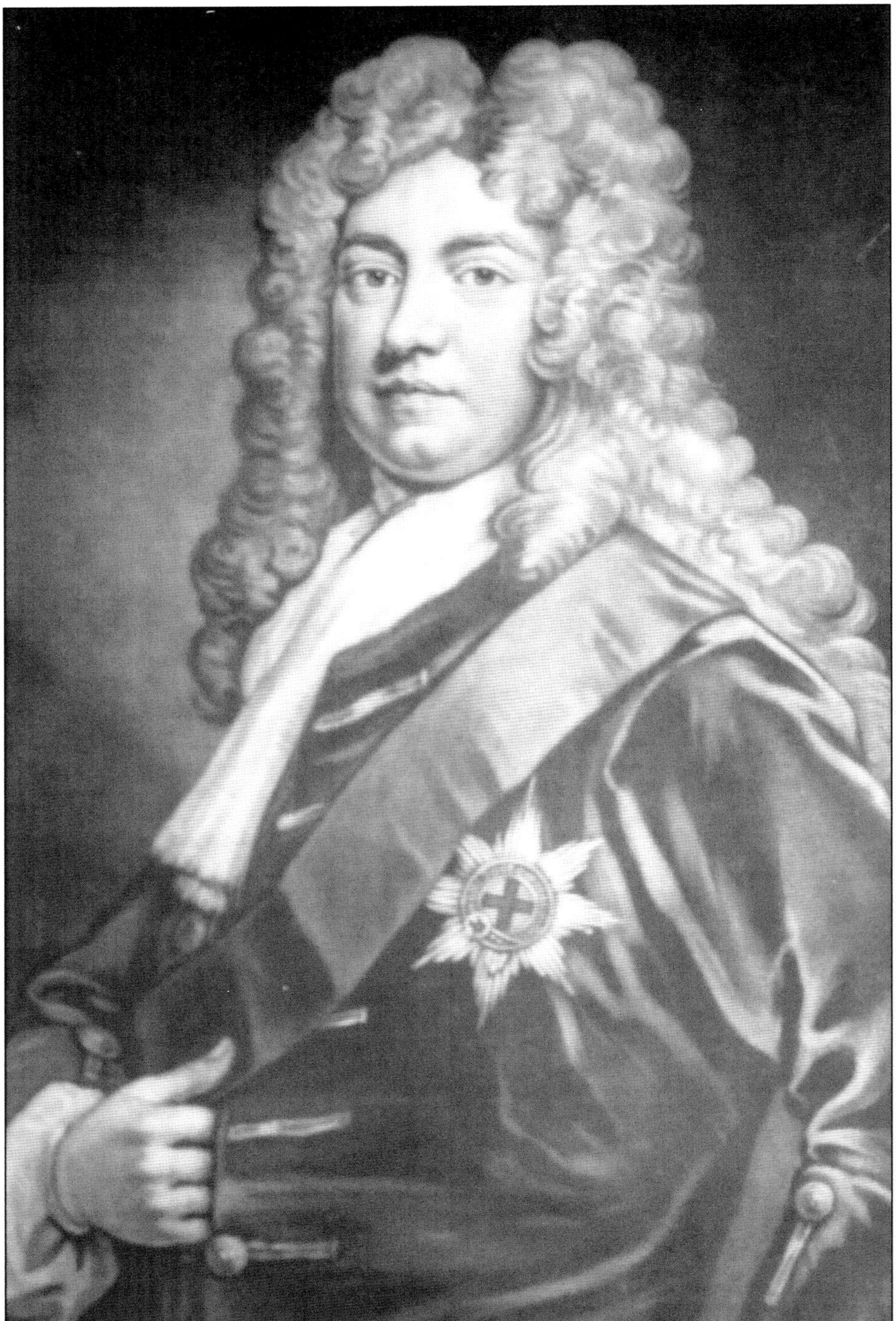

WALPOLE'S NAMESAKE. Sir Robert Walpole was the namesake of the town. He was the prime minister of England from 1721 until 1742 and the first resident of 10 Downing Street, home of England's prime ministers to this day. Prior to his prime ministry, he had served as chancellor of the exchequer (treasury). After his resignation from the House of Commons in 1742 due to ill health, he was named First Earl of Orford, a newly created title, and served in the House of Lords until his death in 1745.

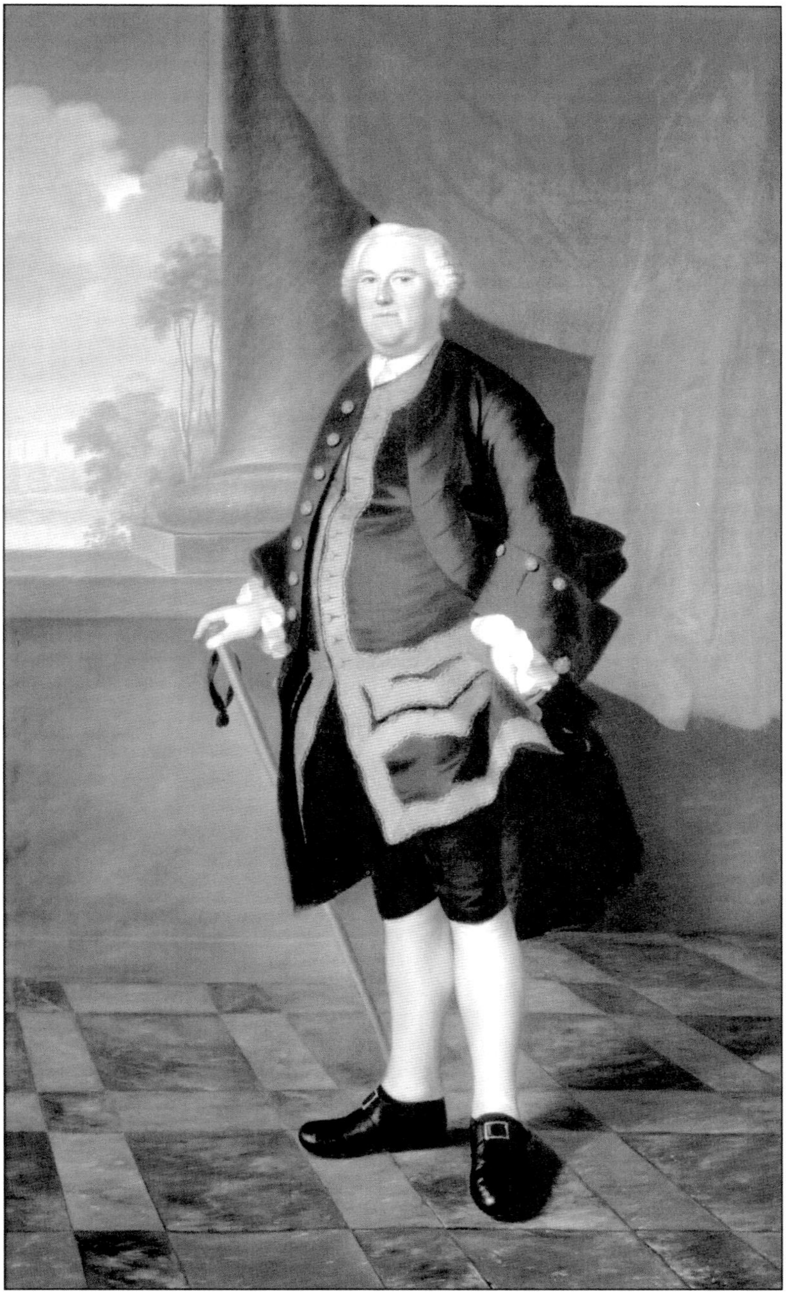

GOV. BENNING WENTWORTH. The royal governor of New Hampshire from 1741 to 1767, Benning Wentworth was the longest-reigning governor in the British Colonial system. He was instrumental in the separation of New Hampshire from Massachusetts in 1738. While in office, Wentworth made over 200 grants of townships, including many in what is now Vermont. Bennington, Vermont, was one of those grants. There was much money to be made from those land transactions and other enterprises. His family became one of the richest in the colonies. Wentworth also granted a township, as a reward for services rendered, to Col. Benjamin Bellows on the Connecticut River in 1752 and named it in honor of Walpole. (Courtesy of New Hampshire Historical Society.)

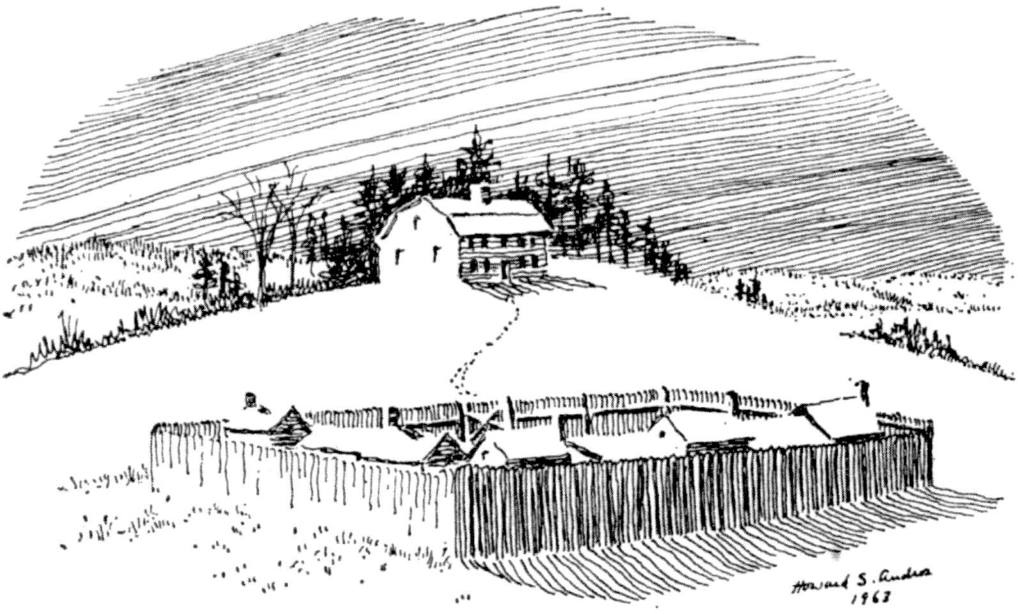

Benjamin Bellows' Fort #471

BENJAMIN BELLOWS'S FORT. Col. Benjamin Bellows "took possession of his Walpole grant, bringing his family here in 1753. About a mile and a half south of Kilburn's cabin [between Cold River and the Connecticut] he erected his dwelling." "It was built sufficiently commodious to be called a fort, and shaped like the letter 'L', being about one hundred feet in the arms and twenty feet broad, strongly built of logs and earth, and surrounded by a palisade." Howard Andros's 1962 drawing (above) may reflect the homestead that Bellows built in 1762 and can be seen as elevated above a fort, looking west toward the Connecticut River. The Bellows homestead today looks much as it did in this drawing, with an additional wing having been added that now serves the public as the Walpole Inn. It has also been known as the Stage Coach Inn, Homestead Inn, and in the 1950s, it served as a nursing home. (Courtesy of Marion W. Andros.)

WALPOLE'S FOUNDING FATHER. There are no known portraits of Bellows, Walpole's founding father. But it is known that he was a true leader of his new community, magnanimous and large in every sense. Taken from woodcuts executed by Thomas Bewick and his school around 1795, Bellows is shown astride his horse, directing work (right). Personal artifacts of the colonel are displayed at the Walpole Historical Society, including this hand-embroidered vest and a homespun stocking of farm-raised flax made by his wife (below). The stocking shows evidence of much mending. The three-by-five-identity card in the lower-right-hand corner provides some perspective of the dimensions of the garments.

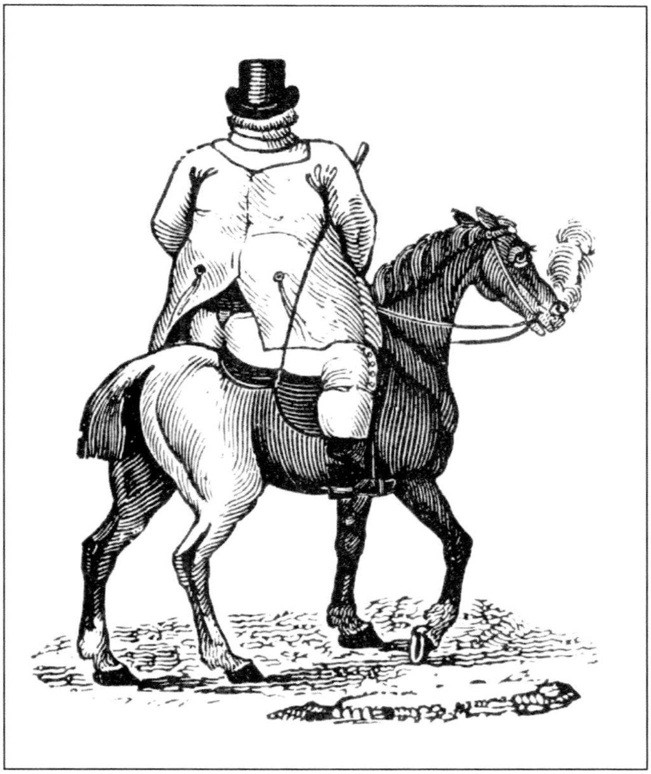

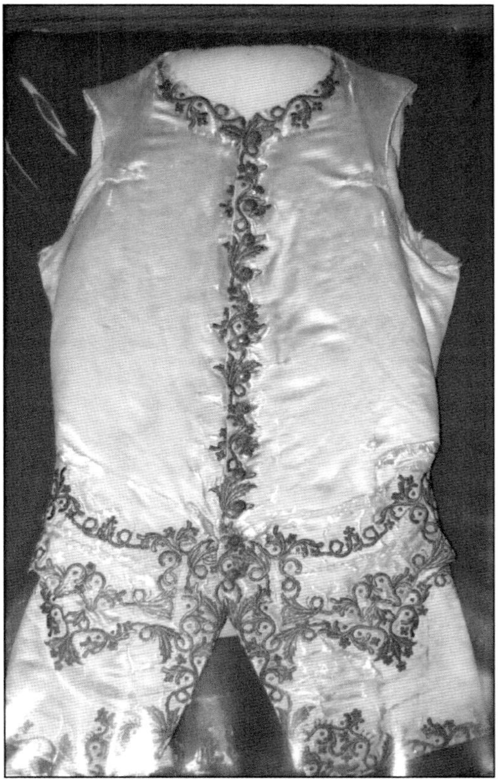

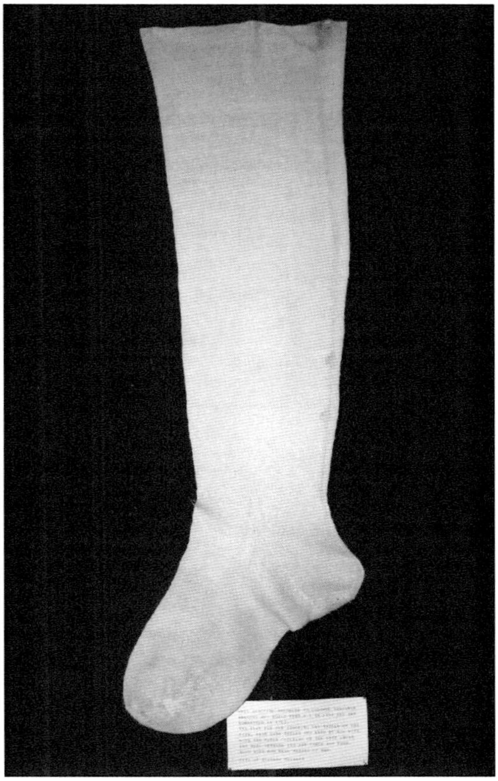

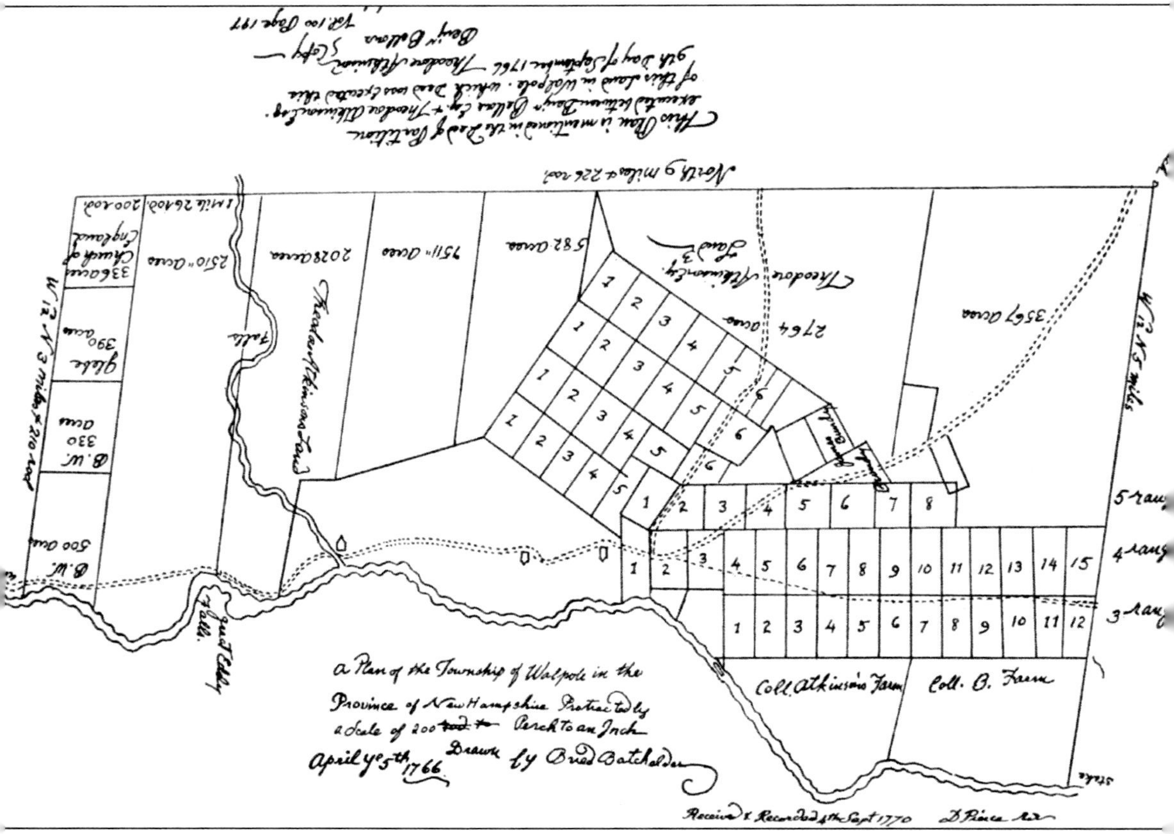

WALPOLE'S EARLIEST MAP. Here is one of the earliest known maps of Walpole occasioned by the subdivision in 1756 by Col. Benjamin Bellows to Theodore Atkinson of "an undivided third of Walpole, including a sawmill, a gristmill, the fort and the house in the fort, all for £500." On September 10, 1766, the two gentlemen filed a memorandum of agreement and partition recorded on September 4, 1770, in the Rockingham County Records, volume 100, page 197, along with this map, showing lots set off at that time.

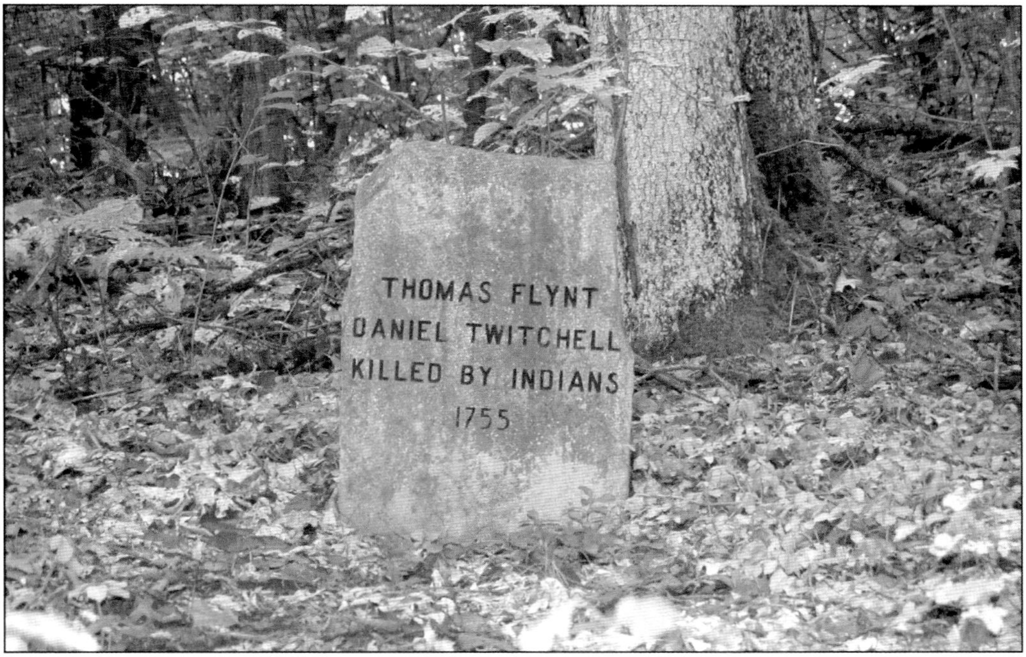

FIRST VIOLENCE. Thomas Flynt and Daniel Twitchell walked to this site north of Walpole Village in 1755 to "procure some ash for oars, and both were shot by the Indians; one was scalped, the other was cut open and his heart taken out, cut in pieces and laid on his breast. Flynt was buried on the spot; Twitchell, having friends, was carried away and buried elsewhere." This was the first violent act over land in Walpole, but others had already occurred in Keene and twice at Great Meadow in Putney, Vermont, as early as July 1745, and also in Swanzey and at Fort No. 4 at Charlestown between 1744 and 1748, during King George's War. Hostilities continued in the Connecticut River valley between 1754 and 1760, during the French and Indian War. The site of Walpole's first settler losses (below) remains today much as it was in those early days of conflict.

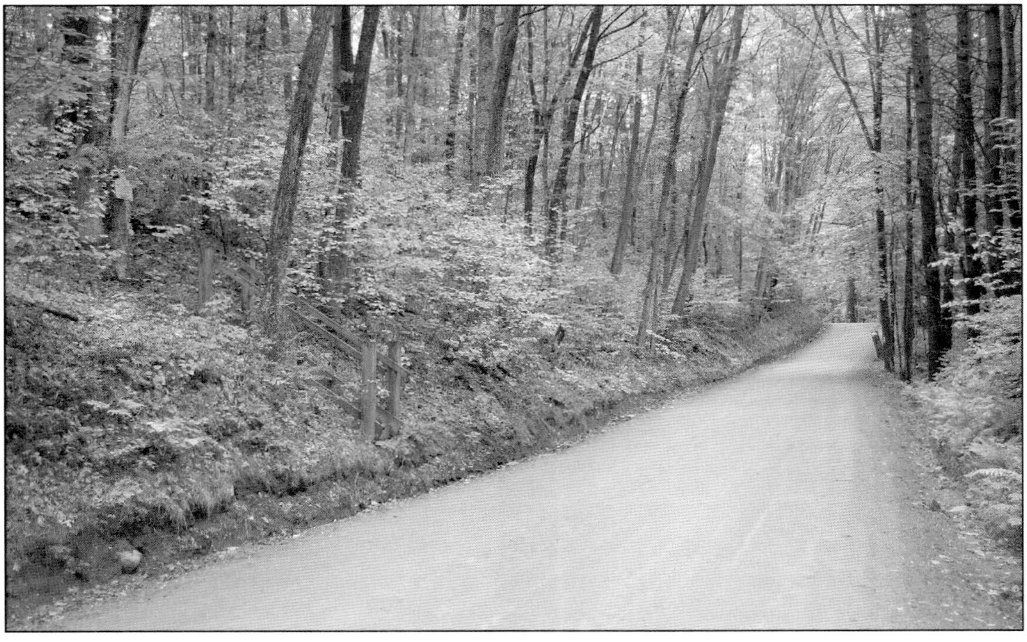

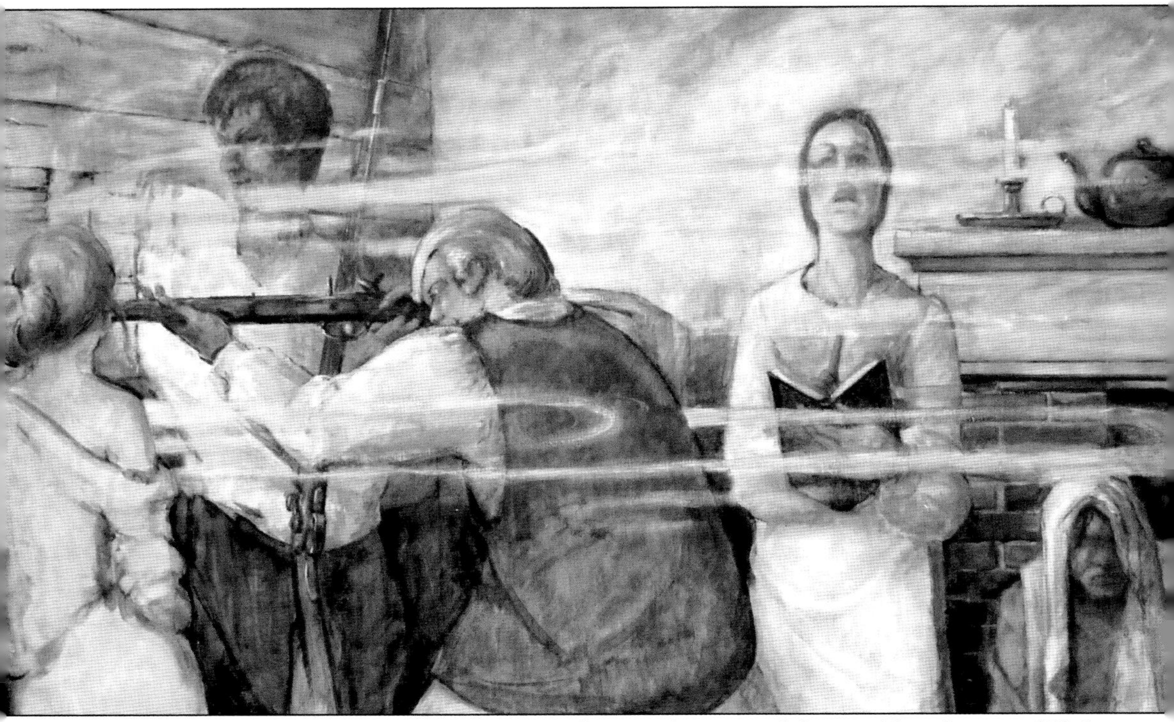

KILBURN UPRISING. In the spring of 1755, intelligence determined that an Abenaki named Philip had been visiting homesteads and asking for food and provisions while assessing the strength of local settlements. Later information from a friendly Native American indicated a large force of warriors had assembled in Canada to wipe out the white population on the Connecticut River. On August 17 of that year, after a brief encounter nearby with Col. Benjamin Bellows and his men, an assault by 197 Abenaki braves (who had been counted by Bellows's men) was launched on the homestead of John Kilburn, his family, a hired man, and son. The attack ensued for six hours while the warriors killed Kilburn's stock and burned his crops. In this painting by William O'Connor, Kilburn and his son can be seen returning fire, while Hannah Fox Kilburn and daughter Hitty supported the men by loading guns and refiring spent lead around them. In the background is Mr. Peak, the hired man, who was wounded and died so early, for want of surgical aid on the sixth day thereafter. (Courtesy of Town of Walpole.)

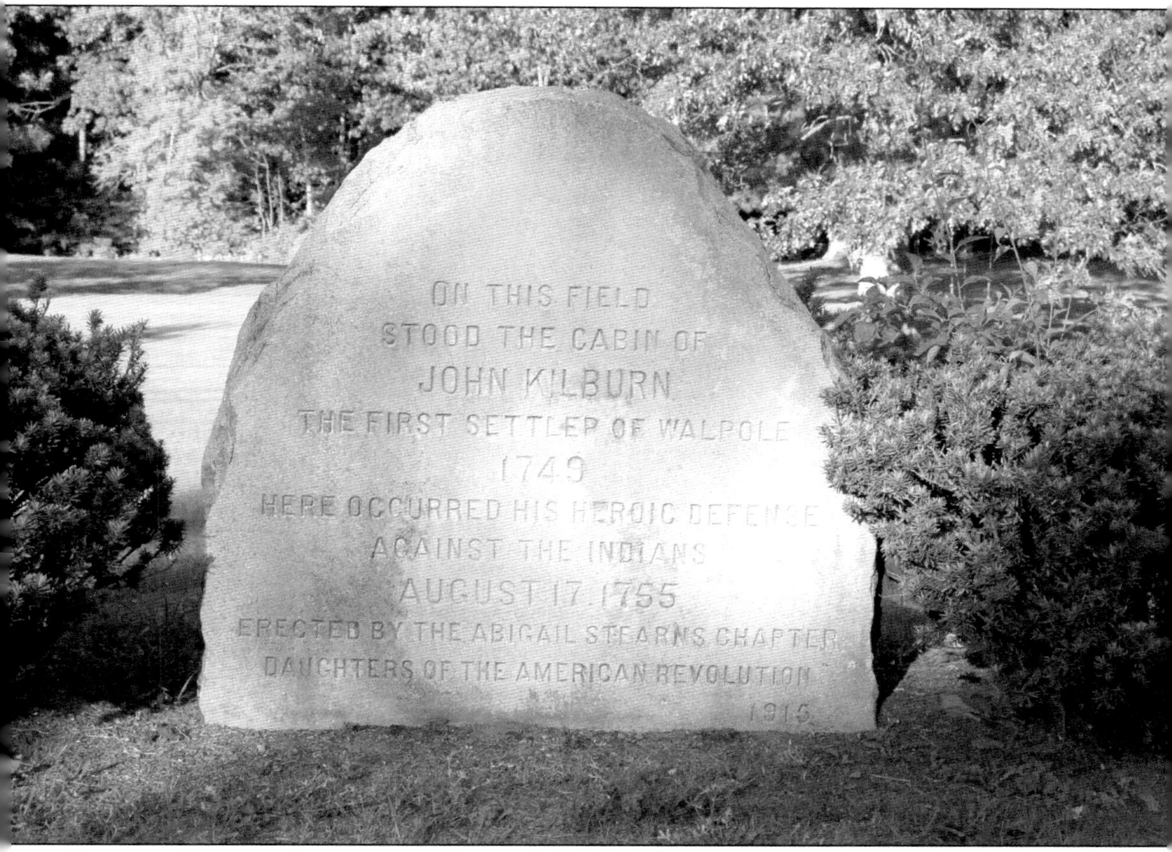

KILBURN UPRISING CONTINUED. Those at Bellows's fort could hear the incessant firing and were much concerned but dared not venture forth. Only at sundown did the warriors retreat, carrying away their wounded and their dead, including Philip, who reportedly was killed with Kilburn's first bullet. In 1848, when work was beginning on the railroad bridge below the Great Falls, an Abenaki warrior's remains were found interred among the rocks with a hole in its skull. The belief is that these were Philip's remains, a renowned Abenaki warrior buried in a place of honor below the falls. Subsequent Abenaki research indicates that the Kilburn Uprising may have been the Abenakis' last major coordinated effort to rid the Connecticut River valley of white settlers. The above monument marks the event and its site near the Connecticut River, just south of Cold River.

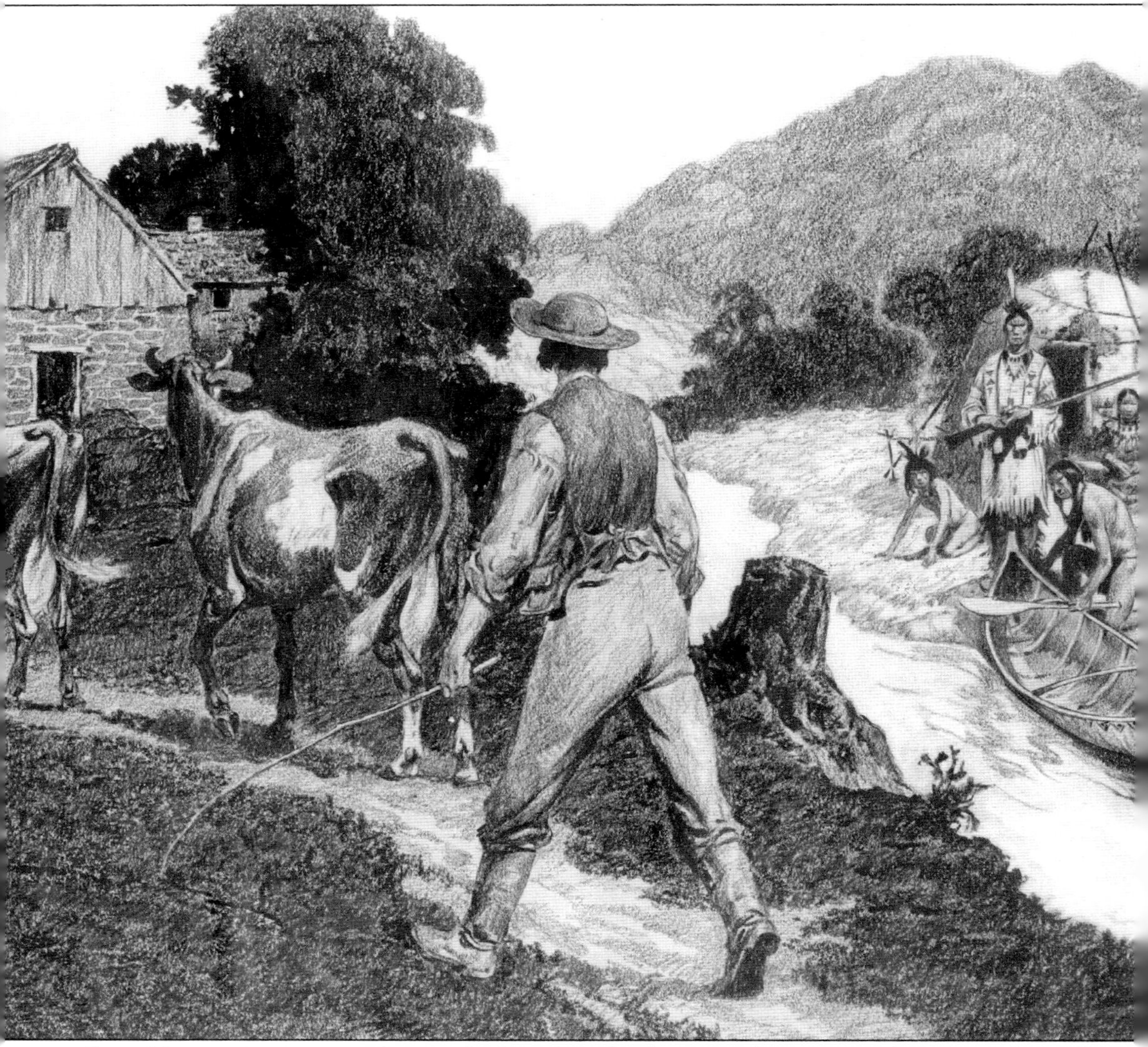

LAST NATIVE AMERICANS. During the French and Indian War, the western Abenaki confronted for the first time an enemy, Rogers Rangers, who was capable of pursuing them to their home base. In the fall of 1759, Rogers was ordered by Maj. Gen. Jeffrey Amherst to destroy the Abenaki Indian stronghold at St. Francis (St. Lawrence River valley in Canada). Raids on Connecticut River valley settlements continued, however. That same year, England defeated the French at Quebec City for control of Canada. In 1760, "some 800 New Hampshire militiamen began cutting a road through the Green Mountains that opened the western Abenaki homeland to direct assault," according to Colin Calloway. Thereafter, the Abenaki, who had been aligned with the French, lived in widely dispersed settlements in northern New Hampshire, in what would become northern Vermont, and in southern Quebec. This 1935 drawing, *Indian Neighbors*, by Roy F. Heinrich, depicts "the last native Indians of record [who] pitched camp in Vermont . . . spent the winter of 1856 on Levi Chapin's meadow in Bellows Falls and then migrated to Canada." (*Indian Neighbors* was commissioned, is trademarked by, and courtesy of National Life Insurance Company.)

Two

A Lively Settlement 1760–1800

Until about 1760, Col. Benjamin Bellows shared the town only with the Kilburns and his own family. In 1762, there were 12 to 15 homes, an unfinished meetinghouse, and three streets laid out—Main, Wentworth, and Prospect. Farms were cleared on the hills surrounding the village, served by a network of roads. In the early days, portions of the valley were forbidding, with wet soil covered by angular boulders and a dense growth of hemlock. By 1771, the population totaled about 500 and was served by three schoolhouses.

After receiving word of the strife in Lexington, Massachusetts, 35 men from Walpole led by Gen. Benjamin Bellows, the colonel's son, rode off to join the battle. Walpoleans also served at Fort Ticonderoga, Saratoga, and Bennington. However, Col. Benjamin Bellows never saw the new nation gain its independence, as he died on July 10, 1777, at the age of 66.

In 1785, the first bridge over the Connecticut River was built below the falls, connecting Walpole with Rockingham in Vermont. It was a hazardous undertaking and brought international fame to its builder. In 1790, the new Prospect Hill meetinghouse was completed, and the town contained the following businesses: a tannery, a bakery, several taverns, stores, a hatter, a tailor shop, a bookstore and printer, a saddle and harness maker, a distillery, a gunsmith, a cabinet maker, an apothecary, and a bell and clock maker.

During this period, many of the disputes over boundaries between New York, New Hampshire, and Vermont were finally settled, as Congress admitted Vermont to the union in 1791.

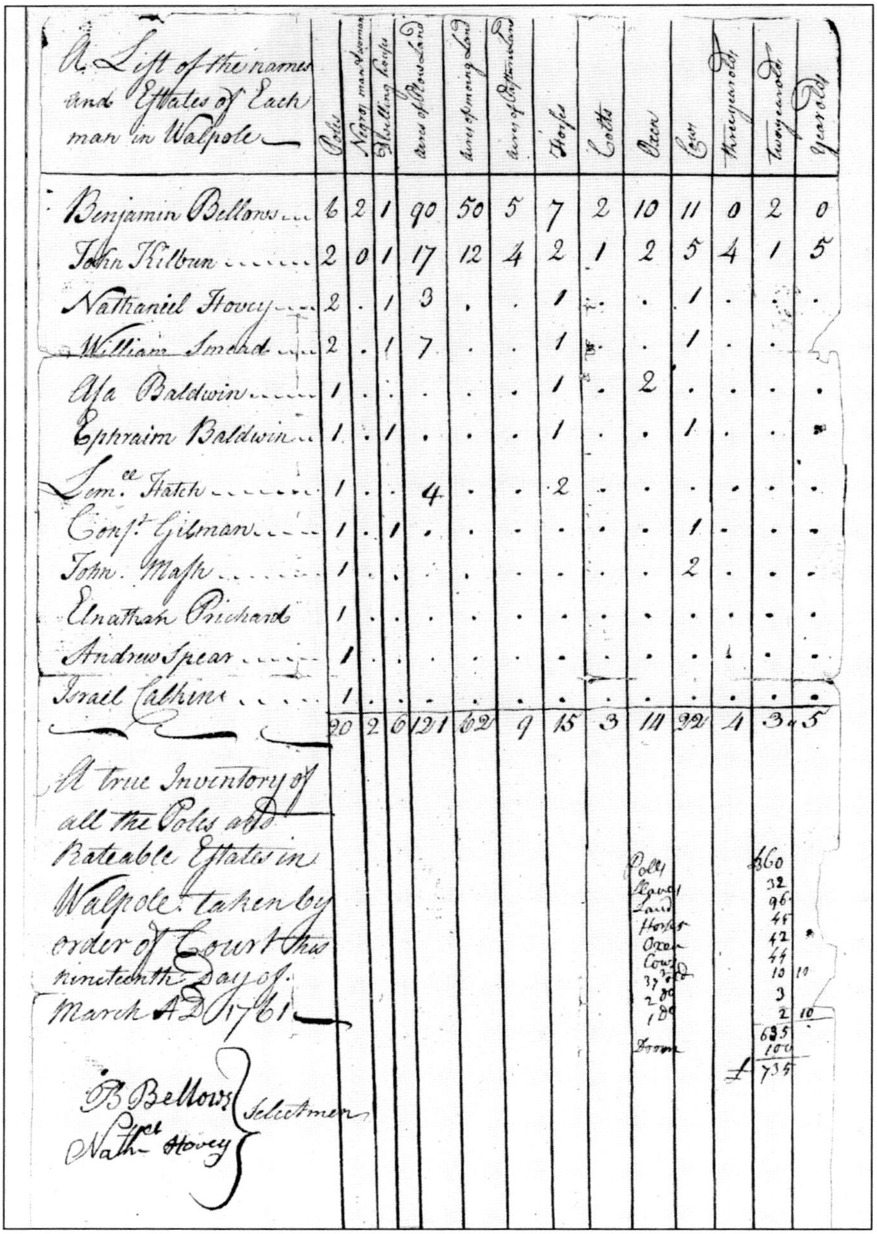

A List of the names and Estates of Each man in Walpole

Name	Poles	Negro man & woman	Dwelling house	acres of Plow Land	acres of mowing Land	acres of Pasture Land	Horses	Colts	Oxen	Cows	three year olds	two year olds	year olds
Benjamin Bellows	6	2	1	90	50	5	7	2	10	11	0	2	0
John Kilburn	2	0	1	17	12	4	2	1	2	5	4	1	5
Nathaniel Hovey	2	.	1	3	.	.	1	.	.	1	.	.	.
William Simonds	2	.	1	7	.	.	1	.	.	1	.	.	.
Asa Baldwin	1	.	.	.	.	.	1	.	2	.	.	.	.
Ephraim Baldwin	1	.	1	.	.	.	1	.	.	1	.	.	.
Lem.ee Hatch	1	.	.	4	.	.	2	.	.	.	.	.	.
Const Gilman	1	.	1	.	.	.	.	.	.	1	.	.	.
John Mash	1	.	.	.	.	.	.	.	.	2	.	.	.
Elnathan Prichard	1	.	.	.	.	.	.	.	.	.	.	.	.
Andrew Spear	1	.	.	.	.	.	.	.	.	.	1	.	.
Israel Calkins	1	.	.	.	.	.	.	.	.	.	.	.	.
	20	2	6	121	62	9	15	3	14	22	4	3	5

A true Inventory of all the Poles and Rateable Estates in Walpole taken by order of Court this nineteenth Day of March AD 1761

B Bellows
Nathl Hovey } Selectmen

INVENTORY, 1761. "A true inventory of all the Poles and Rateable Estates in Walpole, taken by order of Court this nineteenth day of March AD 1761," lists the holdings of 12 men in Walpole. It includes their ownership of poles (a unit of area equal to a square rod or 25.293 square meters), a black man or woman, a dwelling house, acres of plow land, acres of mowing land, acres of pasture land, horses, colts, oxen, cows, three-year olds, two-year olds, and one-year olds. Note that Col. Benjamin Bellows listed six poles and 145 acres of plowed, mowed, and pasture lands. Earlier settler John Kilburn had two poles and 23 acres of land in use. The inventory was signed by the selectmen, including Bellows, who served in that capacity from 1752 to 1773, with the exception of four years. The numbers at the bottom right section of the pages may have been a calculation of taxes owed by Bellows. (Courtesy of New Hampshire Division of Archives and Records Management.)

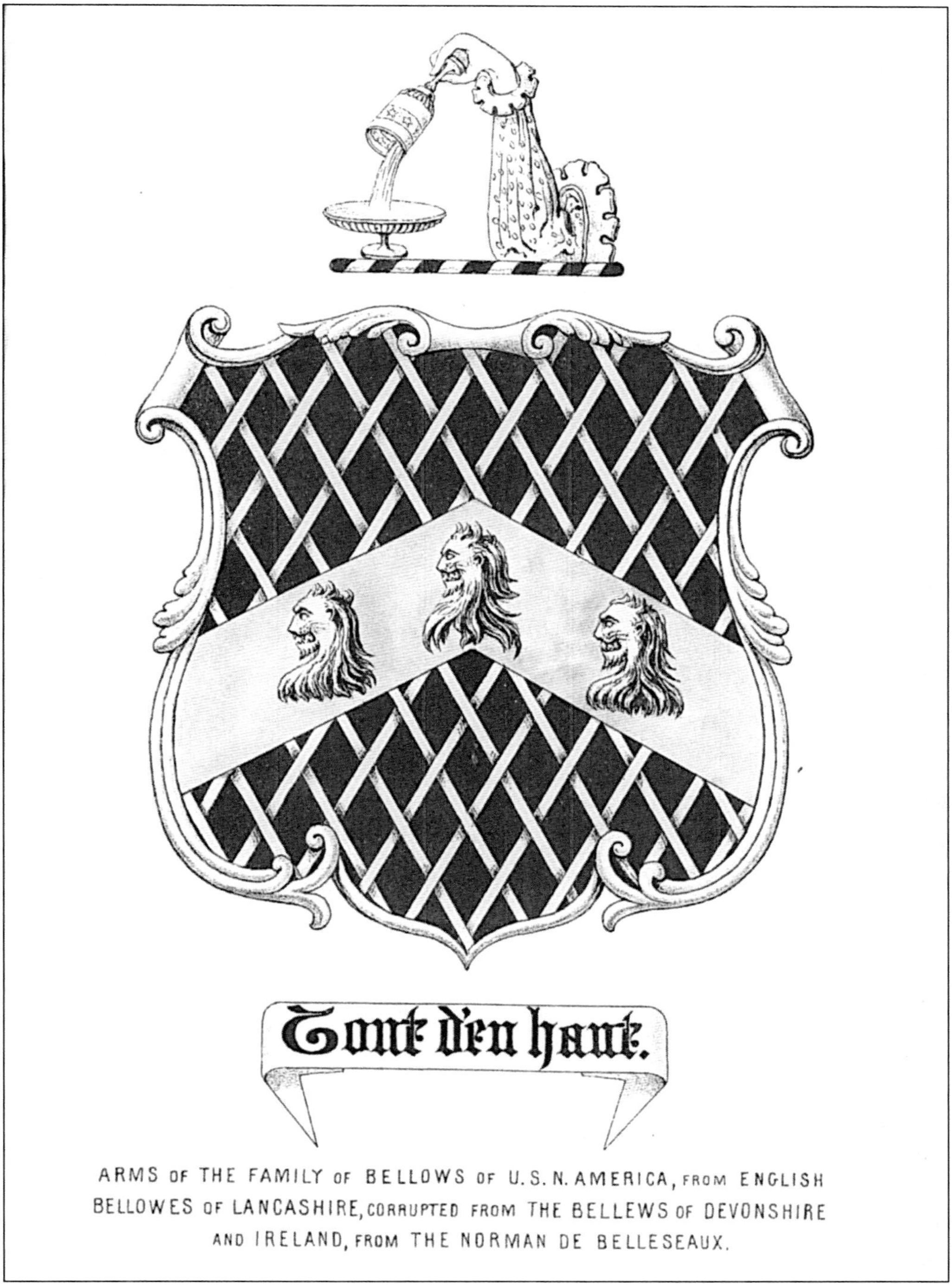

BELLOWS COAT OF ARMS. The Bellows family probably descended from Normans named Belle Eau(x) who came to England with William the Conqueror. The crest on the coat of arms shows an embossed arm with its hand grasping a chalice pouring water (*belle eau*) into a basin. The motto *tout d'en haut* means "all from on high." John Bellows, age 12, arrived in New England from London on April 1, 1635. Col. Benjamin Bellows was his grandson.

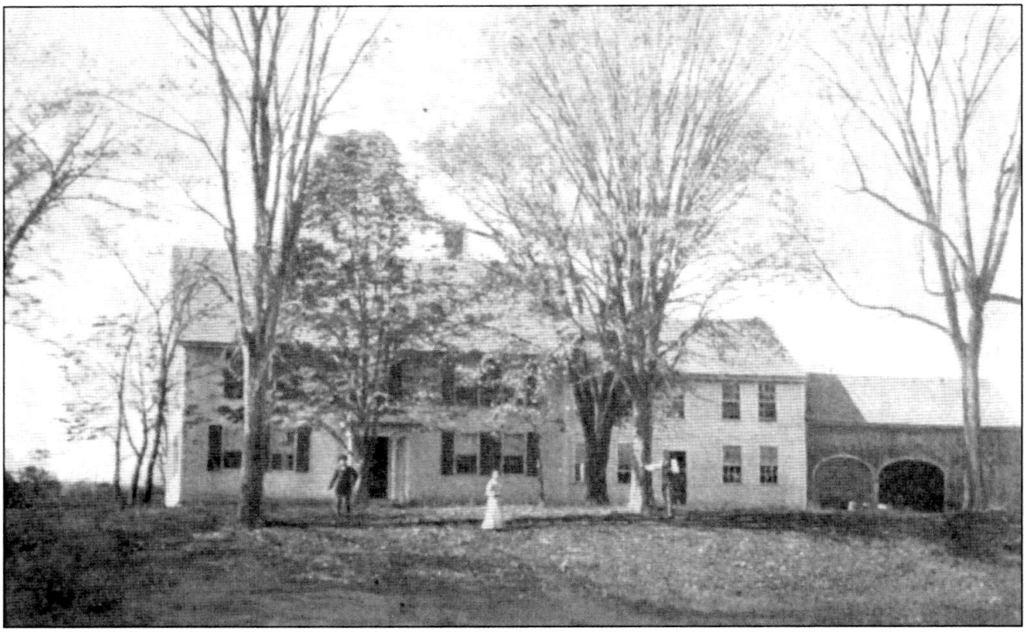

COL. BENJAMIN BELLOWS HOMESTEAD. Col. Benjamin Bellows and his family lived in the fort until his house was completed in 1762. It was the first framed building in town, standing on a rise with a commanding view of the river valley. The site was chosen not only for defense purposes but also because it was surrounded by the most fertile land in the town. The mansion still exists today in its reincarnation as the Walpole Inn.

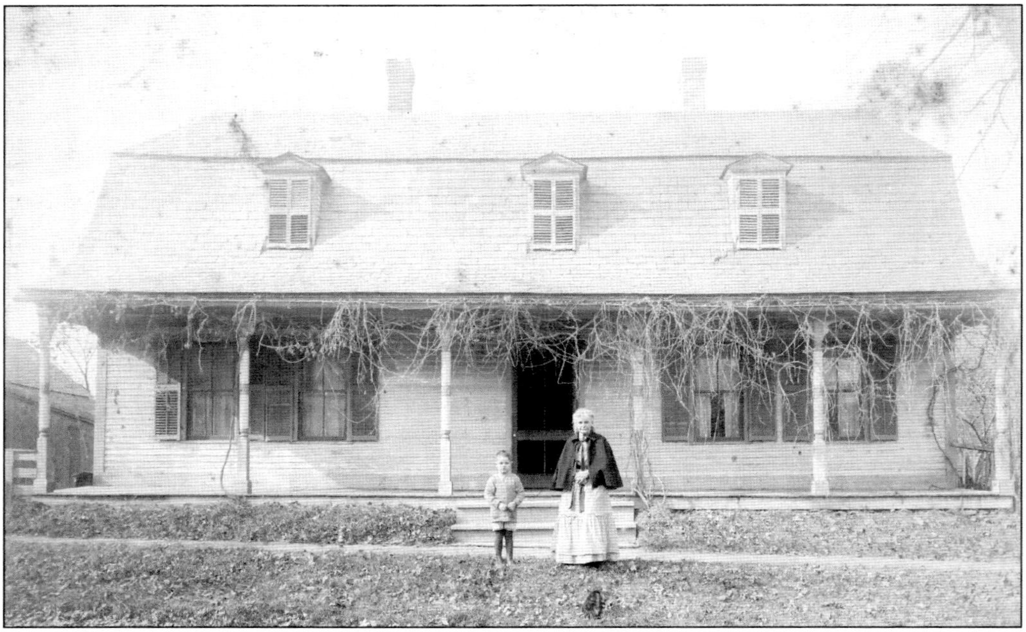

OLDEST HOUSE. The oldest house still existing in Walpole, this North Main Street dwelling was built by Asa Baldwin around 1760 and remains in nearly original condition. Shortly after it was built, it became the parsonage for Rev. Jonathan Leavitt, the first minister in town. Leavitt was dismissed in 1764 after having been seen leading his runaway female slave back to the house with a rope around her neck attached to his saddle pommel.

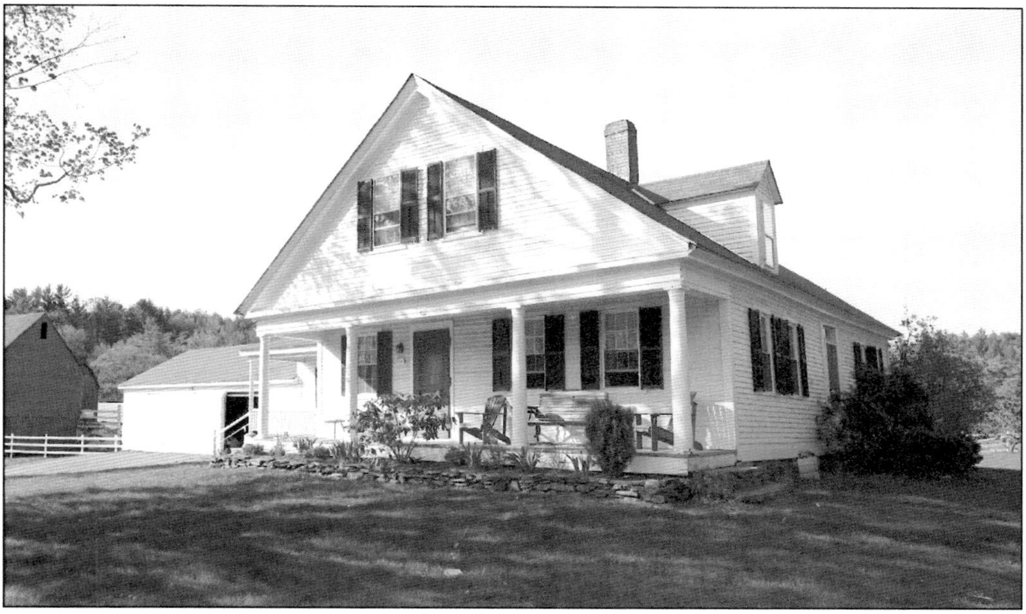

Great Brook Farm. Worked for over 200 years by nine generations of the Graves family, this property was honored in 1976 as a bicentennial farm. Constructed in 1761 by Deac. John Graves on over 400 acres, the house initially faced south on Old State Road. When County Road was built in 1835, the house was turned and moved 100 yards closer to the new road for easier access by horse in heavy snows.

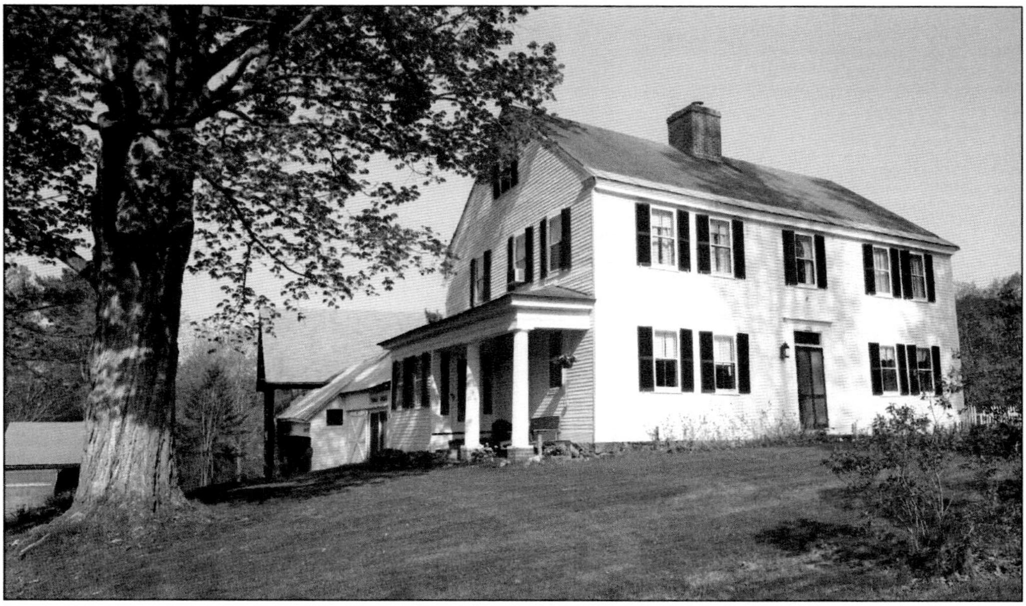

Early Farm House. Built by Jonathan Hall in 1784 then deeded to his son Abraham, this center-chimney Colonial has five working fireplaces, large beams, thick plaster walls and ceilings, and a variety of handsome moldings. There is paneled wainscoting upstairs, and the old kitchen fireplace has a beehive oven on one side. A smoke chamber for preserving meats was built into one chimney. Jonathan, Abraham, and Jonathan Hall Jr. were Revolutionary War soldiers.

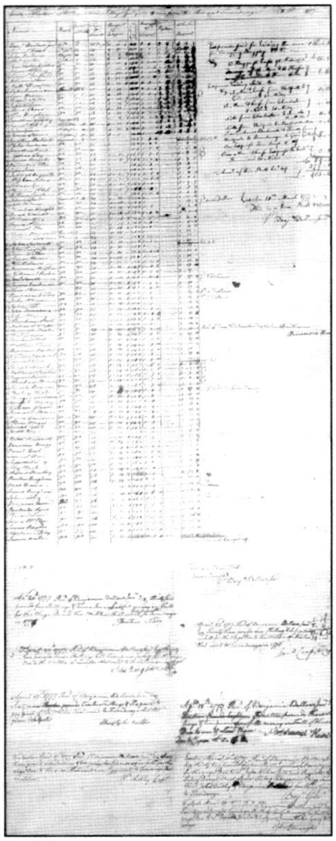

Revolutionary War Muster List. In 1775, upon receiving news of American engagement with British troops at Lexington, Massachusetts, Benjamin Bellows, Col. Benjamin Bellows's second son, led a company of 35 men from Walpole, including his brother John, to join the battle. Benjamin Bellows had received a commission of lieutenant colonel from the British government in 1768 but was a zealous supporter of the American patriots. Not always in the field, he was engaged in raising troops and consulting on military affairs. Twice he marched with his regiment to reinforce troops at Fort Ticonderoga, served under the command of Gen. Horatio Gates at the battle of Saratoga, and was present at the surrender of Gen. John Burgoyne on October 17, 1777. He subsequently became a general and commanded the Third Brigade. There are 36 Revolutionary soldiers interred in the Walpole Cemetery. This muster list is in the archives of the Walpole Historical Society.

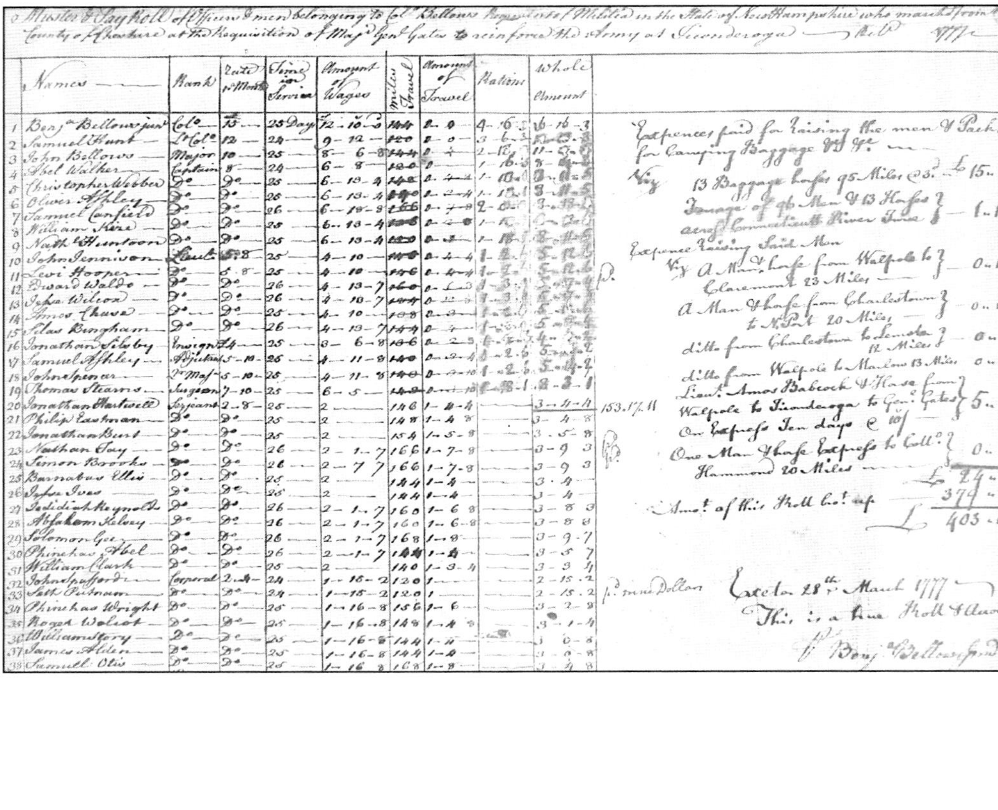

Muster & Pay Roll of Officers & men belonging to Col. Bellows Regiment of Militia in the State of New Hampshire who marched from the County of Cheshire at the Requisition of Majr Genl Gates to reinforce the Army at Ticonderoga — 1777

	Names	Rank	Rate pr Month	Time in Service	Amount of Wages	Miles Travel	Amount of Travel	Rations	Whole Amount
1	Benja Bellows jun	Col°	15	25 Days	12-10-0	144	0-0	4-16-3	16-16-3
2	Samuel Hunt	Lt Col°	12	24	9-12	120	0-0	3-6-3	[illegible]
3	John Bellows	Major	10	25	8-6-8	144	0-4	2-12	11-[illegible]
4	Abel Walker	Captain	8	24	6-8	120	0	1-16-3	[illegible]
5	Christopher Webber	Do	Do	25	6-13-4	142	0-4-4	1-10	[illegible]
6	Oliver Ashley	Do	Do	26	6-13-4	140	0-2-4	1-12-1	[illegible]
7	Samuel Canfield	Do	Do	26	6-18-8	166	0-7-8	2-0	[illegible]
8	William Kere	Do	Do	25	6-13-4	126	0-2-8	[illegible]	[illegible]
9	Nathl Huntoon	Do	Do	25	6-13-4	120	0-2	[illegible]	[illegible]
10	John Jennison	Lieut	5-8	25	4-10	140	0-4-4	[illegible]	[illegible]
11	Levi Hooper	Do	5-8	25	4-10	146	0-4-4	[illegible]	[illegible]
12	Edward Waldo	Do	Do	26	4-13-7	160	[illegible]	[illegible]	[illegible]
13	Josiah Wilcox	Do	Do	26	4-13-7	144	[illegible]	[illegible]	[illegible]
14	Amos Chase	Do	Do	25	4-10	108	0-3	[illegible]	[illegible]
15	Silas Bingham	Do	Do	26	4-13-7	144	0-4	[illegible]	[illegible]
16	Jonathan Sibley	Ensign	4	25	3-6-8	136	0-2-3	[illegible]	[illegible]
17	Samuel Ashley	Adjutant	5-10	26	4-11-8	140	0-2-4	1-2-6	[illegible]
18	John Spencer	Qr Mast	5-10	25	4-11-8	140	0-2-10	1-2-6	[illegible]
19	Thomas Stearns	Surgeon	7-10	25	6-5	142	[illegible]	[illegible]	[illegible]
20	Jonathan Hartwell	Serjeant	2-8	25	2	146	1-4-4	—	3-4-4
21	Philip Eastman	Do	Do	25	2	148	1-4-8	—	3-4-8
22	Jonathan Burt	Do	Do	25	2	154	1-5-8	—	3-5-8
23	Nathan Fay	Do	Do	26	2-1-7	166	1-7-8	—	3-9-3
24	Simon Brooks	Do	Do	26	2-1-7	166	1-7-8	—	3-9-3
25	Barnabas Ellis	Do	Do	25	2	144	1-4	—	3-4
26	Josiah Ives	Do	Do	25	2	144	1-4	—	3-4
27	Jedidiah Reynolds	Do	Do	26	2-1-7	160	1-6-8	—	3-8-3
28	Absalom Kelsey	Do	Do	26	2-1-7	160	1-6-8	—	3-8-3
29	Solomon Gee	Do	Do	26	2-1-7	168	1-8	—	3-9-7
30	Phinehas Abel	Do	Do	26	2-1-7	144	1-4	—	3-5-7
31	William Clark	Do	Do	25	2	140	1-3-4	—	3-3-4
32	John Spafford	Corporal	2-4	24	1-15-2	120	1	—	2-15-2
33	Seth Putnam	Do	Do	24	1-15-2	120	1	—	2-15-2
34	Phinehas Wright	Do	Do	25	1-16-8	156	1-6	—	3-2-8
35	Roger Wolcot	Do	Do	25	1-16-8	148	1-4-8	—	3-1-4
36	William Story	Do	Do	25	1-16-8	144	1-4	—	3-0-8
37	James Alden	Do	Do	25	1-16-8	144	1-4	—	3-0-8
38	Samuel Otis	Do	Do	25	1-16-8	168	1-8	—	3-4-8

Expences paid for raising the men & Pack Horses for Carrying Baggage &c. —
Viz 13 Baggage horses 95 Miles @ 3d — £ 15..8..
Ferrage of 96 Men & 13 Horses across Connecticutt River Twice — 1..16..
Expence raising said Men
Viz A Man & horse from Walpole to Claremont 23 Miles — 0..10..
A Man & horse from Charlestown to No. 4 20 Miles — 0..10..
ditto from Charlestown to Lemster 12 Miles — 0..5..
ditto from Walpole to Marlow 13 Miles — 0..5..
153.17.11 Lieut. Amos Babcock & Horse from Walpole to Ticonderoga to Genl Gates On Express Ten days @ 10/ — 5..
One Man & horse Express to Coll° Hammond 20 Miles — 0..10..
£ 24..5
Amot of this Roll brot up 379..11..
£ 403..16..

pd nine Dollars

Exeter 28th March 1777
This is a true Roll & Accoun[t]
pr Benj Bellows jun

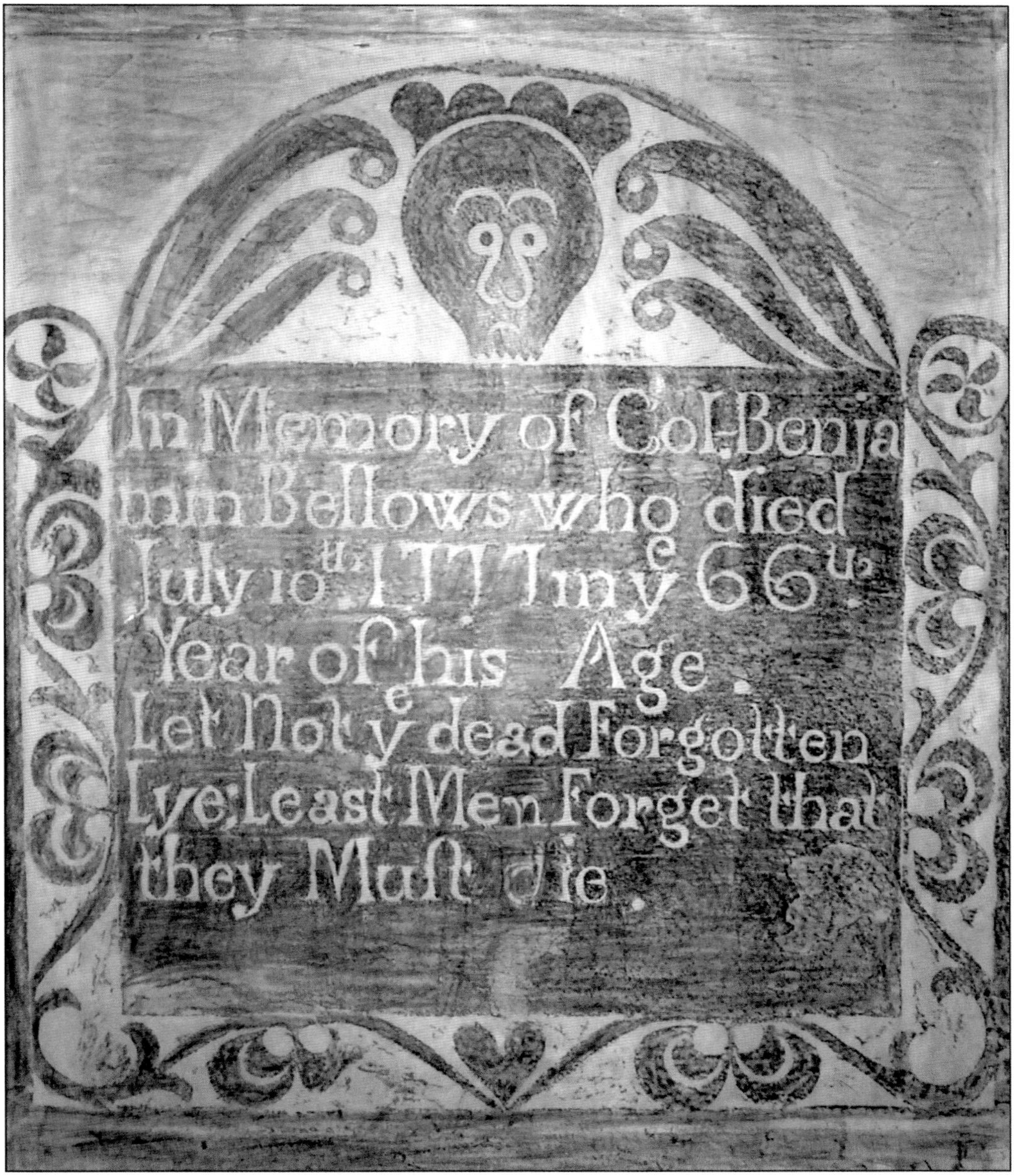

BELLOWS RUBBING. "In memory of Col-Benjamin Bellows who died July 10th, 1777 in ye 66th Year of his Age. Let not ye dead Forgotten Lye; Least Men Forget that they Must die." So reads this rubbing of the gravestone of Bellows in the Walpole Cemetery. He was remembered as a wise, courageous, and honest man with the fortitude to leave familiar surroundings and establish a new home on the frontier. He had the wisdom to found the new town based on law and order and to provide for the church and education. Bellows was tall and in his last years quite stout, weighing 330 pounds. Yet he continued to be active, mounted on his strong sorrel horse, directing the work of his men. In his will, Bellows left to his wife and nine children nearly 4,000 acres of land in Walpole plus property in Westminster, Keene, and other towns.

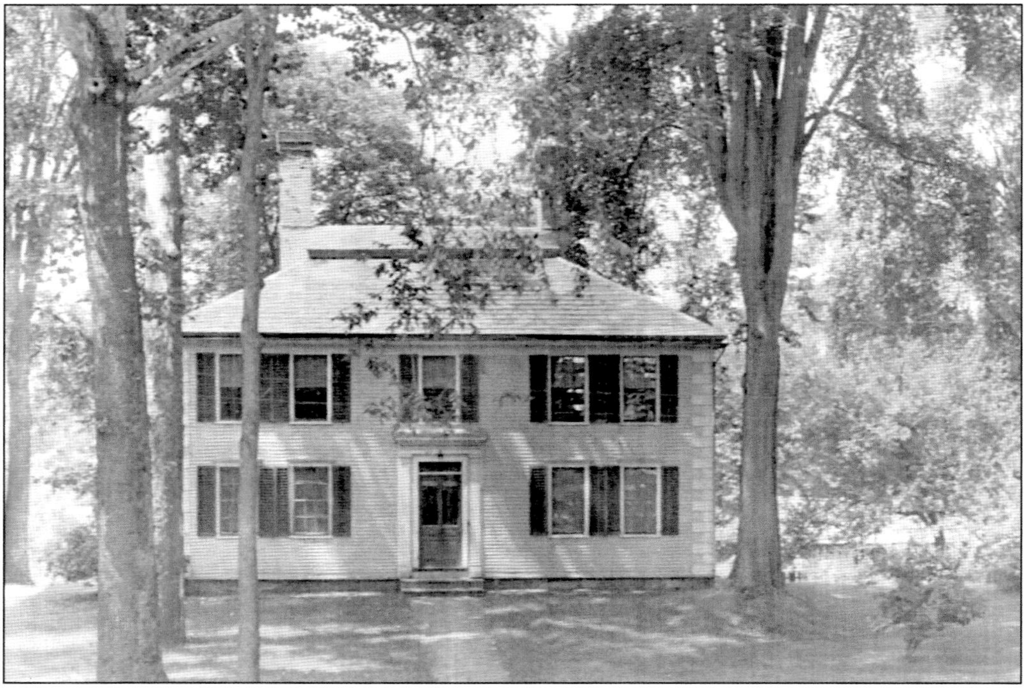

ALLEN HOUSE. Gen. Amasa Allen, who settled in Walpole soon after 1776, built this beautifully proportioned, hip-roofed house on Main Street in 1781. Impoverished when he arrived, Allen started a successful mercantile business in town and died a wealthy man, although childless. He generally arose at 4:30 a.m., according to his neighbors, awakening them by shouting directions to others through the open windows.

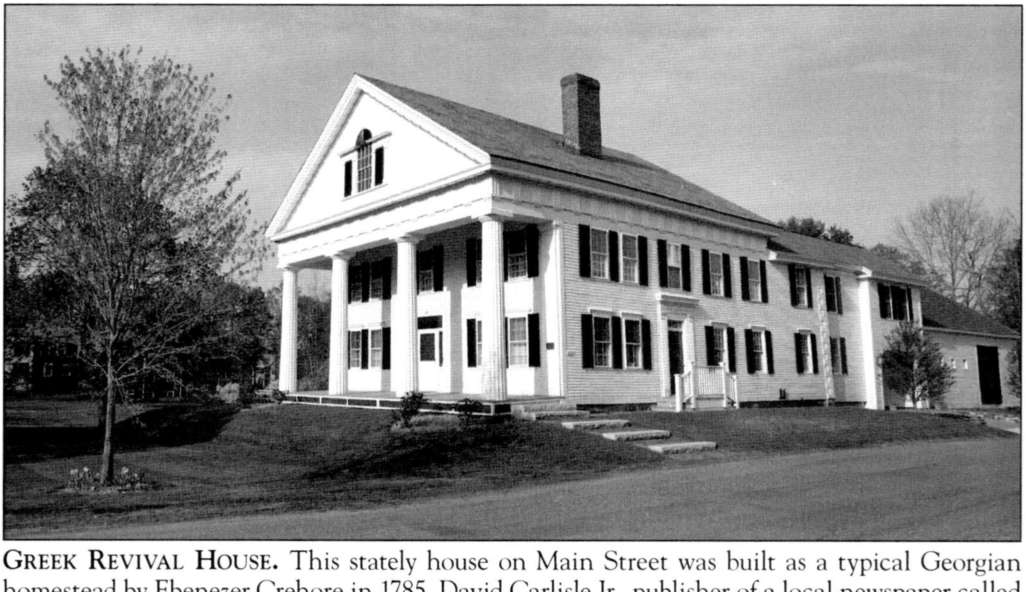

GREEK REVIVAL HOUSE. This stately house on Main Street was built as a typical Georgian homestead by Ebenezer Crehore in 1785. David Carlisle Jr., publisher of a local newspaper called the *Farmer's Weekly Museum*, purchased the house in 1797. Originally hip-roofed with its front entrance on the north side, in the 1830s it was remodeled by the Buffum family in the classical Greek Revival style, with a gable, entablature, and Doric cornice.

First Meetinghouse Site. The first meetinghouse was raised on this property in 1761 but not occupied until 1764 and never completed. Over the next 20 years, the town voted on finishing the structure, but it was eventually abandoned. Josiah Bellows, youngest son of Col. Benjamin Bellows, acquired the acreage and built this home around 1788, enlarging it as necessary for his growing family. Bellows married Rebecca Sparhawk, and when she died, he wed her sister Mary. The two sisters bore 11 children, three of whom later married on the same day. There is original stenciling in the hall and early Zuber's panoramic wallpaper in the parlor. The large ell, added later, housed carriages, housekeeper's rooms, and the summer kitchen. While driving his horse on the Keene road, Josiah met the stagecoach, turned too abruptly, fell from his wagon, struck his head, and died soon after.

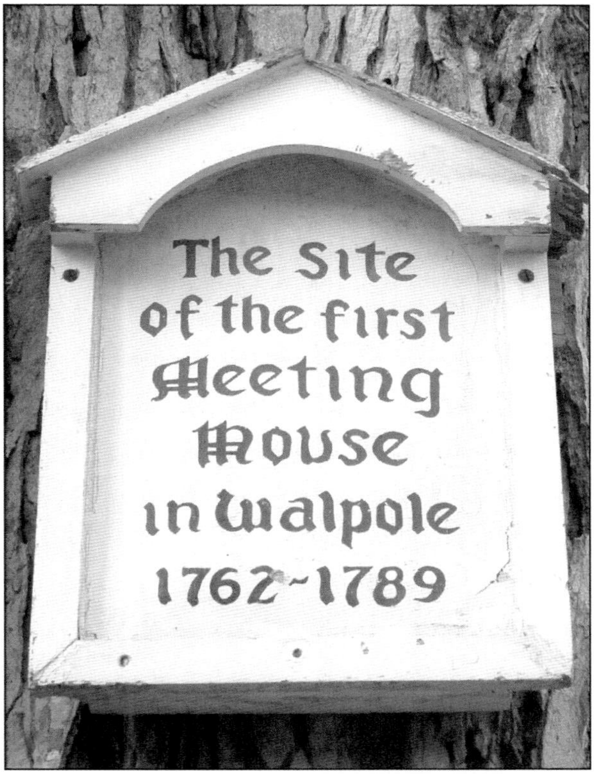

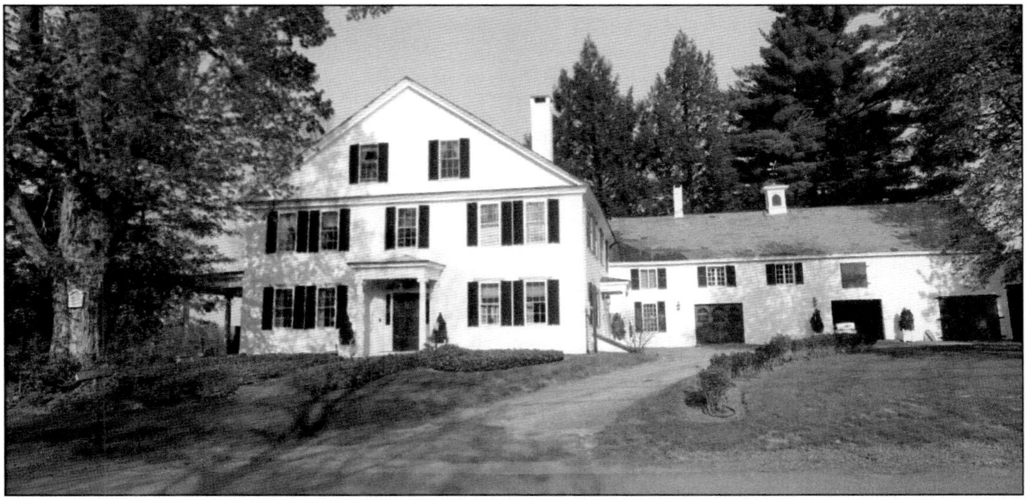

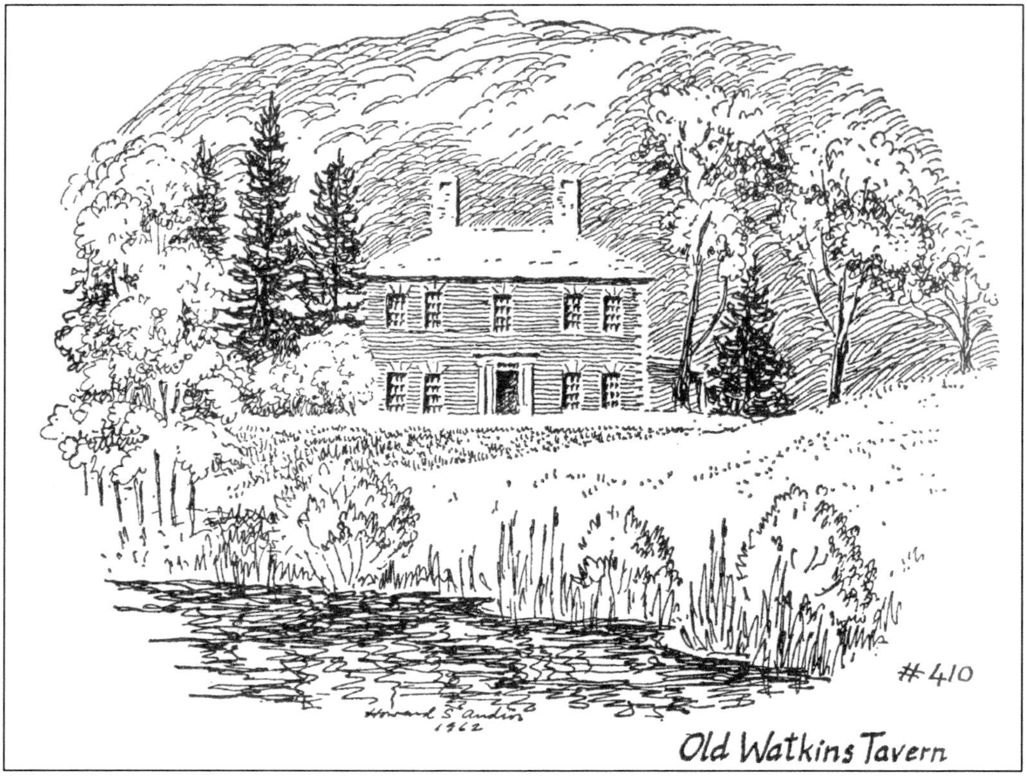

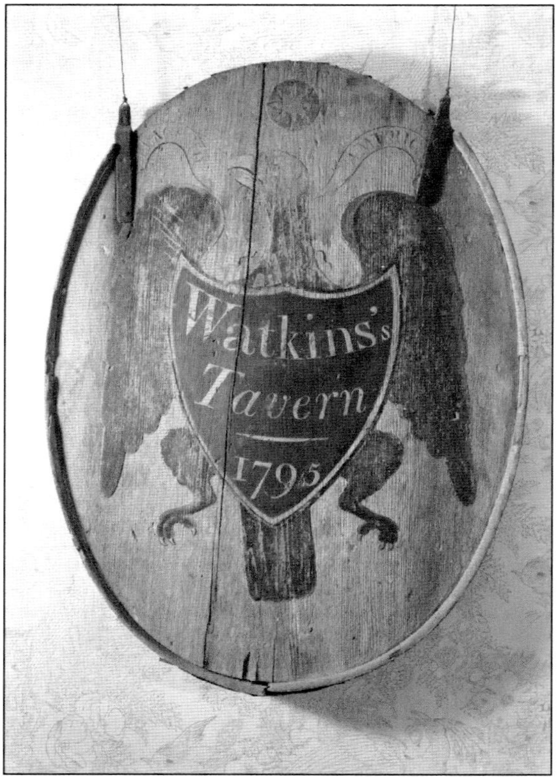

WATKINS'S TAVERN. Alexander Watkins, a tailor by trade, came to Walpole in the 1770s. In 1794, he acquired property near the Prospect Hill meetinghouse and built his home. In 1795, he opened it as a public house. Worship in the unheated meetinghouse was often a day's outing, and in the harsh winters, the tavern became the popular noontime gathering place for many who needed to warm up with a mug of flip after services. Even the pastor could often be found there. Watkins lived here until his death in 1824. Today the building is the clubhouse for the Hooper Golf Club, overlooking a beautiful public course. The original, oval tavern sign (left), a popular shape of the period, hangs on the wall of the clubhouse. The banner held in the beak of the Federal eagle says, "Peace to America." The drawing above was done by Howard Andros. (Above, courtesy of Marion Andros.)

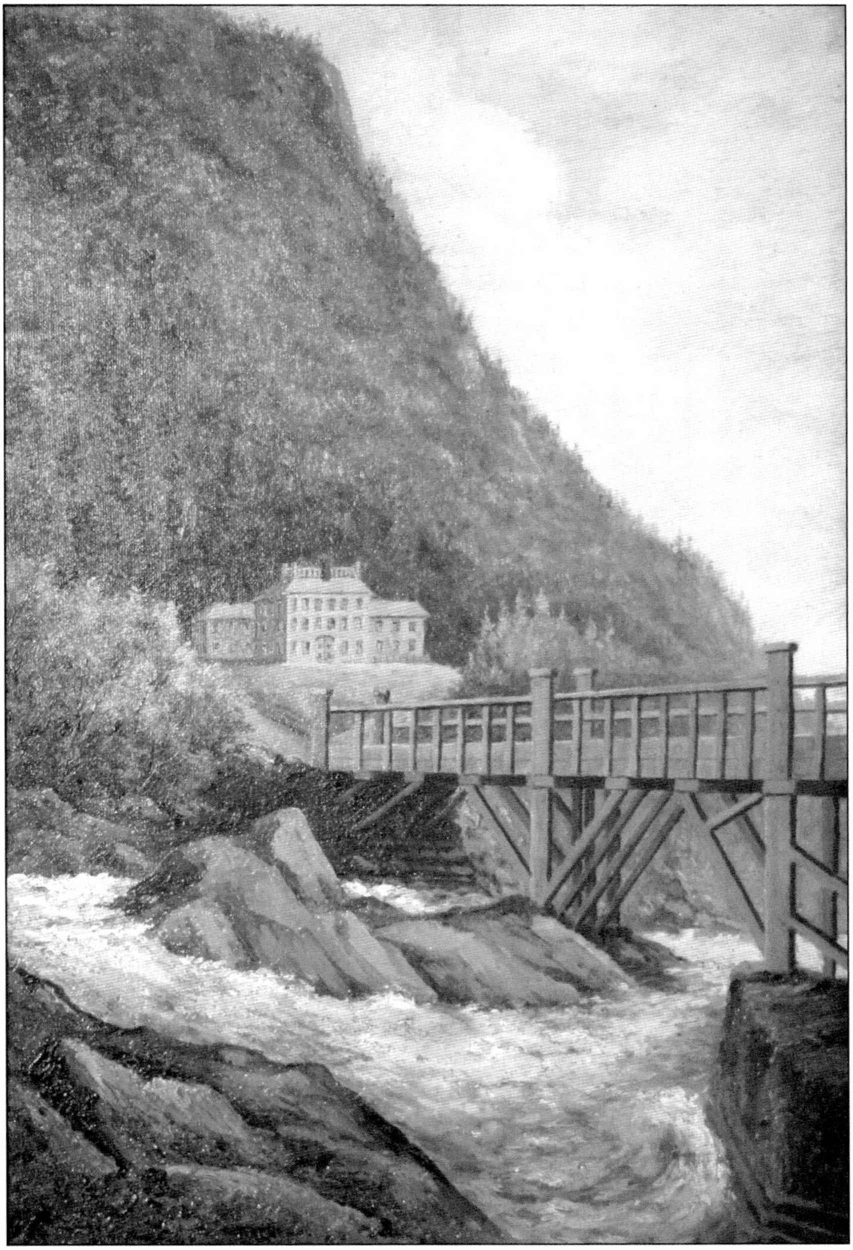

HALE BRIDGE. Seen in this painting by Fred J. Blake, the first bridge over the Connecticut River was built just below the falls, from Walpole to the Vermont shore, by Col. Enoch Hale in 1785. A private toll bridge, it extended 360 feet from the upper end of the falls "to a line between land of said Hale and John Hubbard, Esquire." Built of squared timbers, the roadway was 60 feet above the high-water mark with supports at either end and in the middle. Considered a great engineering feat in its day, it was the only bridge over the river until 1796. At first, tolls were the same as those charged for the ferry. They proved too expensive for early stagecoaches, which stopped at the eastern entrance to allow passengers to walk across the bridge accompanied by their baggage in wheelbarrows. After many efforts to stop this practice, the tolls were eventually lowered. The bridge was replaced in 1840. The Hale mansion is visible in the background.

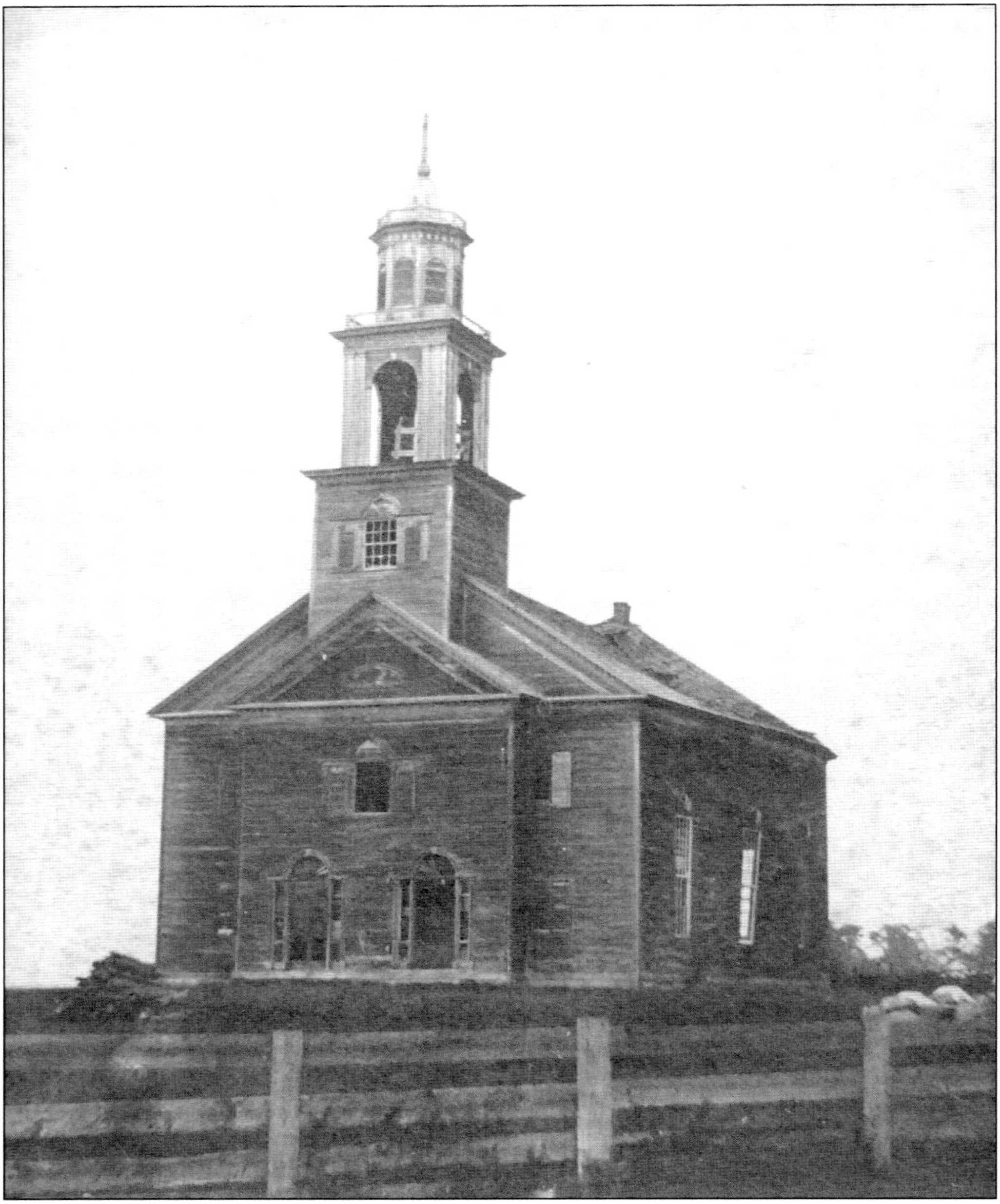

PROSPECT HILL MEETINGHOUSE. In 1786, the town voted to build a new meetinghouse on Prospect Hill to be financed by the auctioning of pews and the sale of public lands and taxes. When the Baptists complained about the taxes, the town gave them a refund. A committee appointed to draw up the plans decided on a dome instead of a spire, removed glass from the old meetinghouse to glaze the new windows, and selected a straw color for the outside. The Church in Walpole was finished in 1792. No sheep were allowed to run on the meetinghouse common, although "neat cattle" could run there from November 15 to May 15. In 1798, the town purchased and installed a Revere bell weighing 936 pounds that was rung at noon and 9:00 p.m. daily and at 9:30 a.m., 10:30 a.m., and 9:00 p.m. on Sunday. The meetinghouse was moved to the village in 1826 and became the town hall. This photograph is from an old stereopticon image in the Walpole Historical Society archives.

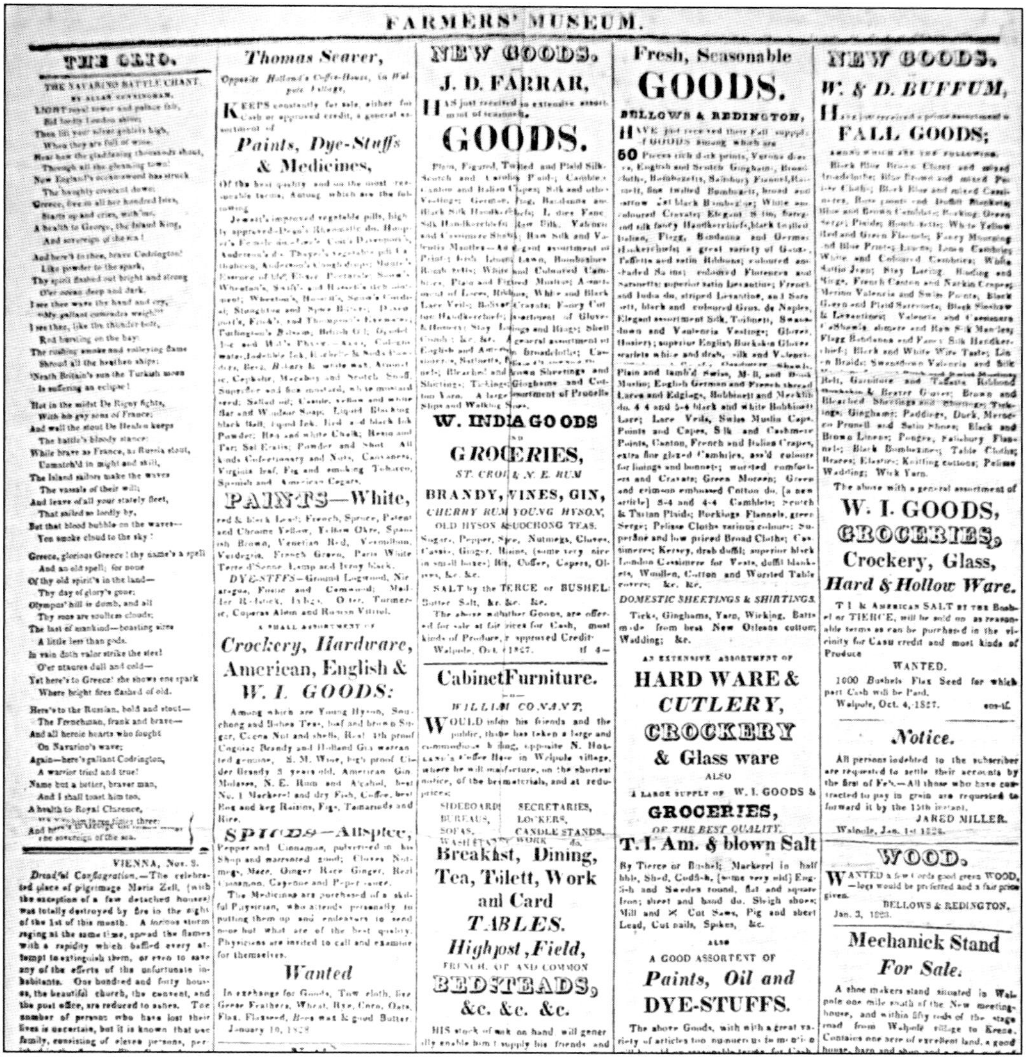
FARMERS' MUSEUM.

THE OLIO.

THE NAVARINO BATTLE CHANT.

Thomas Seaver,

Paints, Dye-Stuffs & Medicines,

PAINTS—White,

Crockery, Hardware, American, English & W. I. GOODS:

SPICES—Allspice,

Wanted

NEW GOODS.

J. D. FARRAR,

GOODS.

W. INDIA GOODS

GROCERIES,

BRANDY, WINES, GIN,

CabinetFurniture.

Breakfast, Dining, Tea, Toilett, Work and Card TABLES.

Highpost, Field,

BEDSTEADS, &c. &c. &c.

Fresh, Seasonable

GOODS.

BELLOWS & REDINGTON,

HARD WARE & CUTLERY,

CROCKERY & Glass ware

GROCERIES,

T. I. Am. & blown Salt

Paints, Oil and DYE-STUFFS.

NEW GOODS.

W. & D. BUFFUM,

FALL GOODS;

W. I. GOODS,

GROCERIES,

Crockery, Glass,

Hard & Hollow Ware.

Notice.

WOOD.

Mechanick Stand For Sale.

FARMER'S WEEKLY MUSEUM. In April 1793, the first issue of the *Farmer's Weekly Museum* was published by Isaiah Thomas and David Carlisle Jr. in a shop on the corner of Main and High Streets. The coarse, dingy 18-by-11-inch paper was printed with inferior, old-fashioned type. Initially, it included short news items, births, deaths, some foreign intelligence, brief poems, an essay or two, and lottery and other advertisements, plus a few "racy" tidbits. Eventually celebrated for its wit and originality, the paper was widely read on both sides of the river, with more than 2,000 subscribers at its height. Thomas, a Bostonian, was a well-known publisher. Carlisle, whose Irish grandfather came to Walpole in its early years from Lunenburg, Massachusetts, had been an apprentice of Thomas. The photograph shows a page from the January 31, 1828, issue.

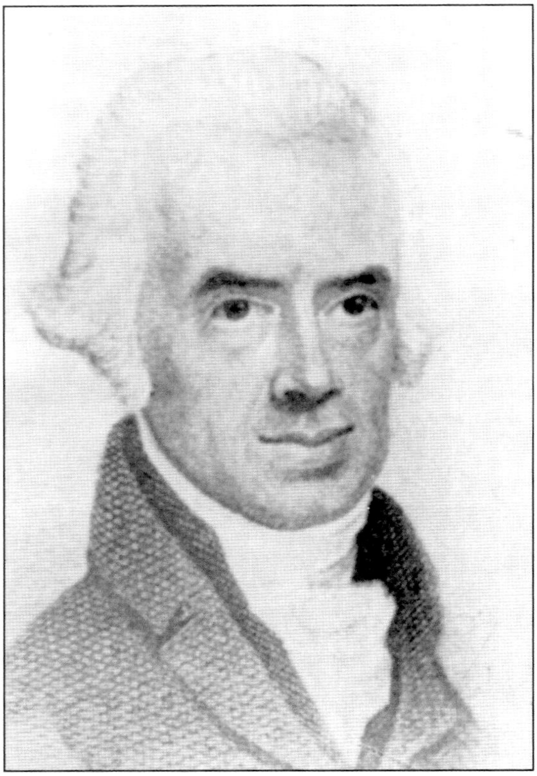

EARLY BOOKS OF ISAIAH THOMAS. Before 1800, book publication was rare in the United States. Yet Isaiah Thomas, LLD, later with his partner, David Carlisle, had a thriving business printing books. One of them, the first American novel reprinted in England, was *The Algerine Captive,* authored by Royal Taylor, a prominent Brattleboro lawyer. Others included A *1794 Almanack and Register for the State of Vermont, The Instructor or Young Man's Best Companion, The Rights of Christians, The Economy of Love, A Shocking Narrative of the Murder of Mr. Joseph Porter,* and *Some Arguments Against Worldly Mindedness.* Thomas, born in Boston in 1749, owned several printing houses. He published the popular *New England Almanac,* and during the American Revolution, he edited the *Massachusetts Spy.* The portrait at left is from the *Granite Monthly;* below are books printed by Thomas, now property of Walpole Historical Society. (Left, courtesy of Historical Society of Cheshire County.)

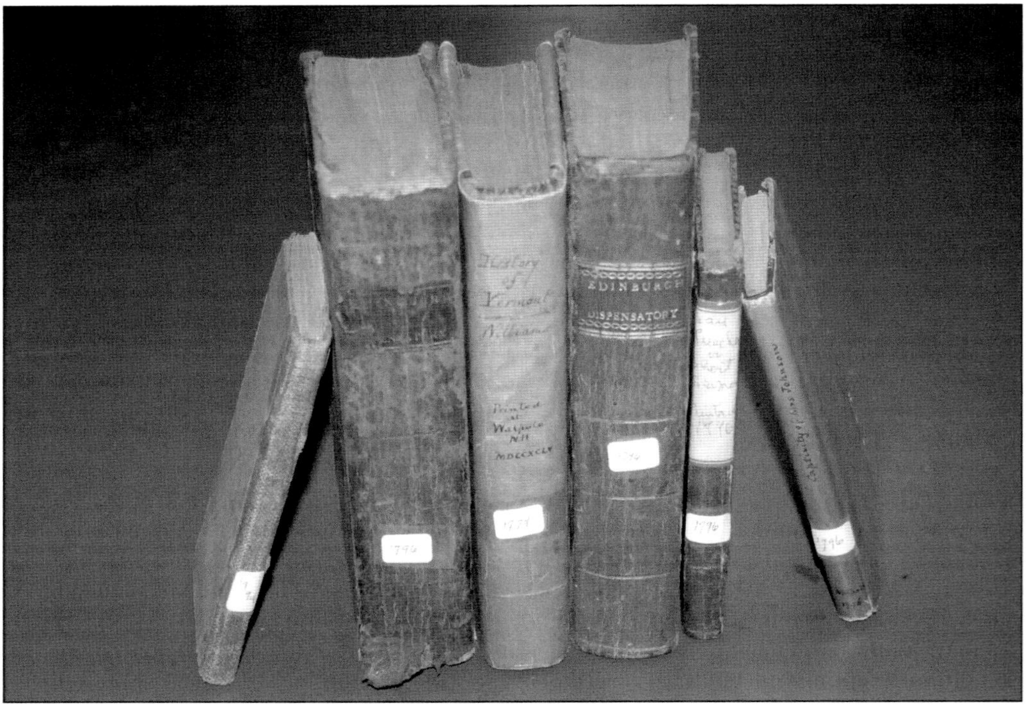

JOSEPH DENNIE AND PRINT SHOP. Joseph Dennie arrived in Walpole in 1795 at the age of 27. A Bostonian, he graduated from Harvard College and practiced law for a short time, then finding law distasteful, he turned to literary pursuits. He assumed the editorship of the *Farmer's Weekly Museum* in its third year. A stylish, eloquent man, his writing style was elegant, especially in the *Lay Preacher* essay series, which was reprinted nationwide. He attracted brilliant writers as contributors, soon earning an enviable reputation for the publication. After the *Farmer's Weekly Museum* failed, he relocated to Philadelphia, eventually starting a literary monthly called *Portfolio*. The portrait at right is from the *Granite Monthly*. Pictured below is the former print shop of Thomas at Main and High Streets, where the *Farmer's Weekly Museum* and early books were produced; today it is a law office. (Right, courtesy of Historical Society of Cheshire County.)

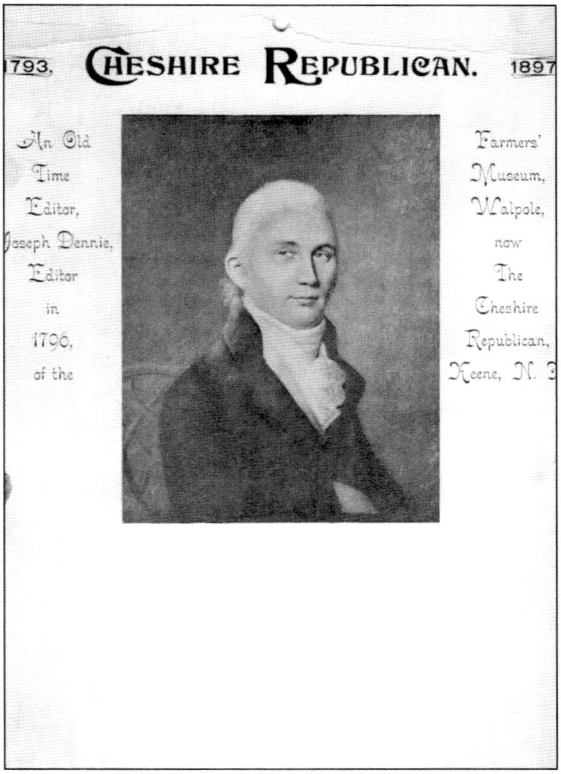

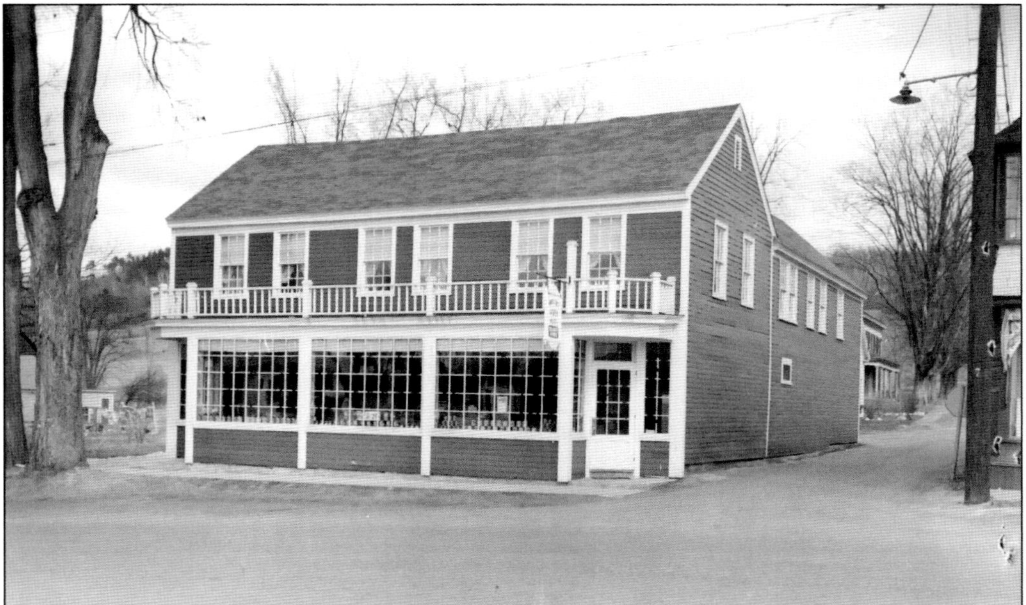

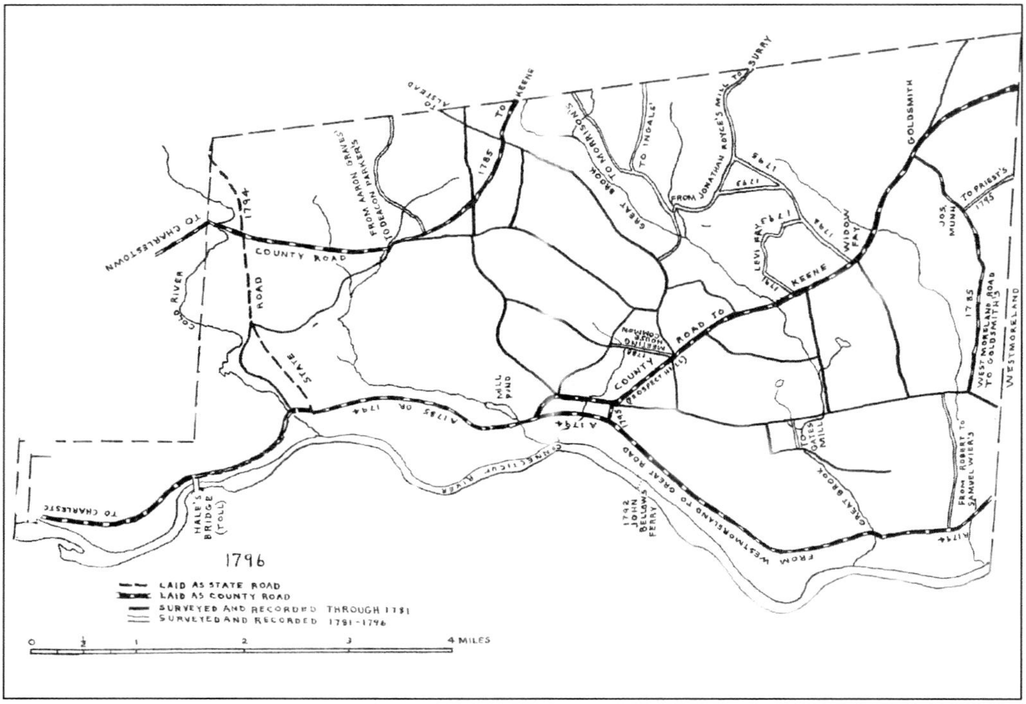

MAP, 1796. This map shows the development of Walpole toward the end of the 18th century. State and county roads were in existence, with a network of others surveyed and recorded. Note the location of Col. Enoch Hale's toll bridge, John Bellows's ferry, and the meetinghouse built on Prospect Hill. The population of the town probably exceeded 1,500, as it grew to 1,743 by 1800.

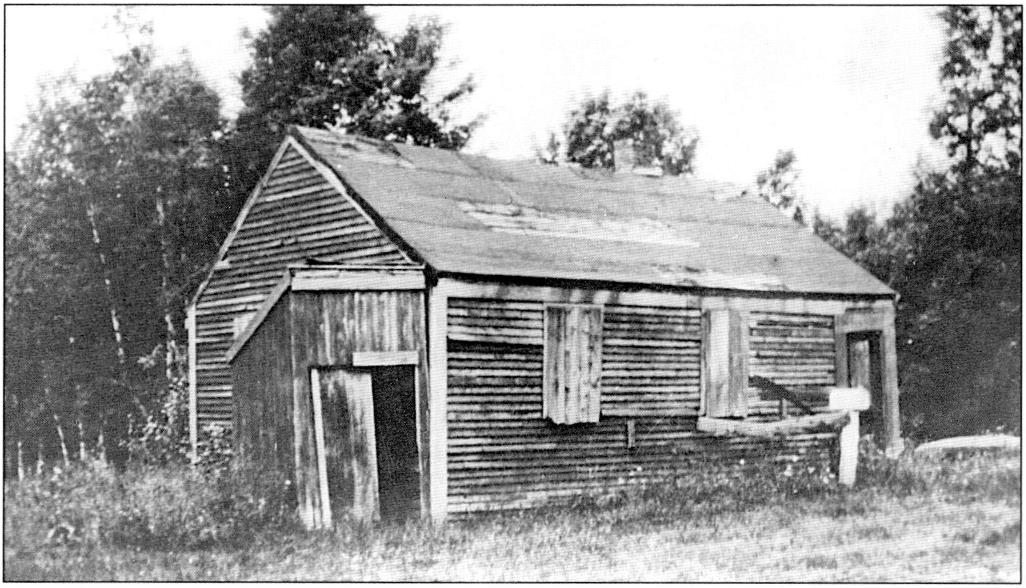

OLD SCHOOLHOUSE. In 1768, Walpole voted to open three schools for the winter. The next year, three school districts were formed, and by 1806, there were 11. A Carpenter Hill deed dated 1798 refers to "school house road," so it is likely this building on the hilltop was in use at that time. It stood on the corner of County and Patnode Roads and accommodated about 30 to 40 students.

Three

Thriving Enterprises and Village Development 1800–1850

In spite of some rough times in the early 1800s caused by serious diseases and weather-related crop failures, Walpole continued to prosper.

Changes in transportation brought growth to the town. The Third New Hampshire and Cheshire Turnpikes connected Walpole to roads in Massachusetts and Vermont. Walpole became a stage and teaming center, as more goods and passengers passed through town. Taverns and inns developed along these routes to serve road-weary travelers. Several new streets were laid out during the early 1800s as the village began to spread outward from the square and common. The Connecticut River continued to handle most of the flow of goods in and out of town, with farm products heading south and manufactured goods coming north. The Cheshire Railroad was built in the late 1840s, with the first train arriving in Walpole on January 1, 1849, en route from Boston to Charlestown.

In 1810, Thomas Collins Drew bought the greater part of what became the village of Drewsville. Given the power of Cold River and Blanchard Brook's rushing waters, Drewsville became a center of manufacturing through the 1830s and 1840s. By 1840, the village boasted three woolen mills, woodworking enterprises and gristmills, two stores, a hotel, a church, and a school.

By 1820, the entire town had 2,020 residents. Most were farmers bartering their products locally. The Prospect Hill Meetinghouse was moved to the village common in the late 1820s, followed by the creation of several new churches in town. Fourteen school districts were created throughout the town. The Walpole Academy was established in 1831.

Local newspapers and stores, where politics were heatedly discussed, allowed residents to express their views on the issues of the day. In 1803, the *Political Observatory* supported Thomas Jefferson, while the *Farmer's Weekly Museum* favored Federalist ideas. Mandatory military training took place until the mid-1840s, when interest in the military decreased. Other organizations, such as the Walpole Detecting Society, later renamed the Walpole Society for Bringing to Justice Horse Thieves and Pilferers, gave townsmen opportunities to serve the community.

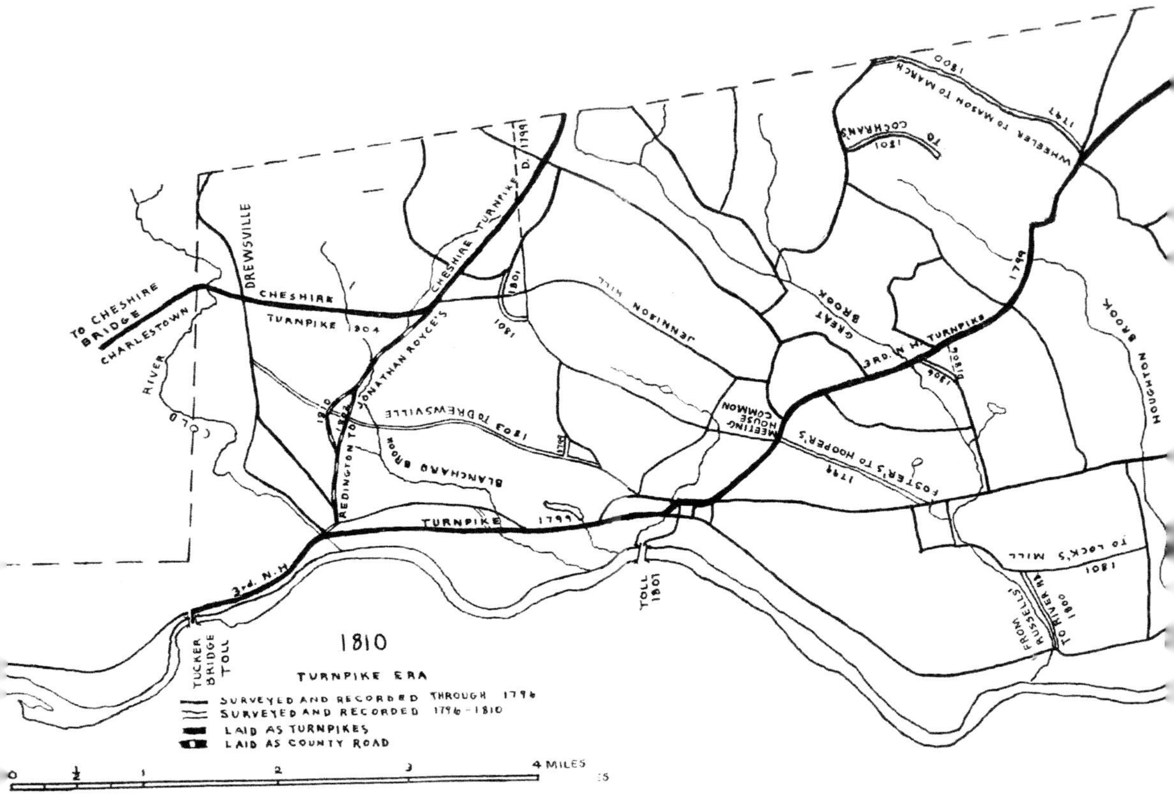

TURNPIKE-ERA MAP. This 1810 map shows the two major turnpikes that passed through Walpole in the early 1800s. Chartered in 1799, the Third New Hampshire Turnpike ran from Walpole along the Connecticut River through Keene to the Massachusetts border. Cheshire Turnpike, chartered in 1804, ran from Charlestown to Keene through Drewsville, spurring economic growth in that village. The Cheshire Turnpike joined the Third New Hampshire in Keene. Both these roads gave area residents easier access to markets in southern New England, where they sold their products and obtained needed manufactured goods. They also gave rise to the development of inns and taverns along their routes. As a result, Walpole became an active stage and teaming center. There was only one tollgate in town, located in Christian Hollow, where County Road and Watkins Hill joined. But the toll roads were very unpopular with local residents, and in 1824, the New Hampshire legislature gave control of the Third New Hampshire Turnpike to the town, dissolving the group of local businessmen who had been its proprietors.

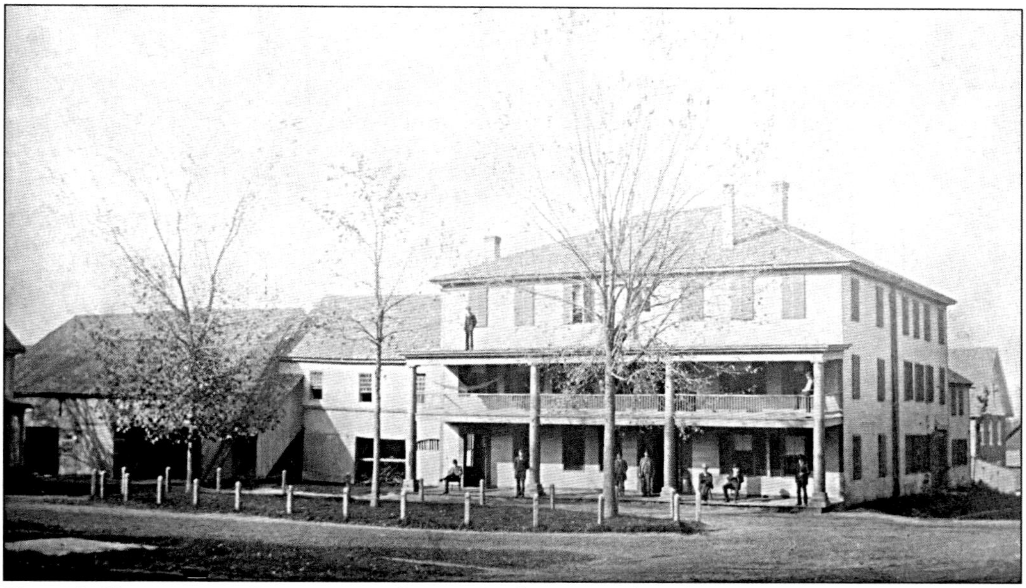

CRAFT'S TAVERN AND STAGECOACH LINES. Craft's Tavern, later known as the Wentworth Hotel, stood at the corner of Main and Westminster Streets in the early 1800s. A popular gathering spot for locals and road-weary travelers, the tavern offered drinks, food, and shelter. A meal there cost 33¢, a price seen as extortionary by many. By the early 1800s, Walpole was a stop on stages traveling between Boston and Burlington, Vermont, or Hanover. It also served to connect points south of Walpole in the Connecticut River valley to these lines. Rates from Boston to the Walpole area ($4.50, later reduced to $2.50) were set by a trio of local businessmen who controlled stage and mail routes through town. The coach below is typical of the time, serving the Marlow-Keene line. (Below, courtesy of Historical Society of Cheshire County.)

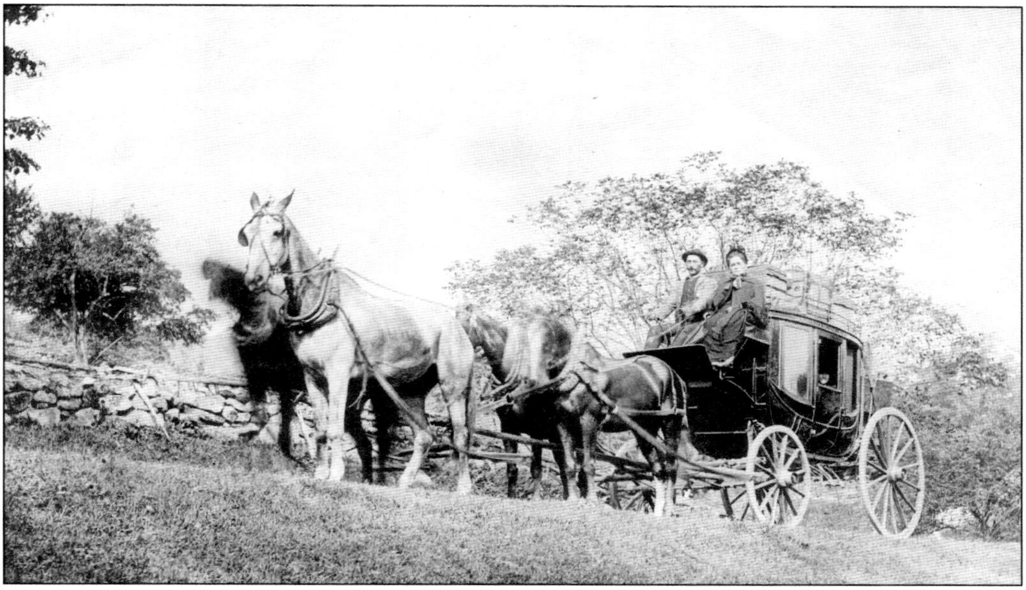

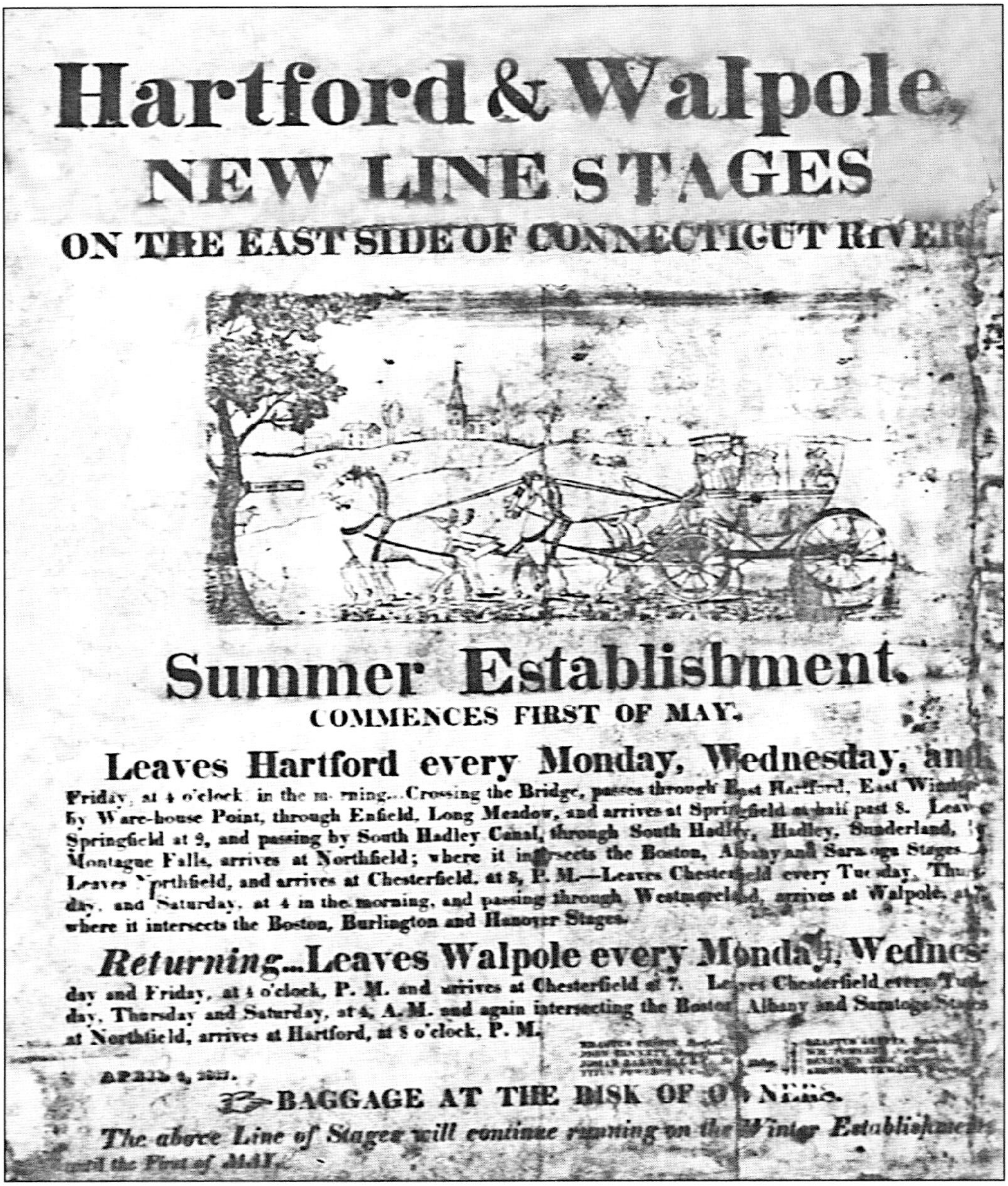

HARTFORD AND WALPOLE STAGE LINES POSTER. This poster, advertising a new summer schedule for a stage line through the Connecticut River valley, was printed on April 1, 1817. It detailed stops through Connecticut, central Massachusetts, and southwestern New Hampshire to Walpole, where this line connected with stages to Boston; Burlington, Vermont; and Hanover. The poster's sketch, the work of engraver Richard Brunton, also appeared on several other New England stage advertisements in this time period.

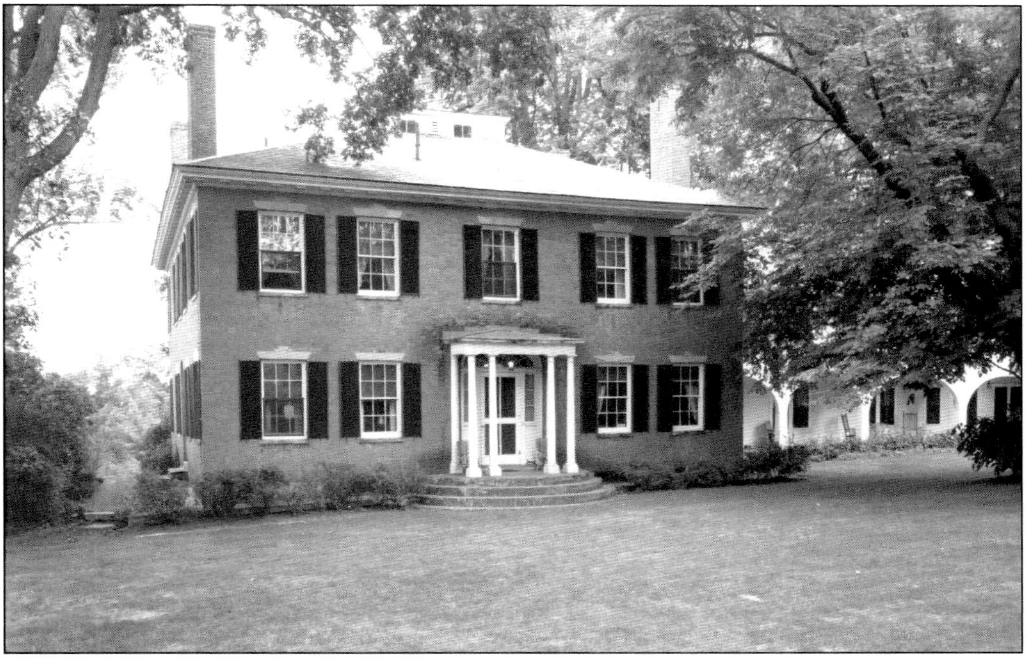

KNAPP HOUSE. This large brick and clapboard mansion was built in 1812 by Josiah Bellows II on a portion of his father's farm. Designed to be the most imposing residence in town, the exterior has changed little. In 1820, Bellows mortgaged the house to his cousin John Bellows, who sold it in 1824 to Jacob Knapp, his brother-in-law. The house remained in the Knapp family until 1927 when it was sold by the Knapp granddaughters. Lucia Alden Knapp, Jacob's daughter-in-law who died in 1924 at the age of 90, is shown below in the music room with its walls covered by the Dufour "Monuments of Paris" wallpaper installed in 1812. The wallpaper was recently removed, cleaned, repaired, and replaced exactly as it was originally. Louisa May Alcott wrote *Under the Lilacs* while visiting in this house.

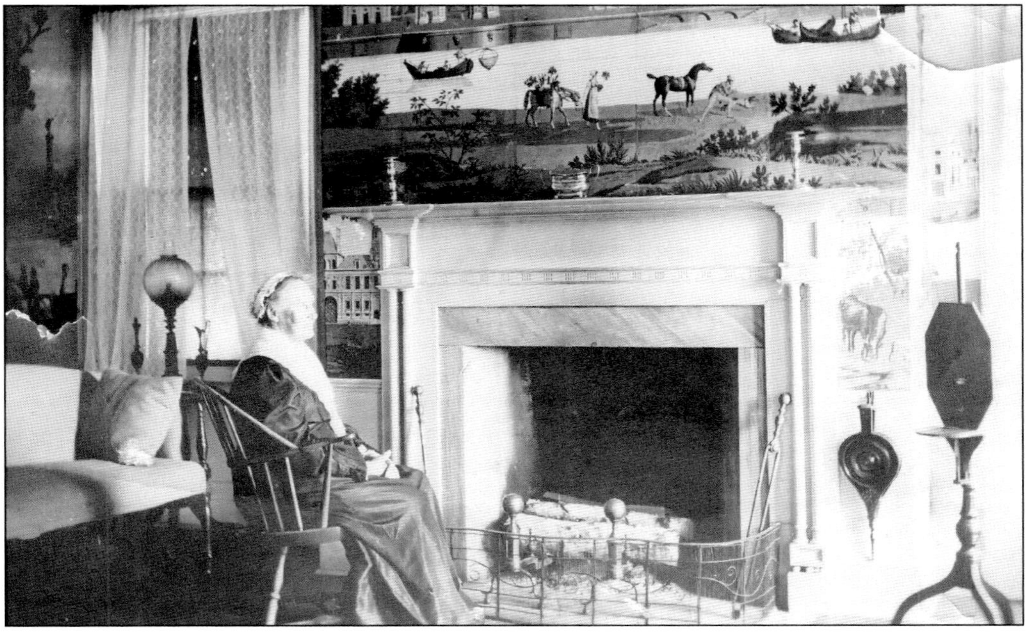

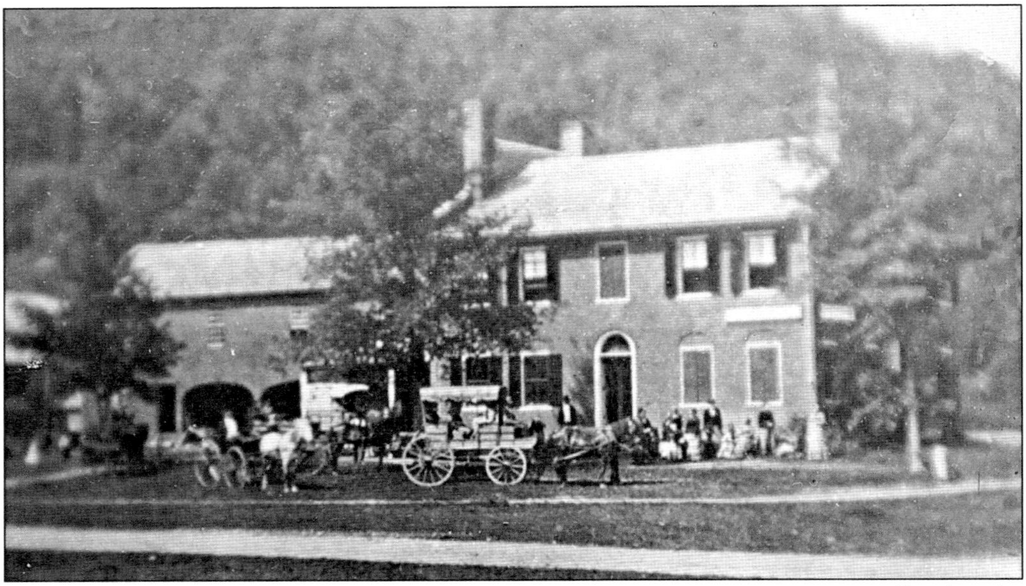

DREWSVILLE. The village of Drewsville had its heyday in the 1830s, growing rapidly after the Cheshire Turnpike brought goods and travelers through and mills developed along Cold River and Blanchard Brook. In 1810, Thomas C. Drew built a hotel known as the Drew Tavern (above) on the northwest corner of the common, using bricks he manufactured in Walpole Village. It became the social center of the village, attracting many well-known figures of the day. In 1875, Thomas Taunt bought the tavern, later renaming it the Mountain House. The Drewsville store, built on the site below about 1814, has been another center of activity for nearly 200 years. In 1819, the post office and the deputy sheriff's office were located here. The building below is a replacement for the store that burned in the early 1930s; the post office remains here.

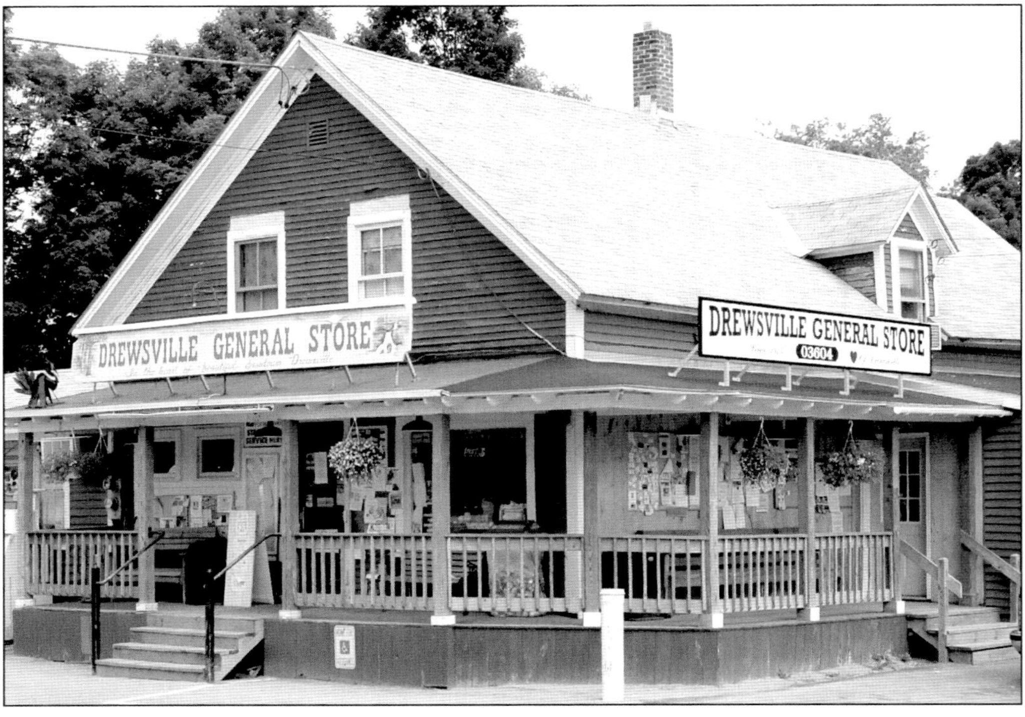

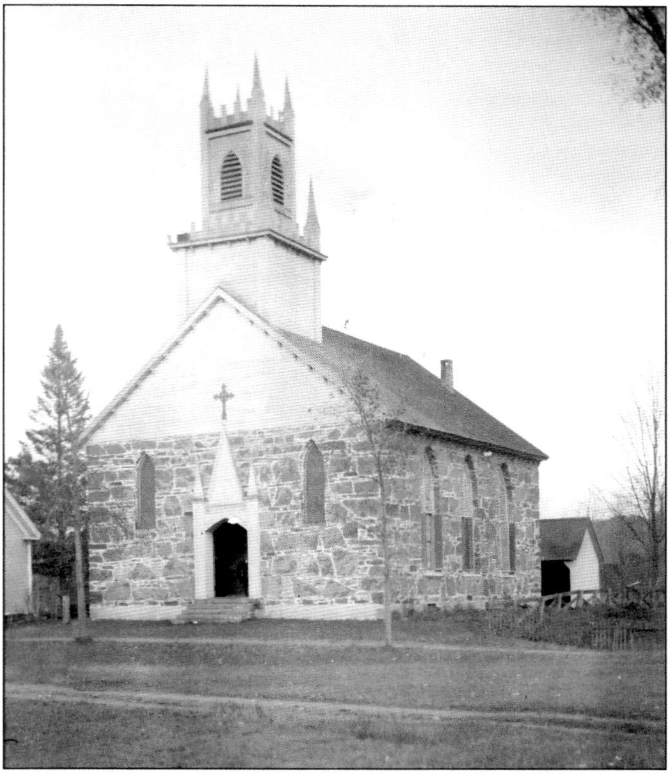

St. Peter's Episcopal Church, Drewsville. In 1834, Drew gave to the Protestant Episcopal Society a lot on the east side of the common. This stone chapel was built and consecrated in 1836, during Drewsville's heyday. In the 1860s, the chapel was altered and repaired. The steeple was removed in recent years because of deterioration. Empty for many years, it now provides worship space for the Seventh Day Adventists.

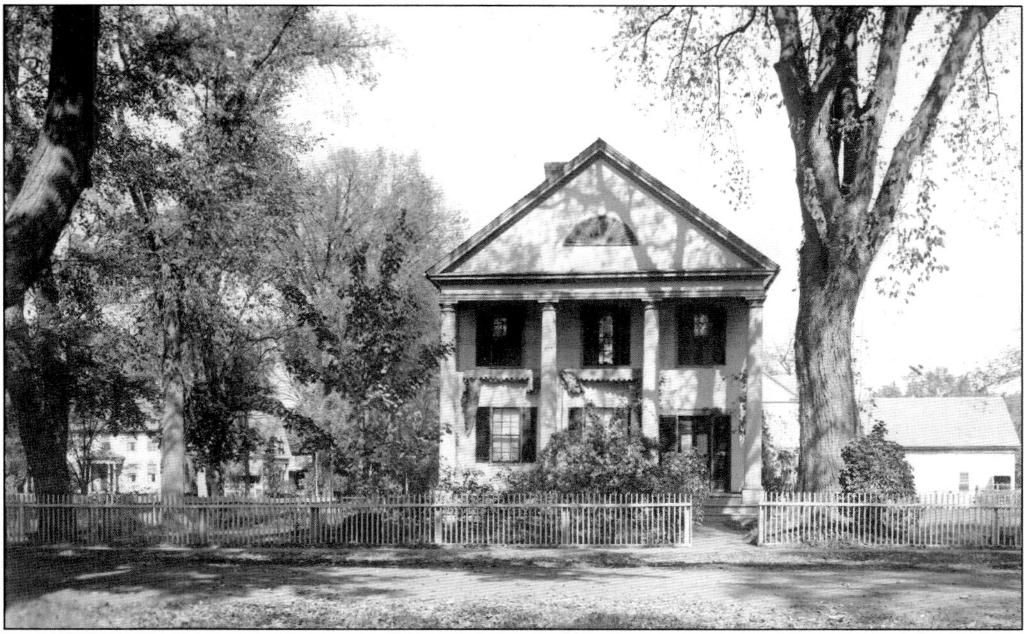

Susan Robeson House. Located at the corner of Elm and Westminster Streets in Walpole Village and designed by Susan Bellows Robeson, granddaughter of Col. Benjamin Bellows, this house was built by Levi Hubbard in the early 1800s. It has been praised as the first house of its type in the village designed for a small family while retaining "the dignity, true worth and charm characteristic of the larger colonial homes of her time."

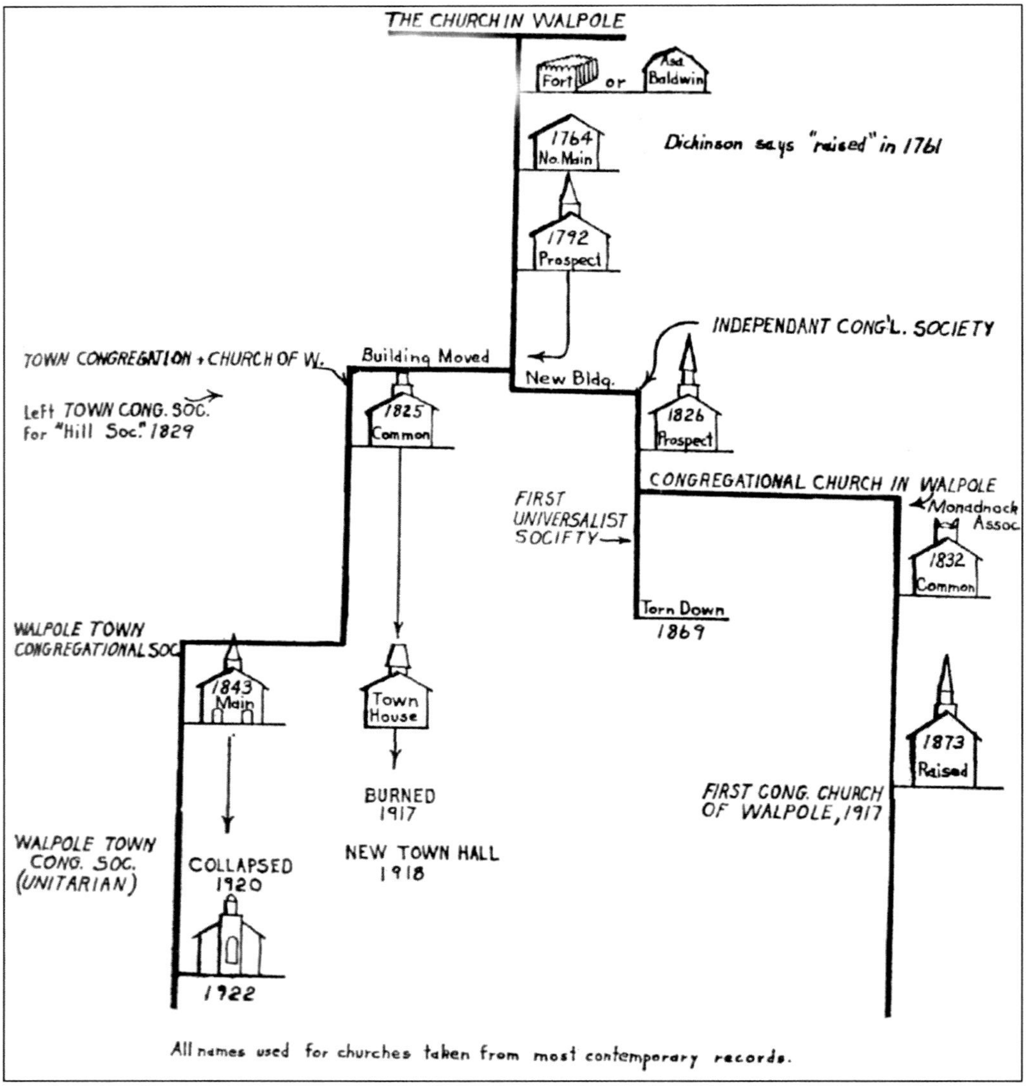

THE CHURCH IN WALPOLE. With the move of the Prospect Hill Meetinghouse down to the village common, the religious differences that had been brewing in the town congregation and Society of Walpole broke out into the open, pitting the Unitarian, Universalist, and Congregational factions against one another. The Independent Congregational Society, opposed to the relocation into the village, decided to build a new church on the Prospect Hill site, completing it in 1826. Ten years later, having lost some of its members to the new First Congregational Church, this "hill" group formed the Universalist Society and used the Prospect Hill church for several years. After standing empty and in poor condition for many years, the Prospect Hill church was torn down in 1869.

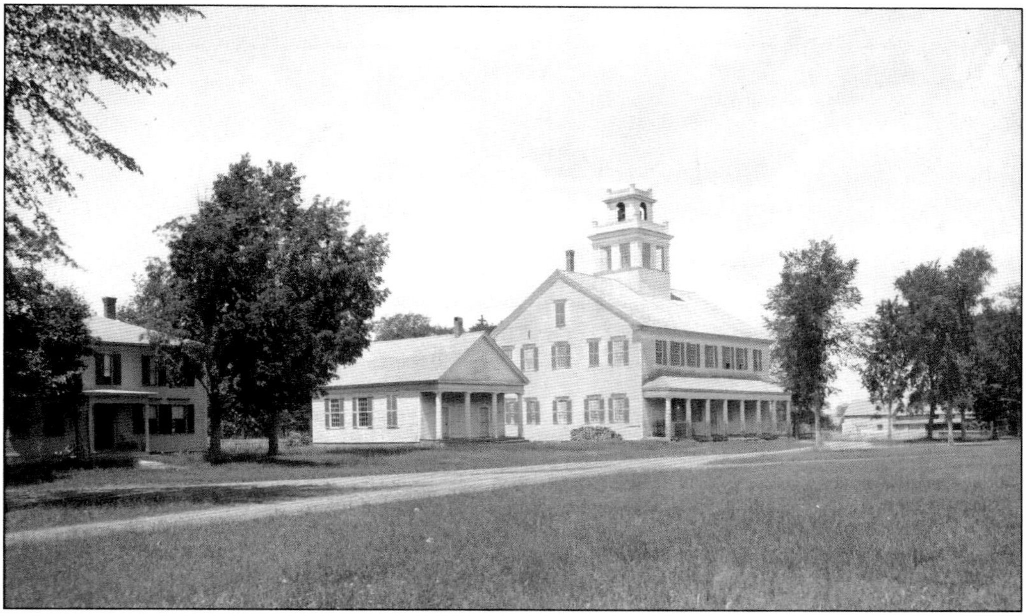

WALPOLE TOWN HOUSE. Originally used as the Prospect Hill Meetinghouse completed in 1792, the town house was dismantled and moved to the common in the 1820s, where it continued to house town meetings and church services until 1844. At that time, total control of the building passed to the town, and renovations were made to better suit municipal needs. Also shown in the photograph is the Methodist church, built in 1845 (now St. Joseph's Catholic Church).

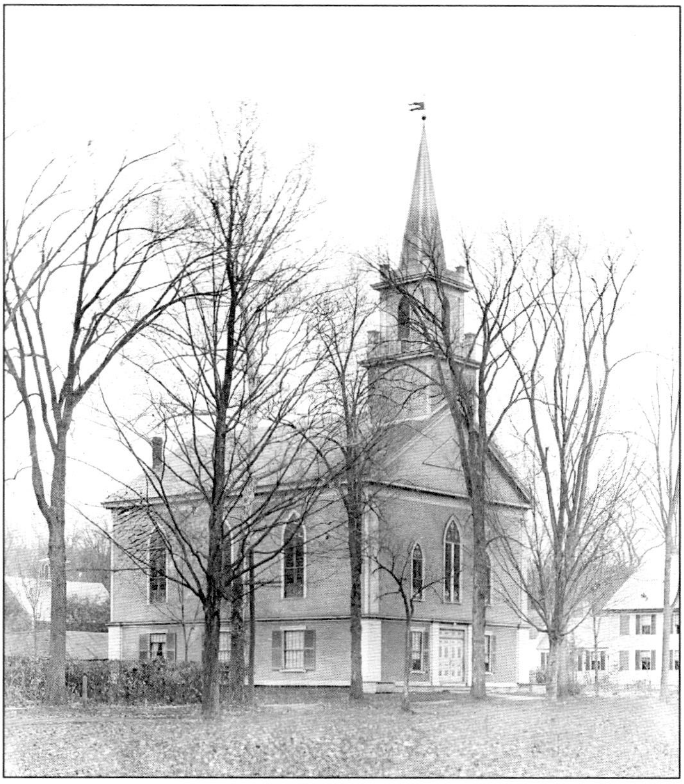

THE FIRST CONGREGATIONAL CHURCH. The Congregationalists withdrew from the "hill" society and formed the First Congregational Church and Society in Walpole late in 1832. Over the next year and a half, they built their church (seen here) just east of the common. In 1873, the building was raised 10 feet and a vestry and kitchen were built underneath the sanctuary.

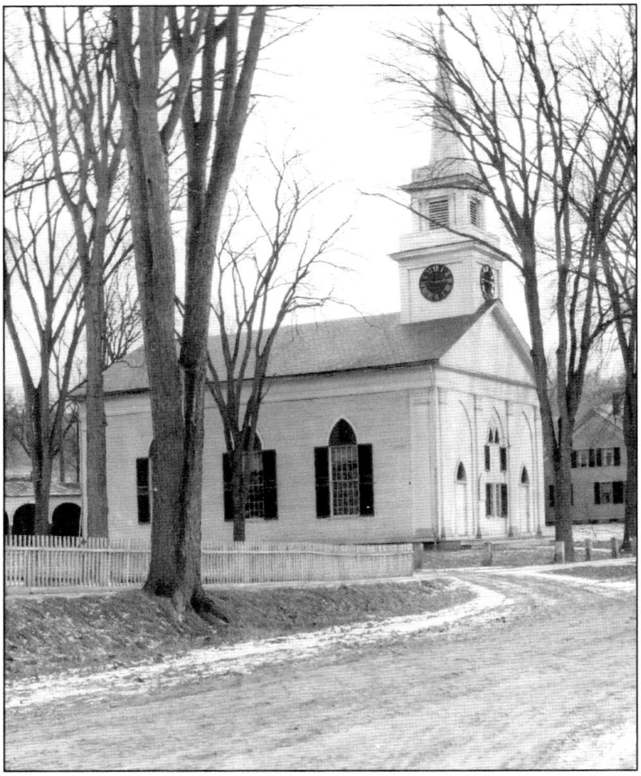

THE UNITARIAN CHURCH. The Walpole Town Congregational Society decided to build its own Unitarian Church (seen here) on Main Street, as the town was taking over the meetinghouse on the common. They obtained land bordering Main, Union, and School Streets and began construction. The church, with horse sheds, was completed in January 1843. The next year, a clock from the academy building was placed in the tower. In the winter of 1920, the building was destroyed by snow load (see chapter 5).

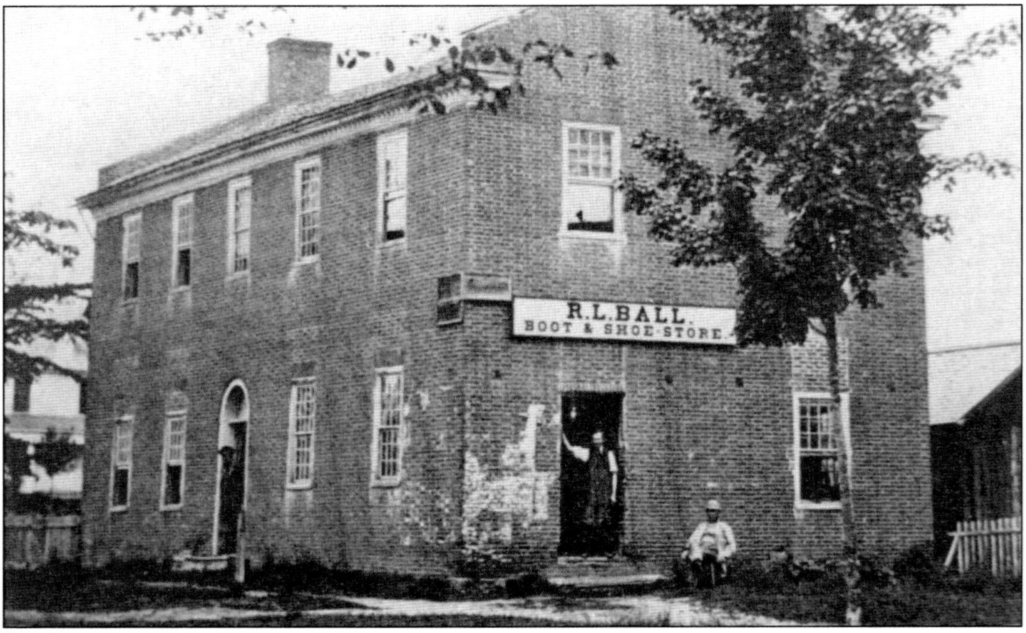

DISTRICT NO. 1 SCHOOL. This school was built in 1807 at the corner of Elm and Westminster Streets, where St. John's Episcopal Church now stands. It contained three classrooms and a second-floor public exhibitions hall. Sanitary facilities were housed in wooden sheds on each end. Younger village students attended here until the village elementary school on School Street was completed in 1854. The building was later used as R. L. Ball's shoemaker's shop.

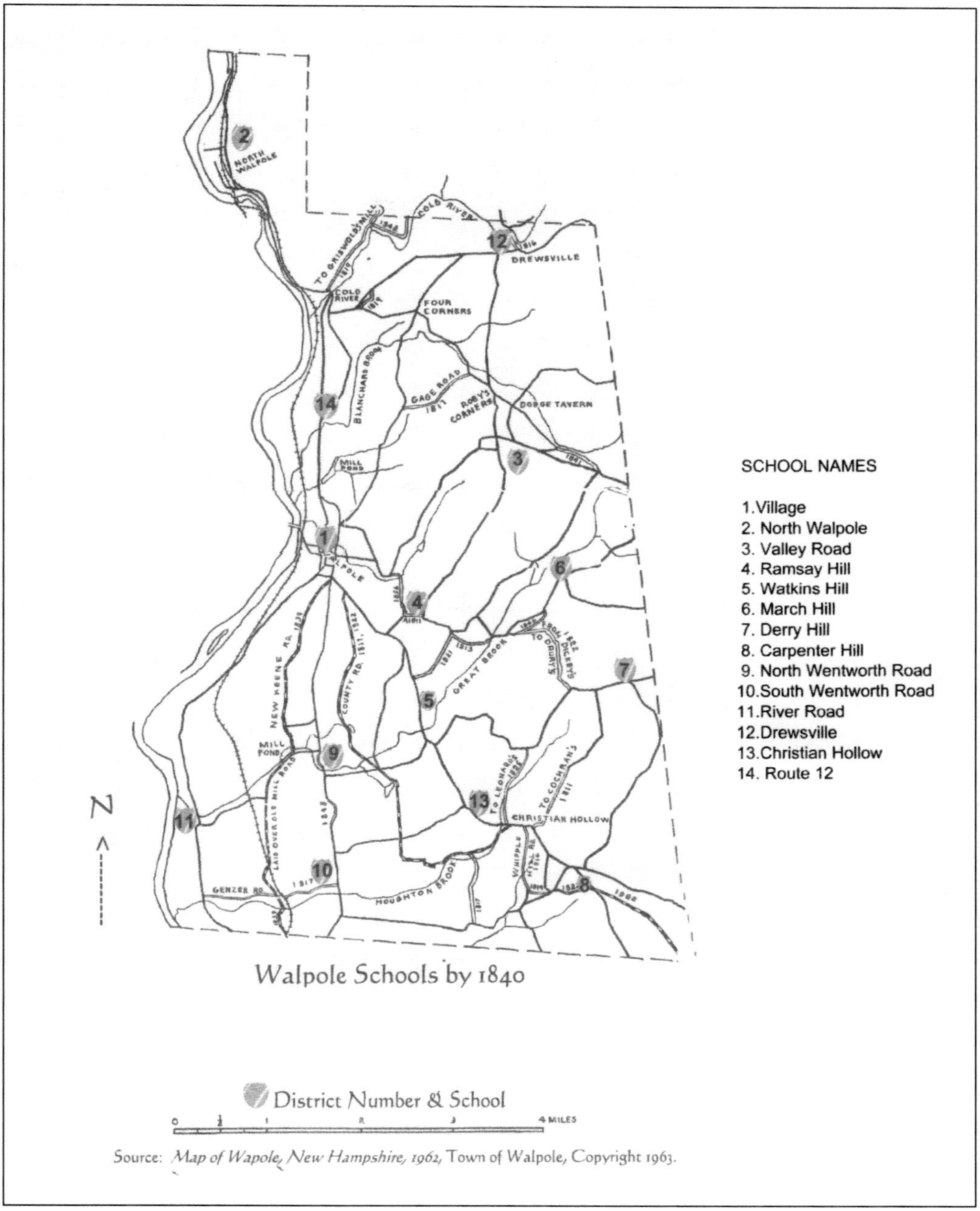

WALPOLE SCHOOL DISTRICTS. In a three-mile-an-hour world, access to public education was by foot or by draft animal and not always easy. By 1840, Walpole had developed 14 school districts within the township to guarantee access, especially in the hill country outside the village proper. The numbering of the districts was in chronological order, so one can see, for example, that Drewsville and the schools along the river valley floor were some of the later. The length of the school year varied from 26 to 34 weeks, with the village school being at the higher end, until the 1888–1889 school year, when all schools required 30 weeks. The districts were self-governing until 1891, when Chapter 64 of New Hampshire state law required all school districts be united under one jurisdiction. Most students were expected to receive 12 years of education; schools were usually taught by one person, often students from Dartmouth College.

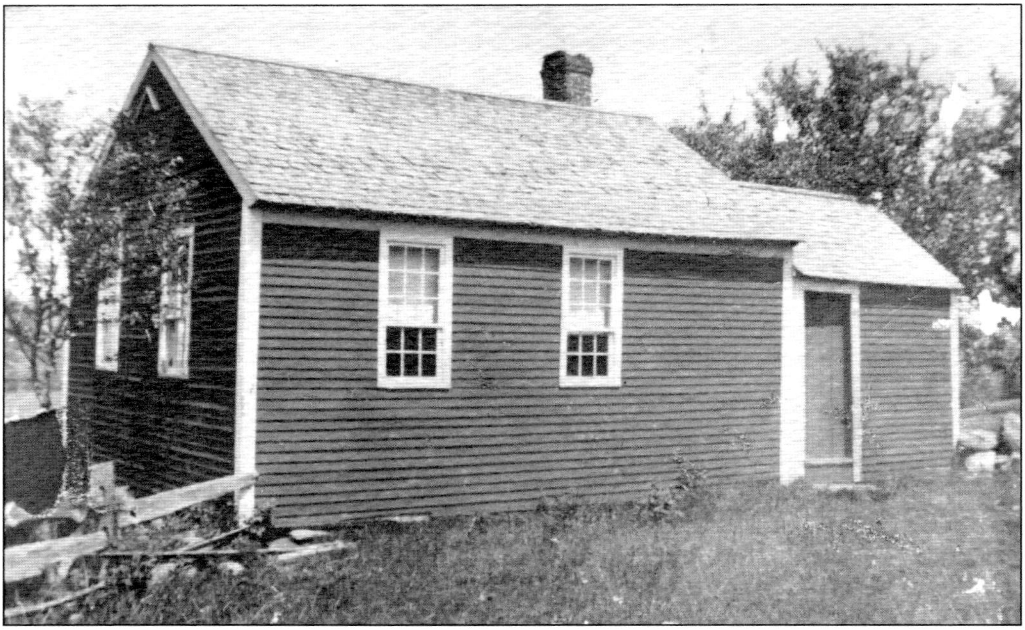

DISTRICT NO. 6 SCHOOL, MARCH HILL ROAD. This district, established in 1796, had its school in two different locations along March Hill Road. The school shown above was the later building, constructed in 1808 directly across from the end of Barnett Hill Road. This school was seen as one with consistently good performance, sparked by active parent involvement. Closed in 1901, the building is no longer there.

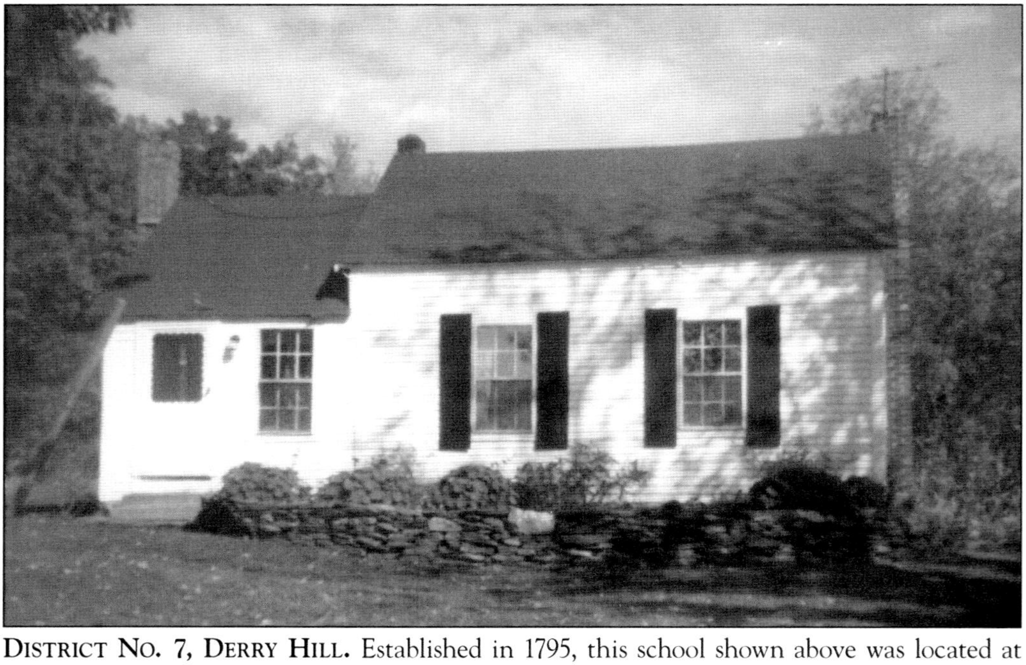

DISTRICT NO. 7, DERRY HILL. Established in 1795, this school shown above was located at the top of Derry Hill. It had a large student population in the early 1800s because of many prosperous farms in the area, but by the 1850s, enrollment had decreased sharply, leading to its closure in 1885. The building was later sold and moved to Maple Grove Farm for use as a herdsman's house.

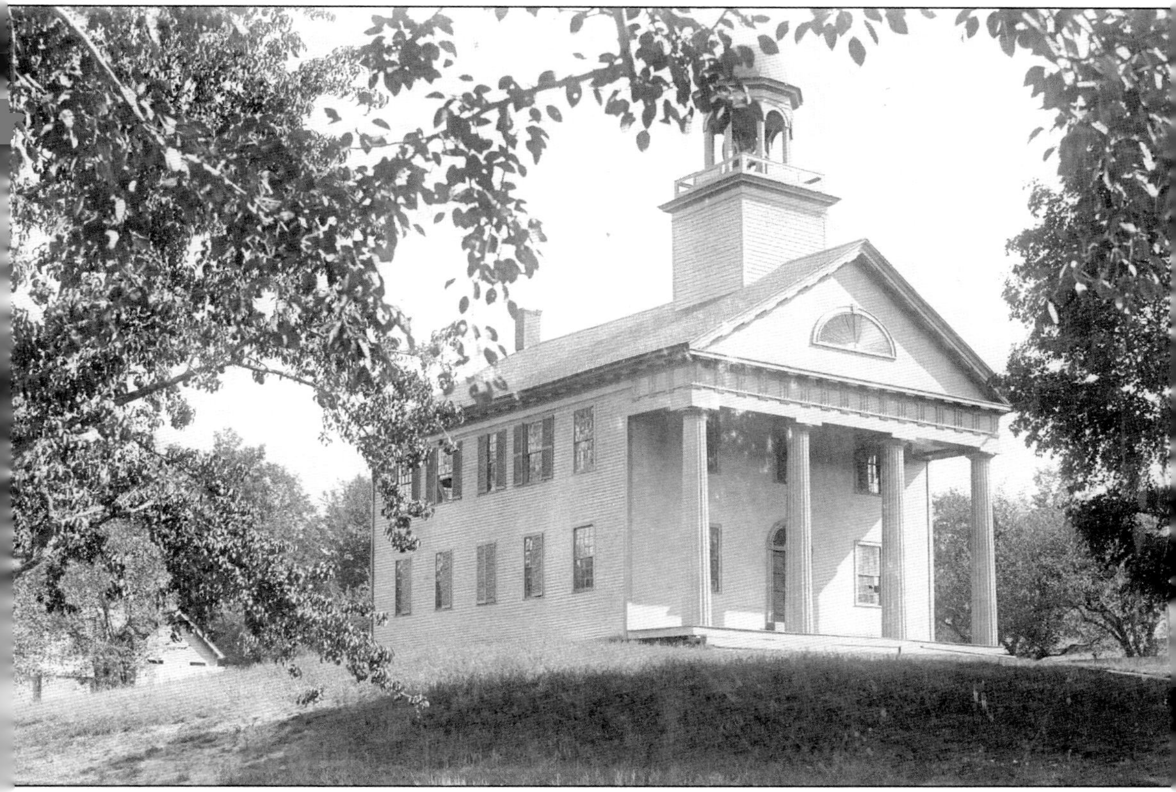

WALPOLE ACADEMY. The old academy building was designed and constructed in 1831 by local carpenter and cabinetmaker Aaron P. Howland. He was influenced by the Greek Revival style, setting the building like a temple on a knoll overlooking Main Street. He designed it with classical columns, a cupola belfry, and large rooms with generous windows. Walpole Academy was a private school until the 1850s, serving boys and girls from both sides of the Connecticut River. Some lived at home, while others boarded in the village. The school's 1837 catalog listed students from the region and claimed a student population of 193. Subjects included Greek, Latin, French, Italian, arithmetic, algebra, astronomy, botany, and grammar. In 1853, the building was purchased by the town and modified for use as a public high school, serving in that capacity until 1950 when the new high school was built on Turnpike Street. The Walpole Historical Society purchased the building in 1950 to serve as its headquarters and museum.

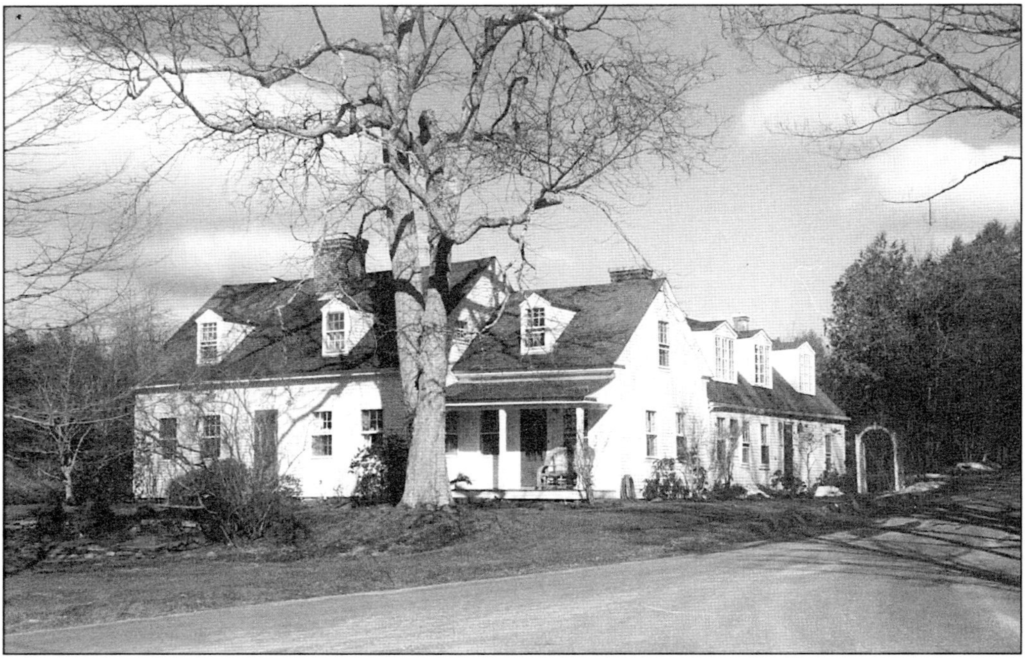

Burns House. In 1820, Seth Hunt, son of Abigail Bellows, sold 35 acres of land to former Vermont senator Stephen Rowe Bradley, who built this house, probably for his grandson Stephen Rowe Bellows, who inherited it in 1831. After changing hands several times, the house was bought in 1983 by Ken Burns, who added a wing and renovated the barn for use as his company's headquarters.

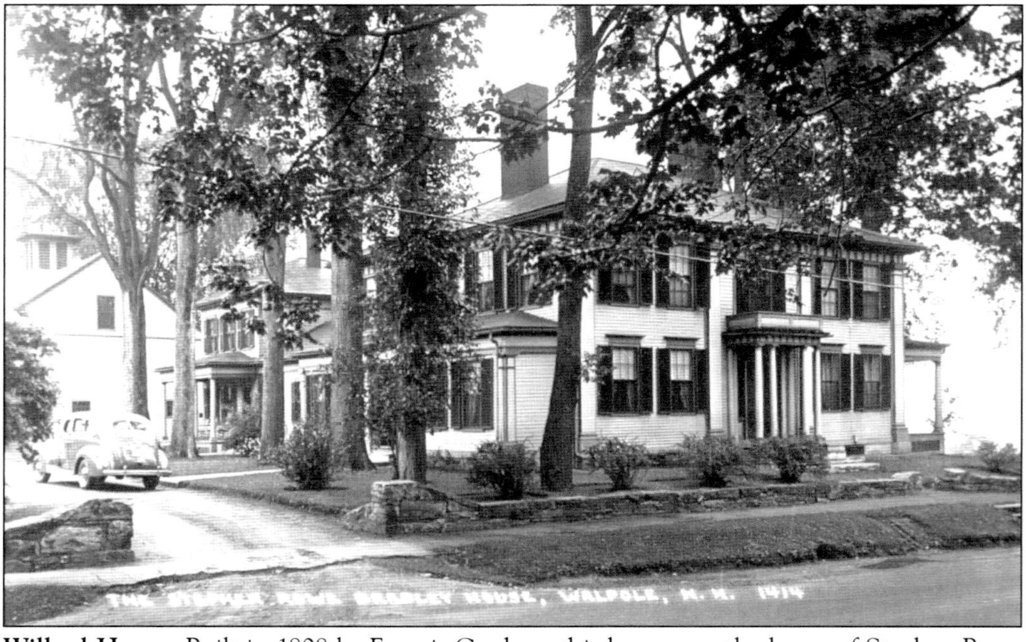

Willard House. Built in 1808 by Francis Gardner, this house was the home of Stephen Rowe Bradley from 1817 to 1830. During the late 1800s, it belonged to the New Hampshire Asylum for the Insane. It came back to the Bradley family in 1913 when it was acquired by Henry K. Willard and is now listed on the National Register of Historic Places.

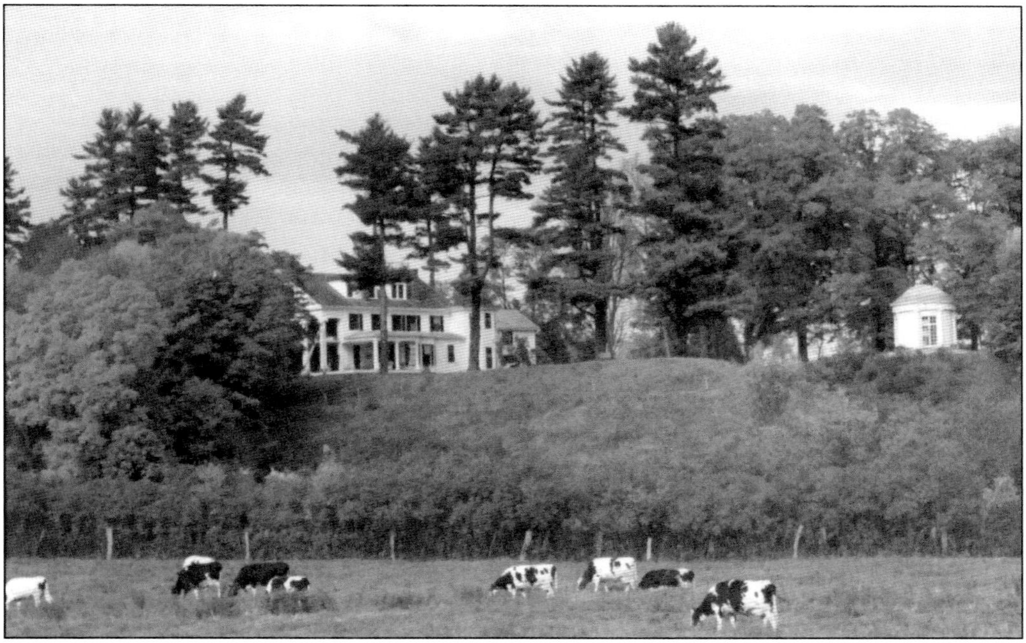

CABOT MANSION OF BOGGY MEADOW FARM. In 1822, Jonathan Mason bought 700 acres near the Connecticut River in Walpole from Col. Josiah Bellows III, and developed Boggy Meadow Farm. In 1832, he completed the first of five houses on the property. The columned mansion shown above was constructed in 1836. William Powell Mason left the property to his daughter Fanny P. Mason in 1901. At her death, she left significant woodlands to the Town of Walpole and the house to her uncle Harry Cabot, who lived there until 1974. Still owned by the Cabot family, Boggy Meadow Farm remains a working farm and the home of Boggy Meadow cheeses. The cheese shop (below) occupies a 1770 farmhouse, one of the earliest on the property.

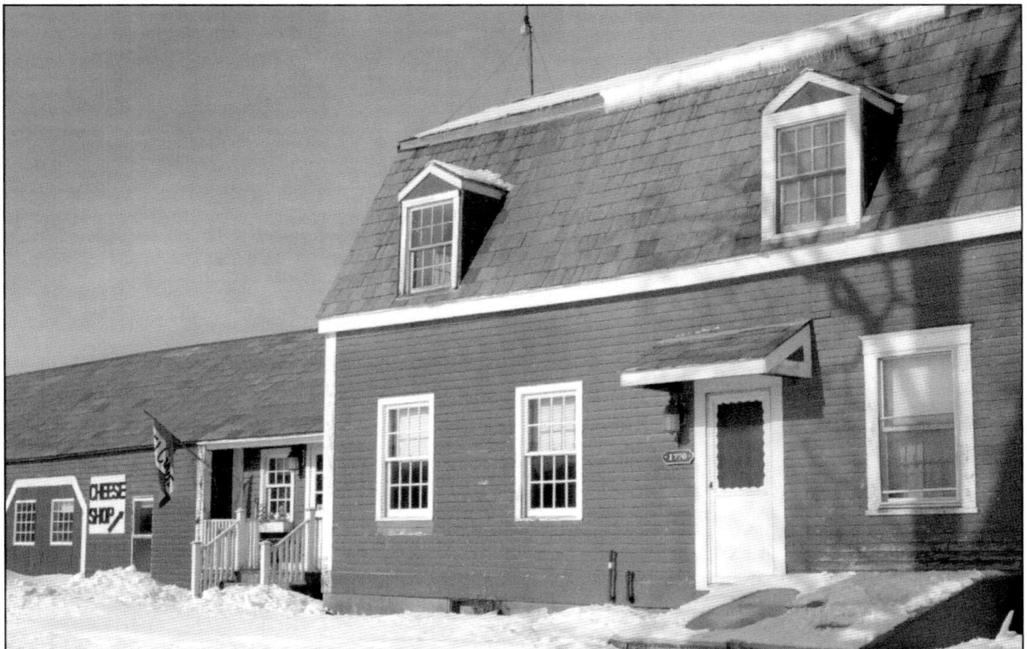

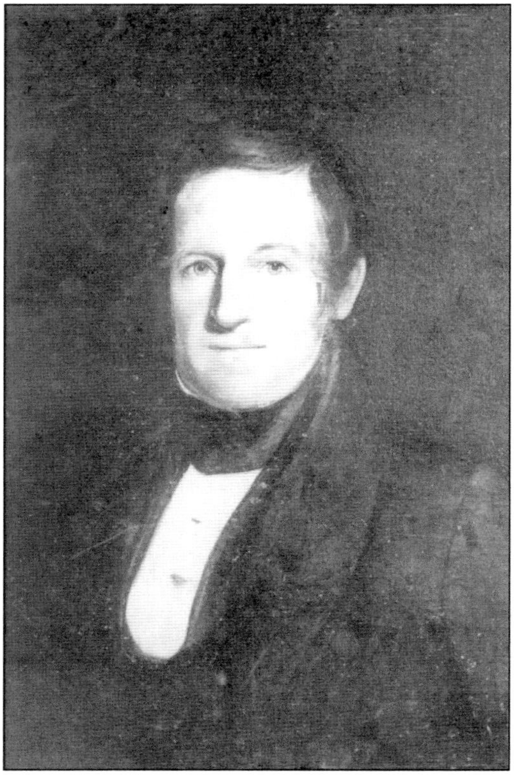

COL. JOSIAH BELLOWS III. Josiah Bellows III was born in Walpole on November 25, 1788, son of Josiah Bellows II and Rebekah Sparhawk. Known as "Handsome Si," he was popular, active, and influential in town affairs. During the War of 1812, he led a company of Walpole men in defense of Portsmouth. In 1813, he married Stella Czarina Bradley, daughter of Stephen Rowe Bradley. She died in 1833, followed quickly by their four children. He was married again in 1840 to Mary Ann Hosmer, widow of Walpole native Dr. Alfred Hosmer. Their son Josiah Grahme Bellows was born on July 24, 1841. The colonel died on January 13, 1842. His North Main Street home (below) remained in the Bellows family until the 1940s.

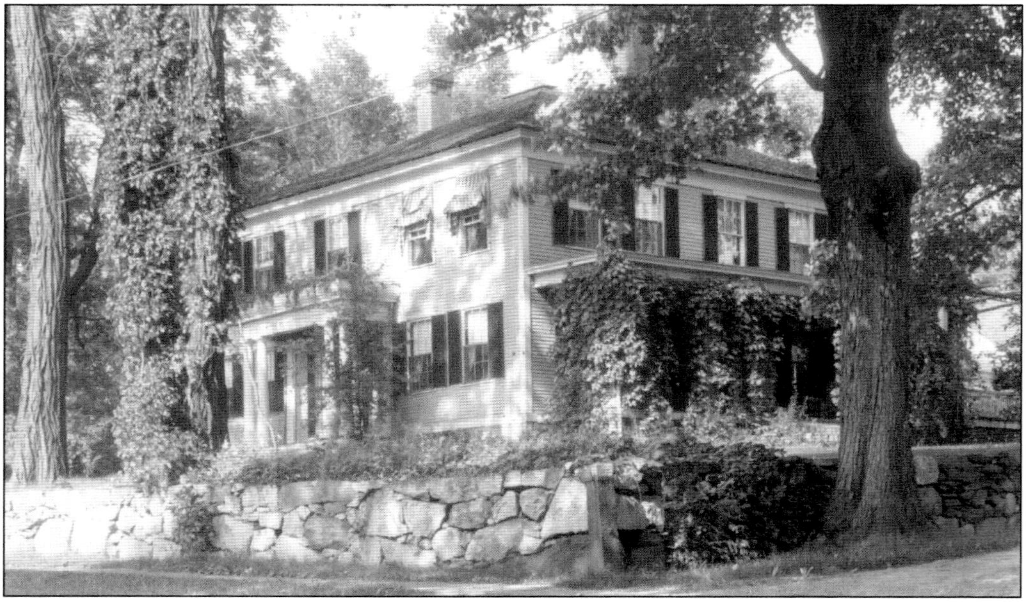

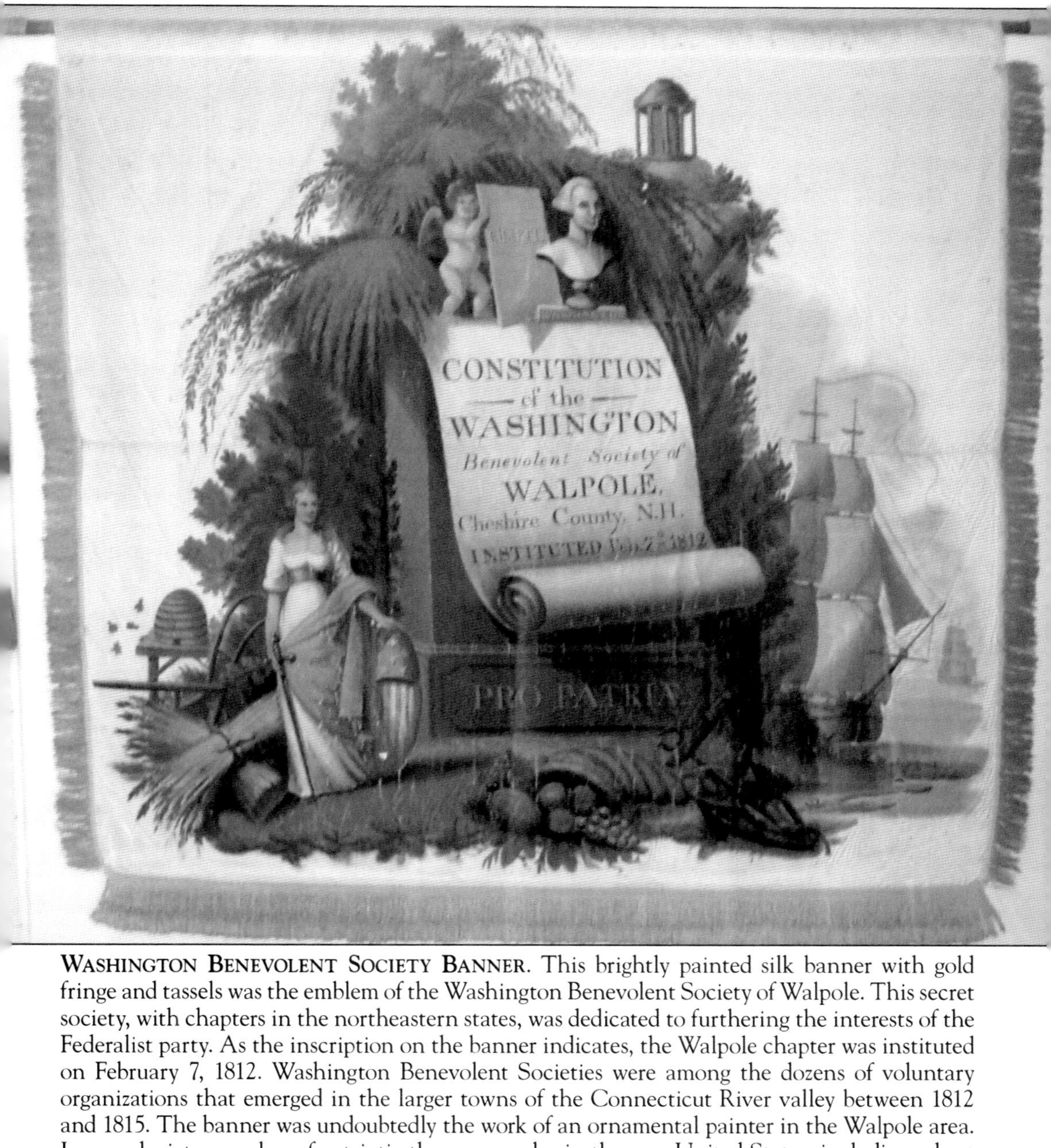

WASHINGTON BENEVOLENT SOCIETY BANNER. This brightly painted silk banner with gold fringe and tassels was the emblem of the Washington Benevolent Society of Walpole. This secret society, with chapters in the northeastern states, was dedicated to furthering the interests of the Federalist party. As the inscription on the banner indicates, the Walpole chapter was instituted on February 7, 1812. Washington Benevolent Societies were among the dozens of voluntary organizations that emerged in the larger towns of the Connecticut River valley between 1812 and 1815. The banner was undoubtedly the work of an ornamental painter in the Walpole area. Images depict a number of patriotic themes popular in the new United States, including a bust of George Washington, Columbia standing with sword and shield near agricultural symbols, and a cornucopia leading the eye to anchor and ships, symbolizing commerce.

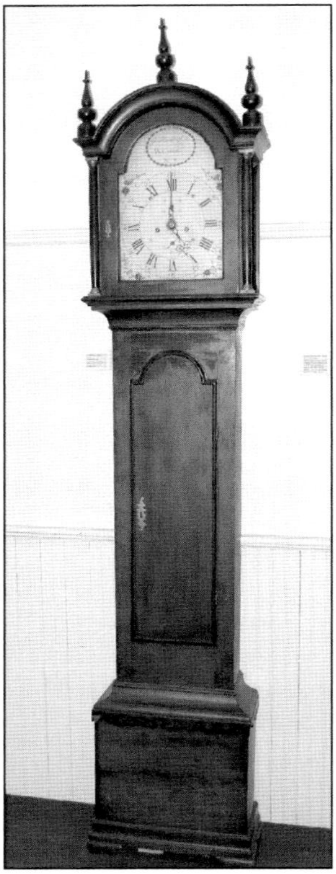

GURDON HUNTINGTON, CLOCK MAKER. Gurdon Huntington (1763–1804) was a goldsmith and clock maker who moved to Walpole with his wife and child in 1789. In addition to plying his trade, he served as Walpole's postmaster. Several examples of Huntington's clocks are known to exist in private collections in the United States, as well as some scientific instruments. One such clock, signed by Huntington, is part of the Walpole Historical Society's collection.

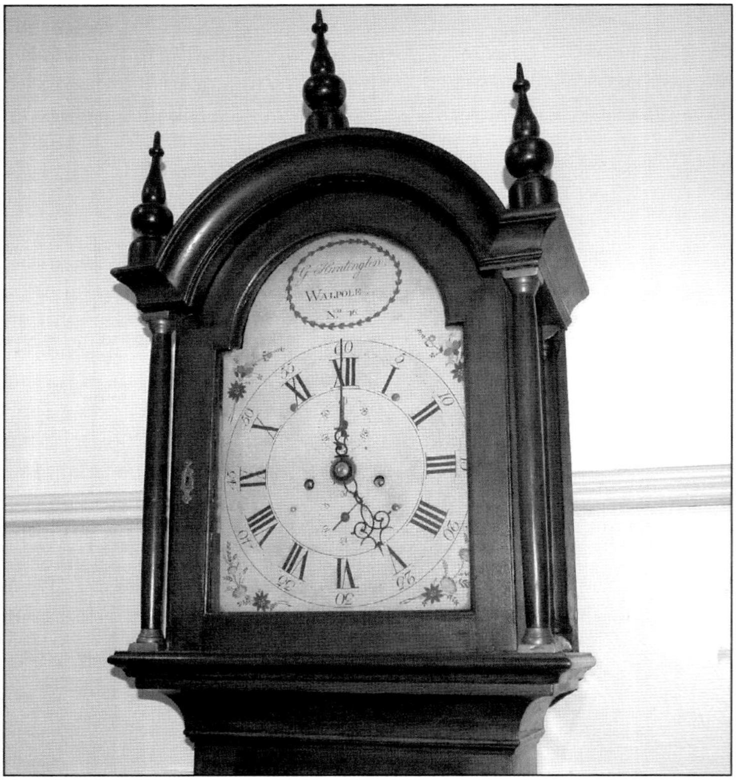

WALPOLE SOCIETY

FOR BRINGING TO JUSTICE

HORSE THIEVES AND PILFERERS

ORGANIZED IN 1816. INCORPORATED 1835.

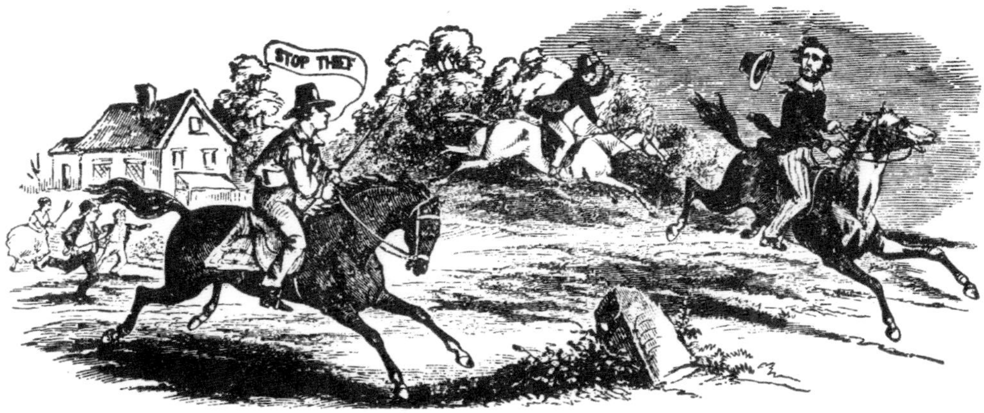

WALPOLE SOCIETY FOR BRINGING TO JUSTICE HORSE THIEVES AND PILFERERS. The Walpole Detecting Society, founded with 89 members in 1816, was chartered in 1835 as the Walpole Society for Bringing to Justice Horse Thieves and Pilferers. In 1880, clotheslines and hen roosts were added to property protected by the group. Officers, elected annually in January, include a president, clerk, and treasurer, a committee of three, and 12 riders. The committee's duty was to investigate applications for help and to send out the riders to pursue stolen horses and thieves. The society did do some searches and returns, with its last official business in 1926. It remains a social organization open to any gentleman resident of Walpole who pays the $2 lifetime membership fee and signs the bylaws. The group holds a banquet every two years for members and invited guests.

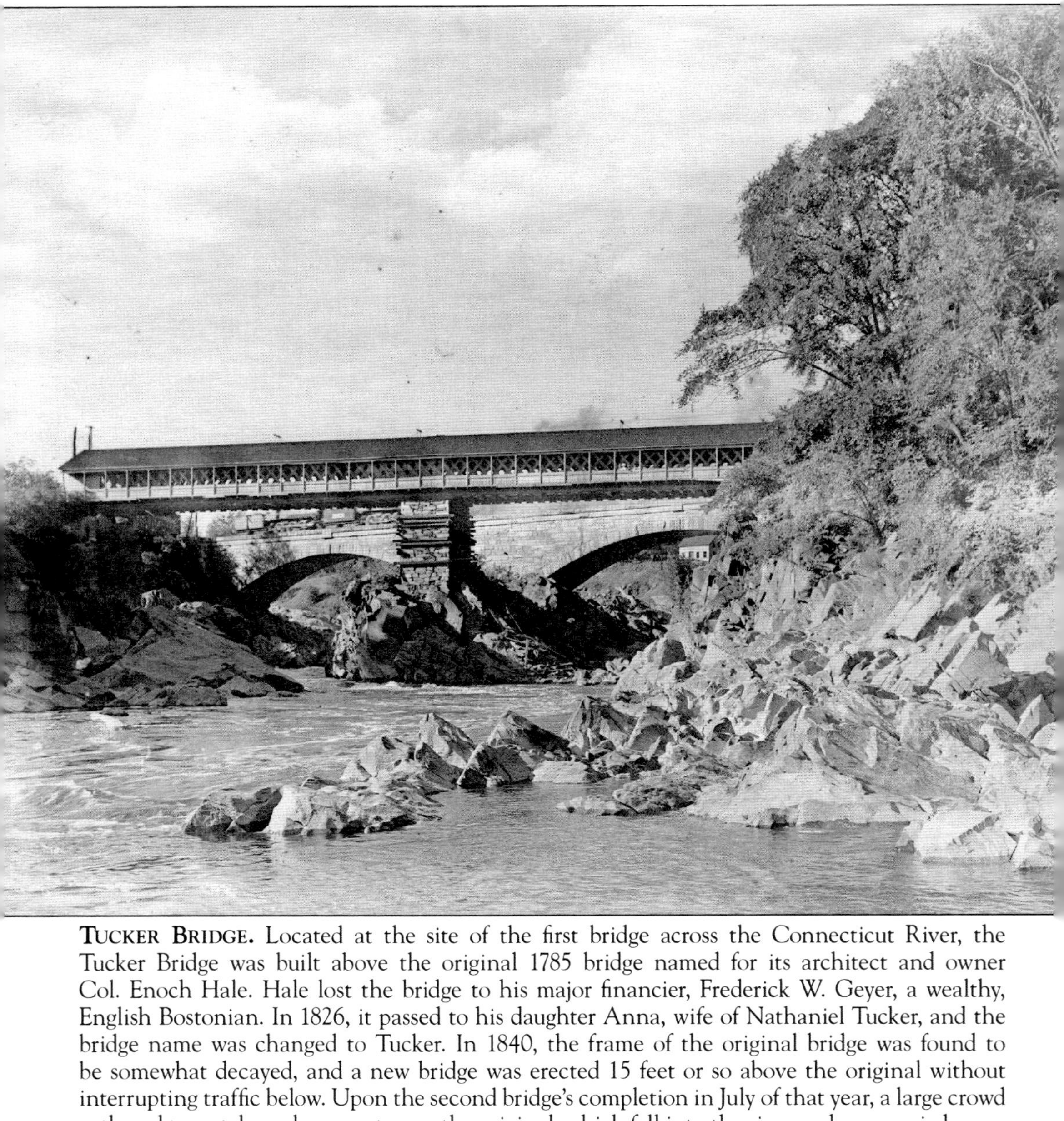

TUCKER BRIDGE. Located at the site of the first bridge across the Connecticut River, the Tucker Bridge was built above the original 1785 bridge named for its architect and owner Col. Enoch Hale. Hale lost the bridge to his major financier, Frederick W. Geyer, a wealthy, English Bostonian. In 1826, it passed to his daughter Anna, wife of Nathaniel Tucker, and the bridge name was changed to Tucker. In 1840, the frame of the original bridge was found to be somewhat decayed, and a new bridge was erected 15 feet or so above the original without interrupting traffic below. Upon the second bridge's completion in July of that year, a large crowd gathered to watch workmen cut away the original, which fell into the river and was carried away. This picture of the (second) Tucker Bridge is from about 1915 and provides perspective of the deep gorge below the Great Falls, which both bridges spanned. Behind the Tucker Bridge is the Fitchburg Railroad bridge, which was built about 1849, replacing an earlier, wooden structure with a stone-arch base.

Four

Civil War and Recovery 1850 to 1900

In the second half of the 19th century, Walpole flourished. Growth and popularity of railroads broadened its physical and cultural horizons. The new village of North Walpole emerged. The railroads also brought visitors to town, and inns were built to house them. By the end of the century, bicycles and even automobiles were seen on the as-yet-unpaved streets, and the telephone had made its debut.

Businesses in Walpole were bustling. "In the village are seven stores, one hotel and three meeting houses . . . There are two shoe manufactories, one shirt manufactory where about 250 hands are engaged, one carriage factory, besides some 12 or 15 other shops . . . Drewsville had several handsome residences, two stores and several manufacturing establishments. The population was 2,034, with 12,771 sheep, 1,538 neat stock and 370 horses," according to *New Hampshire As It Is* in 1856.

As a result of this prosperity, Walpoleans sought entertainment. Performances by local choral groups, theatrical troupes, and dancers were commonplace. Winter sleigh rides were a popular diversion. There were numerous dances, for which the lower floor of the town hall was advertised as "free from dripping creosote from the stove pipe." Also thriving were reading clubs, Shakespeare clubs, Dickens clubs, and a Sorrel Club, where a group of young women blackened their faces, wore pants, and performed minstrel shows for their own amusement.

All was not gaiety, however. On the morning of April 12, 1861, when news of the firing on Fort Sumter arrived in Walpole, the mood change was instantaneous, "and the whole north rose as one man." In the summer of 1862, with more soldiers needed, Walpole started to raise a company of enlisted men. The town took on the look of a garrison, with camps dotting the common and streets resounding with martial fife and drum music," according to Josiah G. Bellows in his *Reminiscences*. There were 185 soldiers credited to the town, including volunteers and substitutes. Nine died of disease, four were killed outright, eight were wounded, and six were missing. Dr. Henry W. Bellows of Walpole conceived the idea of the U.S. Sanitary Commission and was joined in the mission by several townspeople.

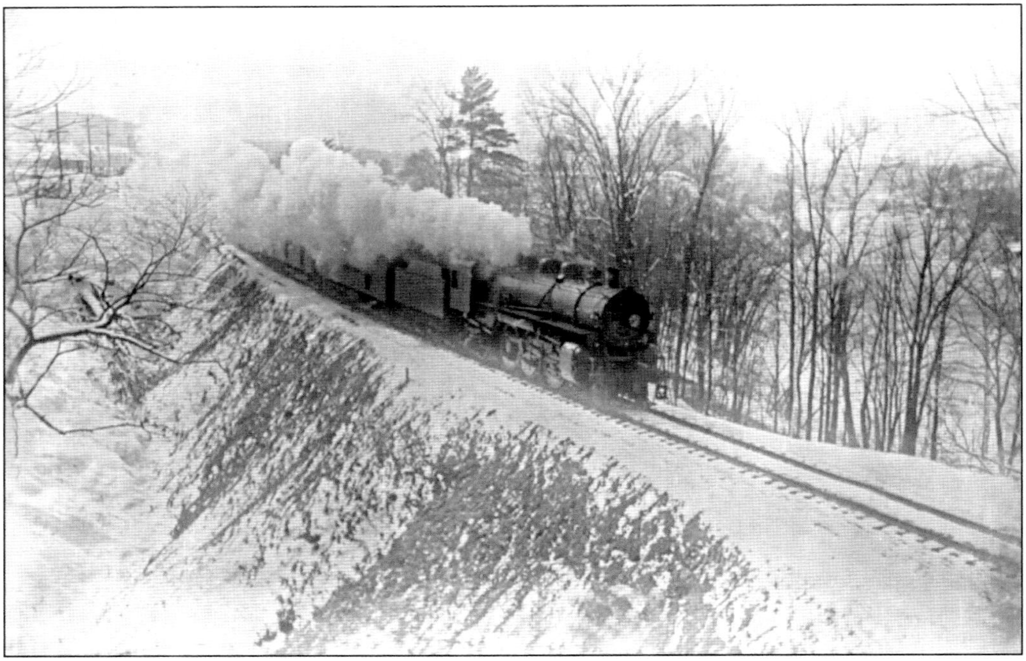

CHESHIRE RAILROAD AND WALPOLE DEPOT. Above, an unidentified steam engine runs toward Walpole depot along the Connecticut River. The first locomotive over the Cheshire Railroad in the fall of 1848 was run up from Keene as far as the end of the track in Westmoreland. Two four-horse teams drew it, dismantled, by the incomplete section in Walpole and set it up just over the Charlestown line. The first train ran over the line on January 1, 1849, with a trainload of excursionists from Boston to Charlestown. Below is an early photograph of the Walpole depot at the foot of Depot Hill on Westminster Street. Seen in the background is the Westminster Covered Bridge under construction in 1870.

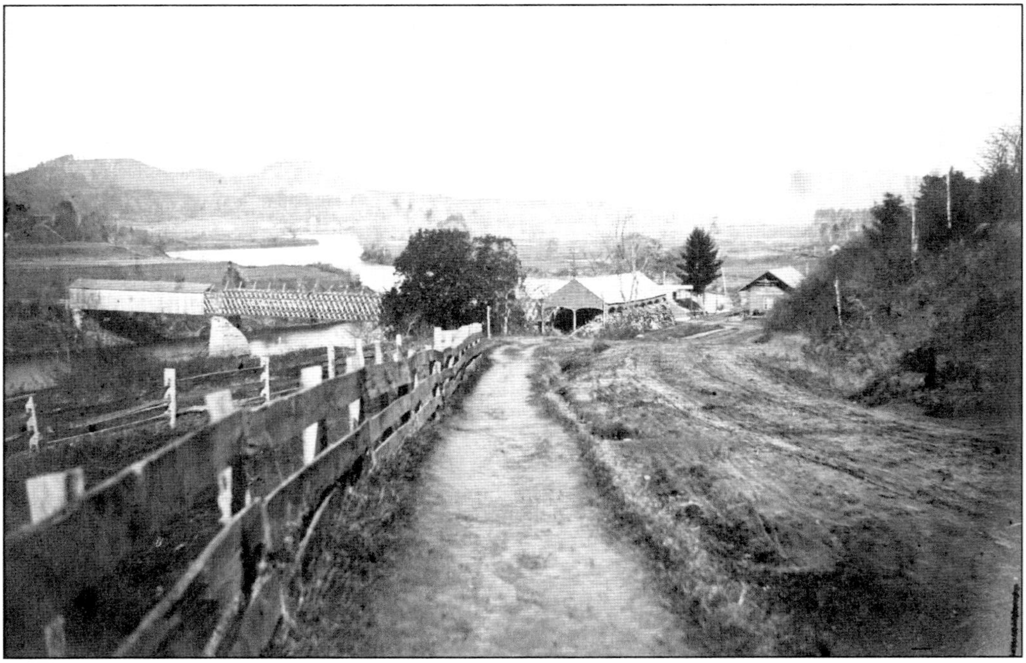

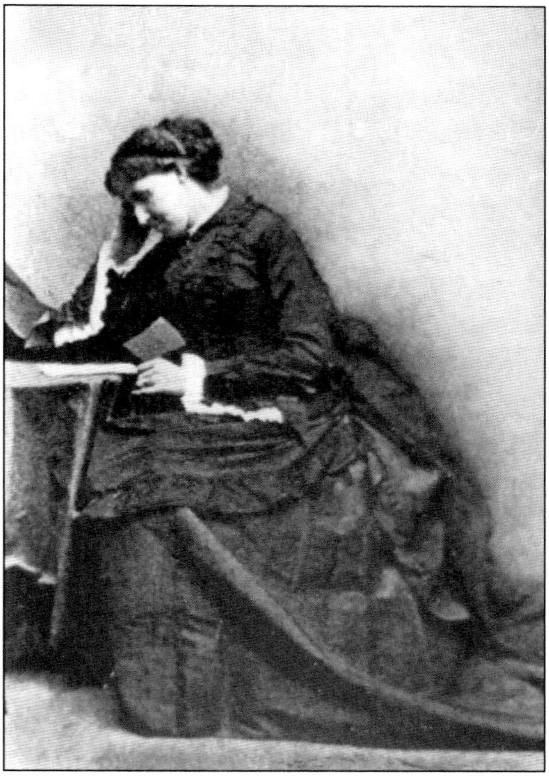

DRAMATIC PROGRAMS. Louisa May Alcott (right) and her family lived with her uncle Benjamin Willis in Walpole for several years, arriving about 1850. Her poem *Under the Lilacs* was written while staying at the Knapp house, where lush lilac hedges still grace the home. Her book *Little Women* is descriptive of the lives of the young Alcott sisters when they lived in Walpole. A favorite reading/resting place for Alcott along Mad Brook is now named Alcott Falls. Alcott took part in local theatrical productions that were staged in various homes throughout the town. The program below, dated 1855, lists her and her sister as cast members.

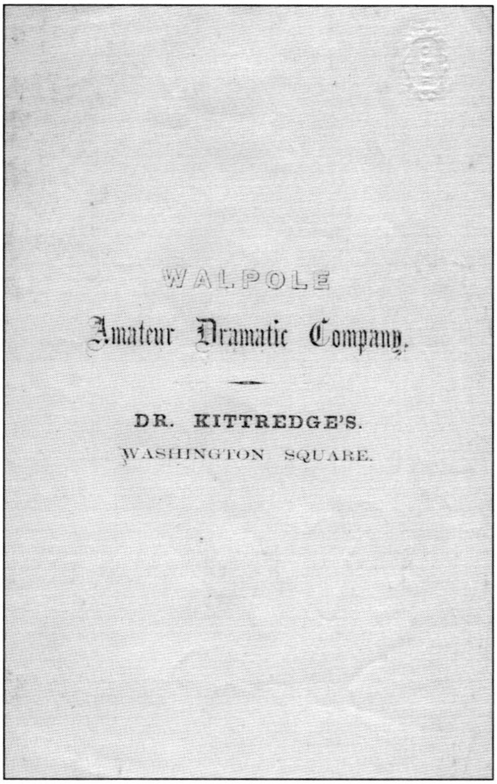

WALPOLE

Amateur Dramatic Company.

DR. KITTREDGE'S.

WASHINGTON SQUARE.

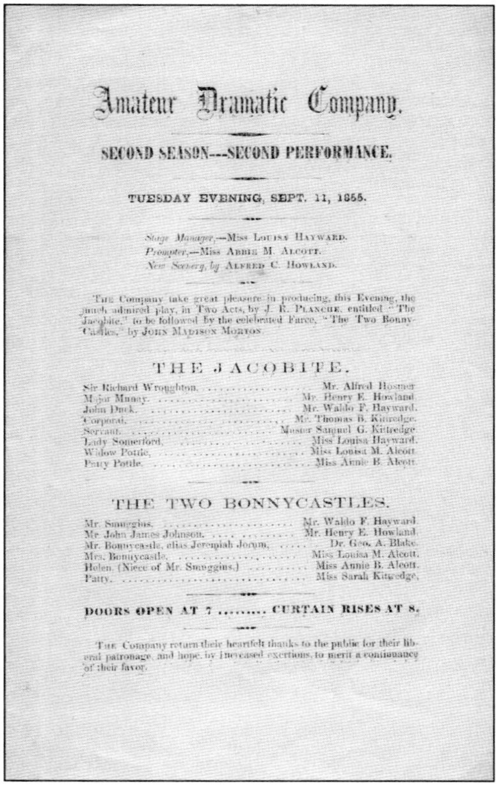

Amateur Dramatic Company.

SECOND SEASON---SECOND PERFORMANCE.

TUESDAY EVENING, SEPT. 11, 1855.

Stage Manager,—Miss Louisa Hayward.
Prompter,—Miss Abbie M. Alcott.
New Scenery, by Alfred C. Howland.

The Company take great pleasure in producing, this Evening, the much admired play, in Two Acts, by J. R. Planche, entitled "The Jacobite," to be followed by the celebrated Farce, "The Two Bonny-Castles," by John Madison Morton.

THE JACOBITE.

Sir Richard Wroughton, ... Mr. Alfred Hosmer
Major Murray, ... Mr. Henry E. Howland
John Duck, ... Mr. Waldo F. Hayward.
Corporal, ... Mr. Thomas B. Kittredge.
Servant, ... Master Samuel G. Kittredge.
Lady Somerford, ... Miss Louisa Hayward.
Widow Pottle, ... Miss Louisa M. Alcott
Patty Pottle, ... Miss Annie B. Alcott.

THE TWO BONNYCASTLES.

Mr. Smuggins, ... Mr. Waldo F. Hayward.
Mr John James Johnson, ... Mr. Henry E. Howland.
Mr. Bonnycastle, alias Jeremiah Jorum, ... Dr. Geo. A. Blake.
Mrs. Bonnycastle, ... Miss Louisa M. Alcott.
Helen, (Niece of Mr. Smuggins,) .... Miss Annie B. Alcott.
Patty, ... Miss Sarah Kittredge,

DOORS OPEN AT 7 .... CURTAIN RISES AT 8.

The Company return their heartfelt thanks to the public for their liberal patronage, and hope, by increased exertions, to merit a continuance of their favor.

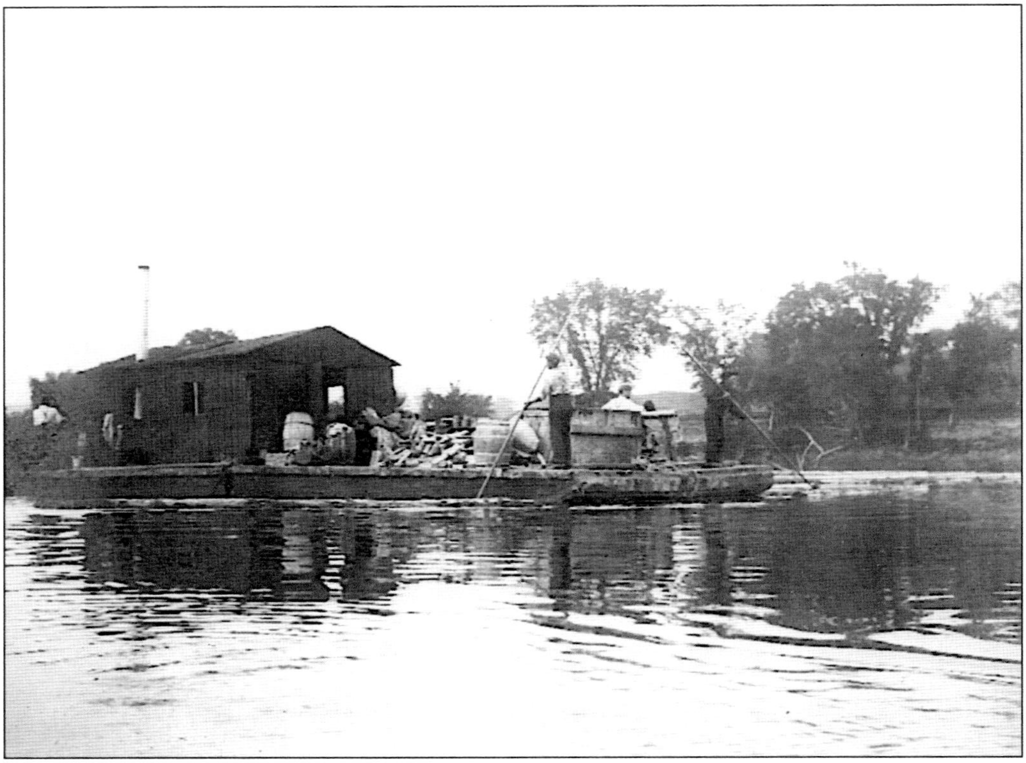

FERRIES. The Connecticut River was a watery obstacle to trade between the towns of Westminster and Bellows Falls in Vermont and Walpole. In the mid-1800s, bridges were built to span the river, but ferries still carried passengers from shore to shore. The photographs show ferrymen poling their laden ferry from Halls Crossing in Walpole to Westminster, Vermont.

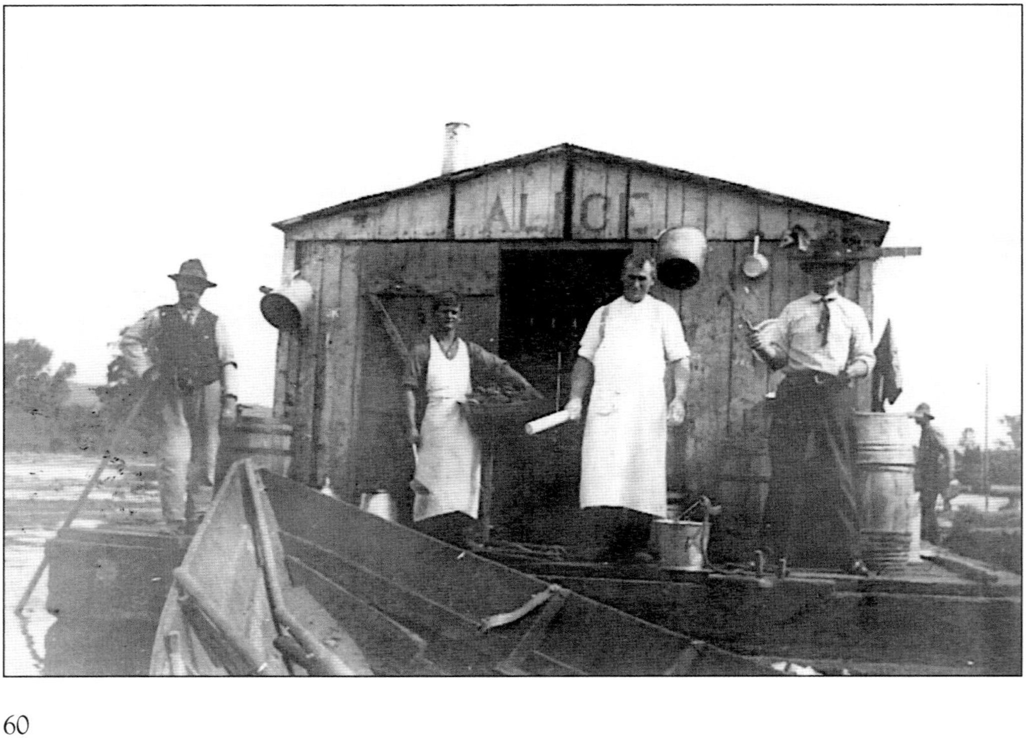

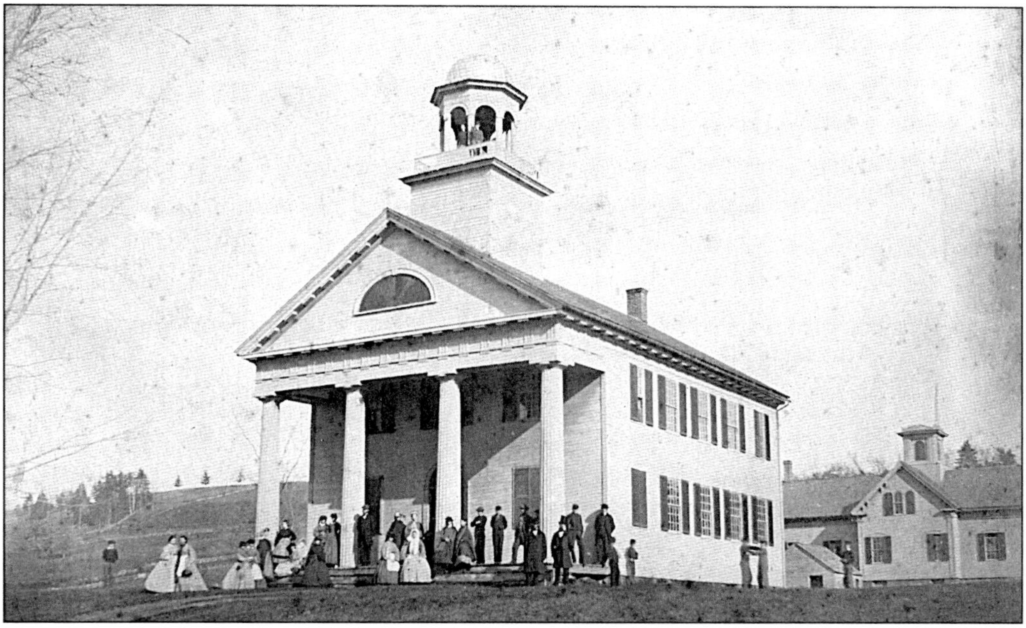

The Academy, 1860. Here is yet another view of the Walpole Academy building, now the home of the Walpole Historical Society. At the time of this photograph in 1851, it was recently purchased by the town of Walpole for public education. Note this photograph was taken prior to construction of the rear addition and the reforestation of the town. The historical society museum has an extensive collection of clothing from this and later periods in Walpole history.

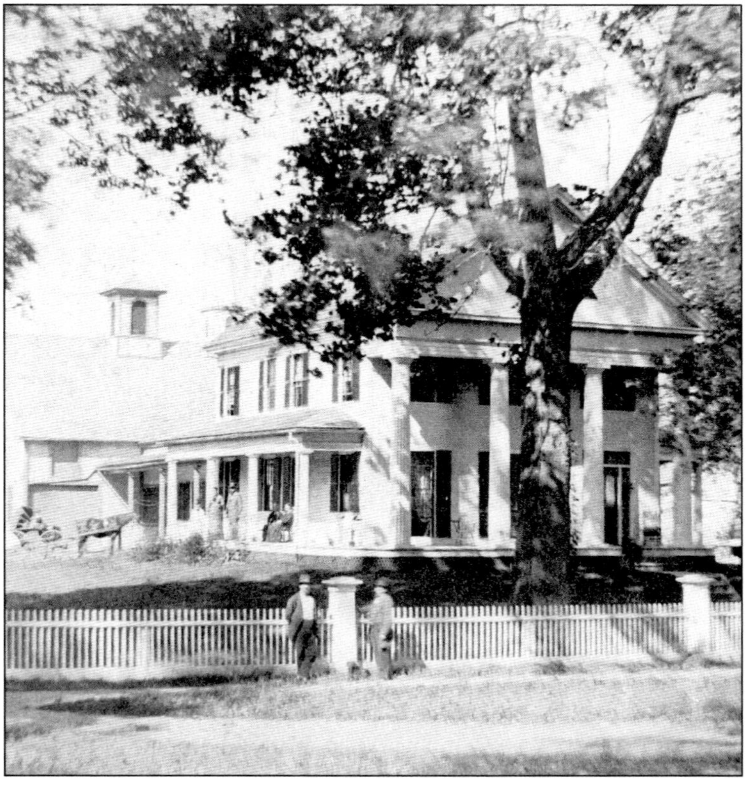

Peck House. Philip Peck, a clerk in Buffum's mercantile store, built this Greek Revival home in 1840. Sold in 1846 to Henry Foster, the house changed hands several times until 1875, when Dr. Winslow Porter and his family bought it and lived in it for many years. The home is across the street from the Buffum house and the Walpole Historical Society, both also fine examples of the Greek Revival style of architecture that was fashionable in this period.

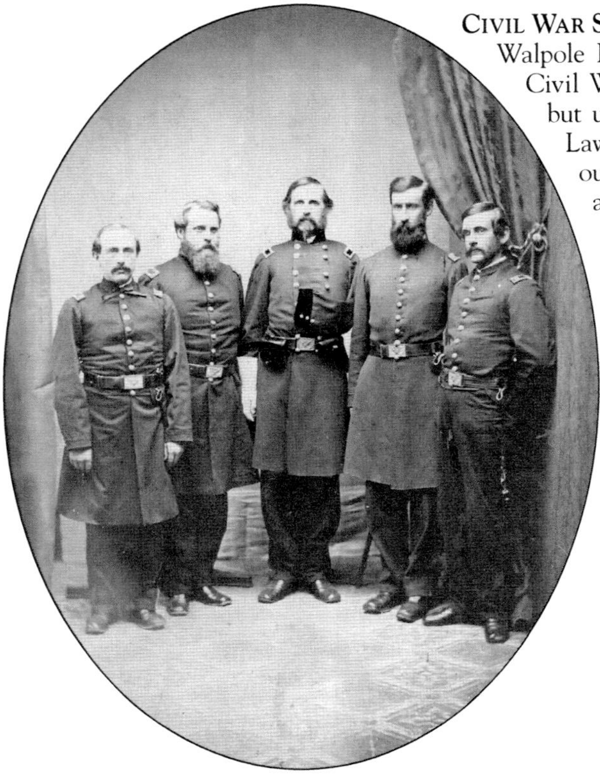

Civil War Soldiers This photograph, found in the Walpole Historical Society archives, shows five Civil War soldiers, presumably from Walpole but unidentified. Walpole soldier Benjamin Lawrence was one of 27 Union soldiers—out of an original 600—left standing at the battle of Aldie. He later died of wounds received in the fight. Fifty-eight residents of Walpole enlisted in the Civil War; another 20 from Walpole enlisted in out-of-state regiments.

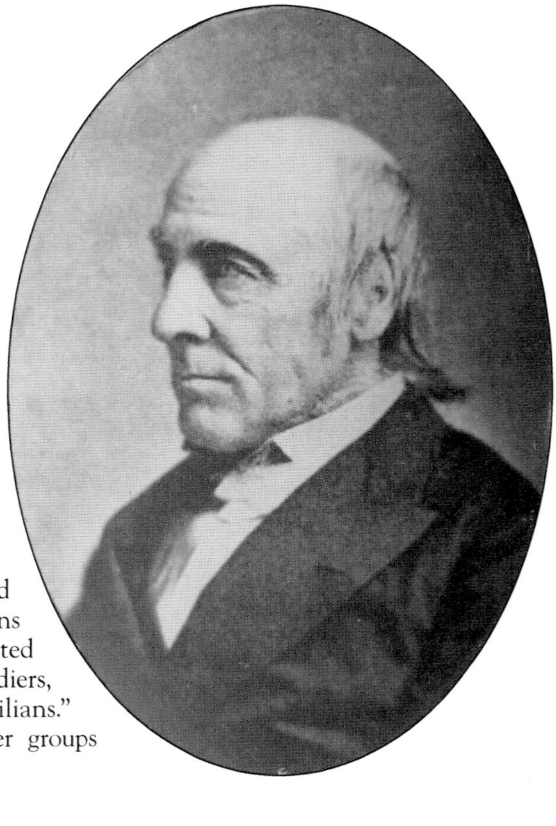

U.S. Sanitary Commission. Walpole's Dr. Henry W. Bellows was the renowned pastor of All Soul's Church in New York City. He conceived the U.S. Sanitary Commission at the start of the Civil War and was its president, recruiting several Walpoleans for important posts. The commission, dedicated to preventing spread of disease among soldiers, was "organized . . . run, and funded by civilians." Churches, ladies' organizations, and other groups volunteered desperately needed goods.

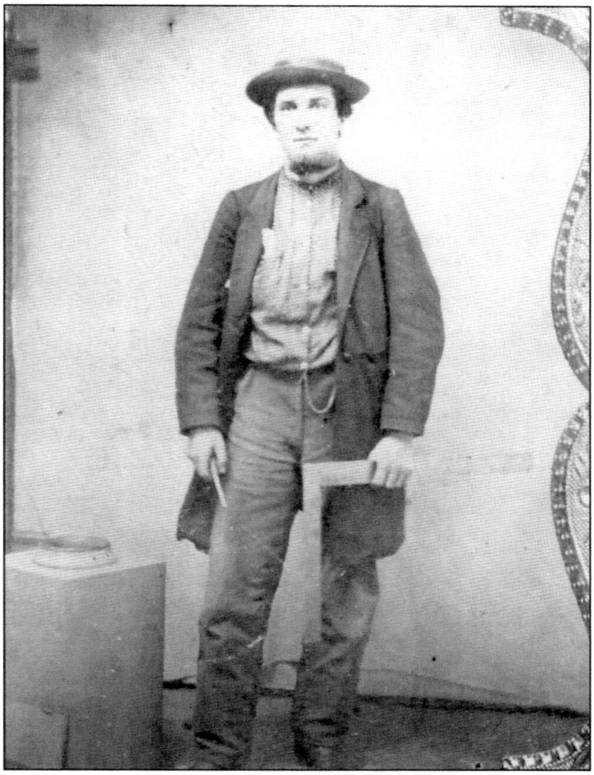

THERON BURT. Grandson of Revolutionary War soldier Moses Burt, Theron Burt was born in 1836 and died in 1863. He was married to Mary Collins and was a woodworker by trade. Interestingly, Holland Burt, a renowned Walpole cabinetmaker, was no relation. Cabinet- and furniture making were common in Walpole, due to the number of waterpowered sawmills that have existed here since 1756. (Courtesy of Historical Society of Cheshire County.)

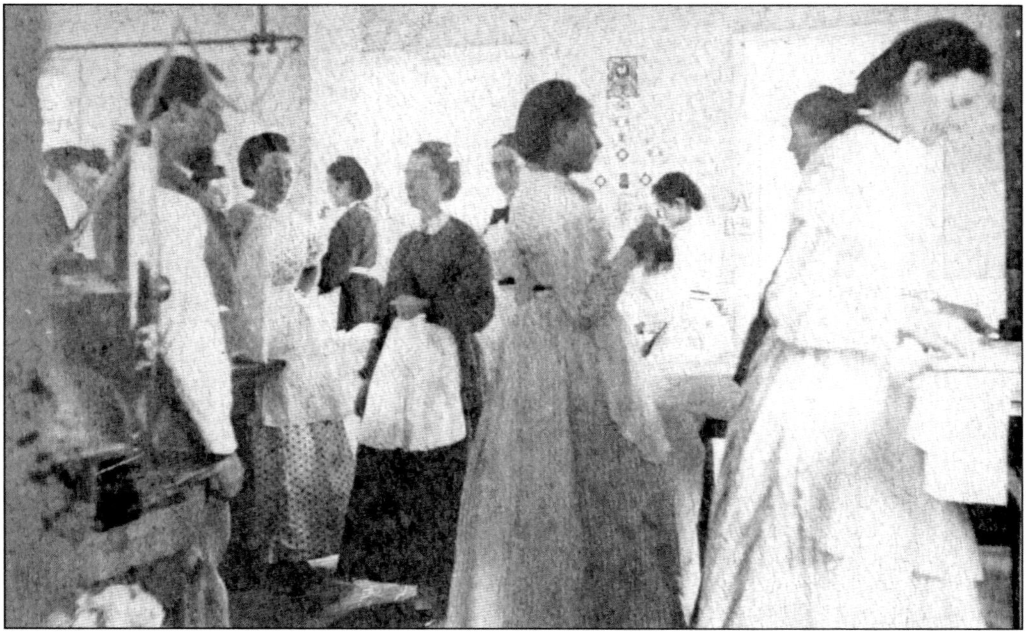

WALPOLE SHIRT FACTORY. In 1864, the Bates and Aldrich Company began the manufacture of shirts, employing "some sixty females and half a dozen males in their factory, besides a large number of seamstresses living in and out of town. They paid their help liberally . . . and a great share of employees' earnings was spent in town," according to George Aldrich. In their day, they were the largest manufacturer of shirts exclusively in the country. The company closed in 1876.

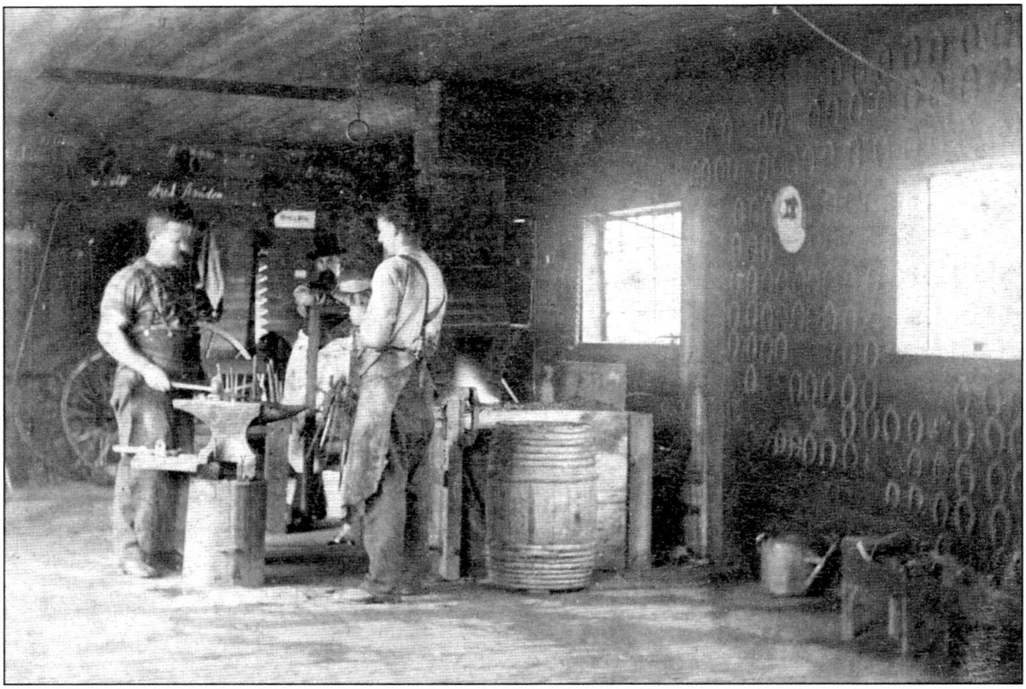

Blacksmith and Livery. The blacksmith shop interior (above) is unidentified but one of several in Walpole. Many of Walpole's larger farms had "smithies" of their own. The blacksmith shop below was located at Turnpike and North Streets. Situated at a busy intersection of two major routes, north to Canada and south to Boston, Walpole's blacksmiths, stables, carriage makers, and liveries flourished during the late 1800s. The Turnpike Street shop also doubled as the town jail of lockup from 1888 to 1952. After its demolition in 1952, the lockup was in the basement of town hall or at the county jail.

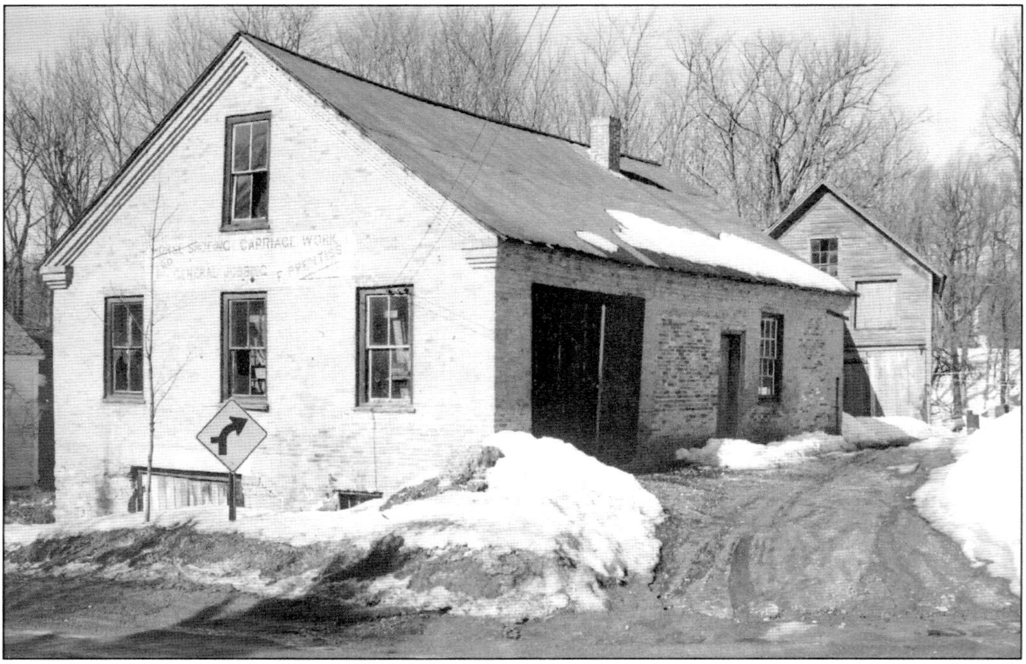

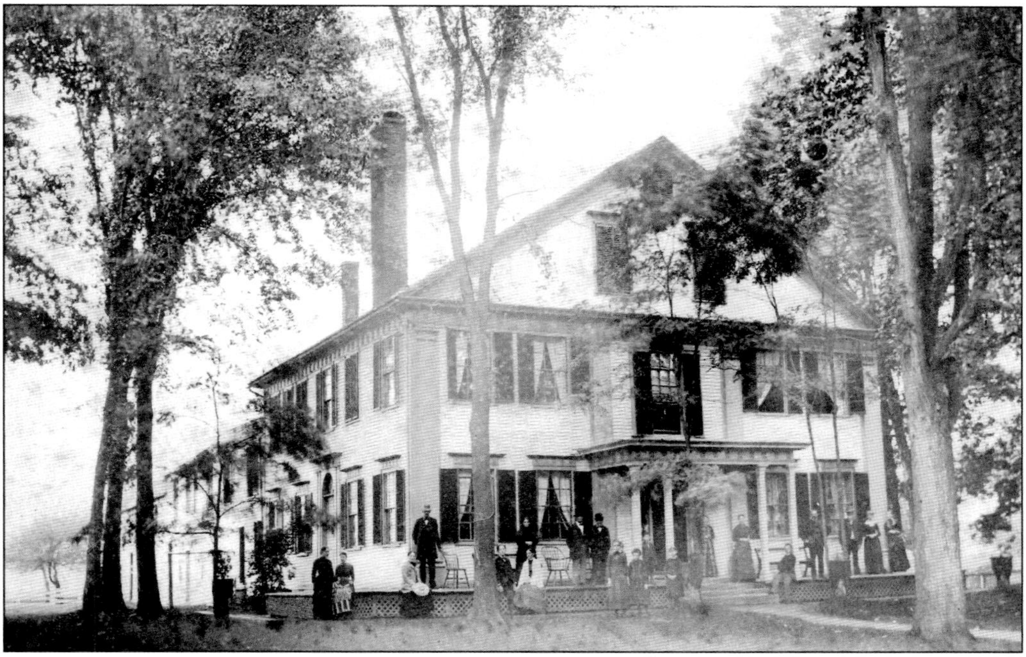

THE ELMWOOD. This home, located on the Walpole common, was built by David Stone in 1811. It has served as a summer boardinghouse for tourists (at times named the Elmwood and later the Old Colony Inn). The upstairs balcony (added after this photograph was taken) was where author James Michener wrote parts of his book *Hawaii*.

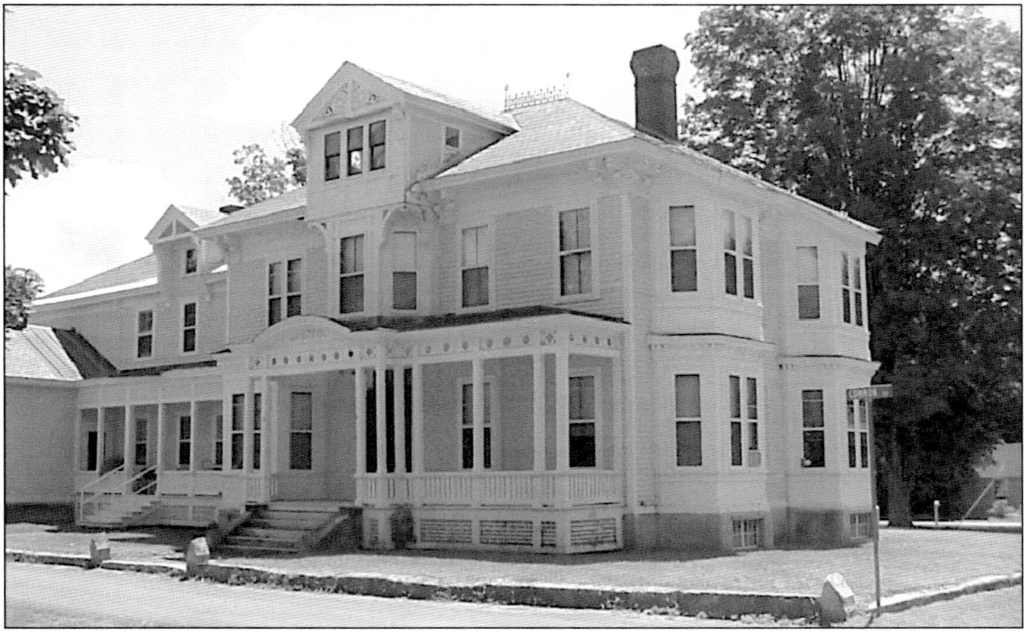

THE MANSION, DREWSVILLE COMMON. The Lovell and Lathrop families owned or sold at least seven Drewsville properties between 1850 and 1890. When the families combined, Sarah Lathrop-Lovell built the Drewsville mansion in 1880 on the site of her parents' home on the old Cheshire Turnpike at the head of the common. This home is a sample of the vernacular stick style, seldom used in the region.

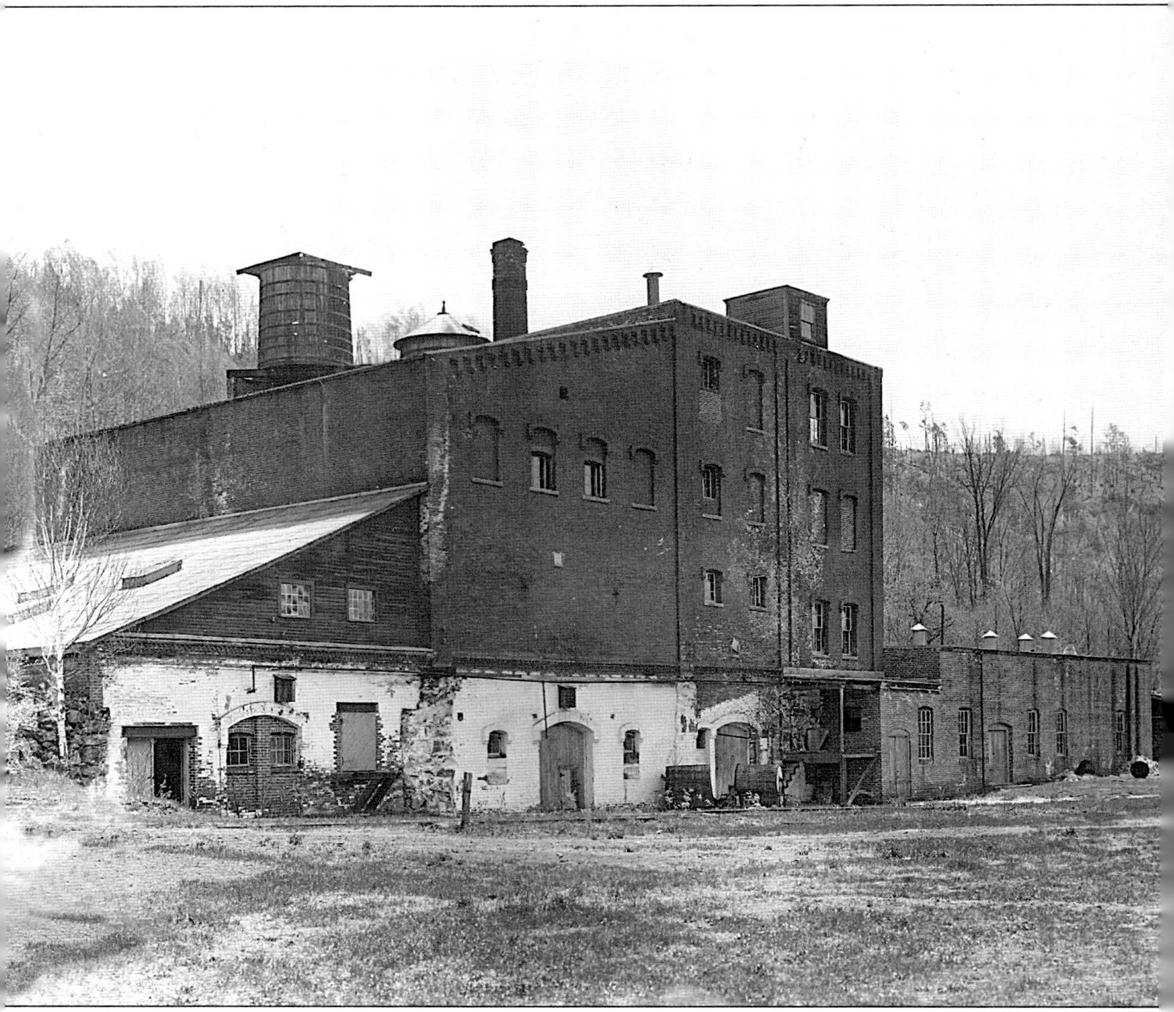

MOUNTAIN SPRING BREWERY. In the spring of 1877, Walker, Blake and Company erected a large beer brewery, five stories high and made of brick, on Cold River. It was built after a model shown at the centennial in Philadelphia and was the first of its type in the country. The 1880 Walpole history notes, "The business is in successful operation, employing eleven hands constantly, making about 15,000 barrels beer annually." It was first named the Fall Mountain brewery, but in 1893, the name was changed. After several changes in ownership, by 1904, it was defunct. It is said that one Easter Monday morning, the brewery was set afire, and the beer was allowed to run from the great vats into the river. Coincidentally, the temperance movement was active at the time.

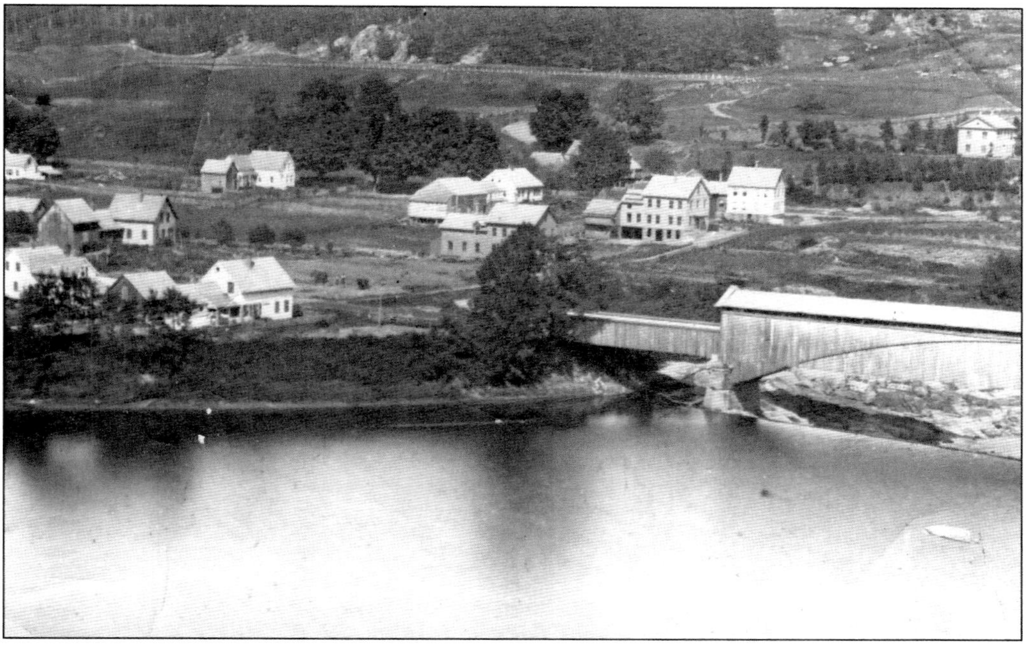

NORTH WALPOLE. Situated on the east bank of the Connecticut River at the foot of Mount Kilburn is the village of North Walpole. The photograph above, taken before 1882, and the one below, taken between 1882 and 1912, shows the remarkable growth that took place at the end of the 19th century. The construction of the railroad through North Walpole brought Dutch and Irish immigrants to the region. In the early 1900s, new Americans from Poland and Italy followed. To the right, above, is the North Walpole and Sullivan Railroad covered bridge built over the Great Falls. In the springtime during the 1890s, this section of the river could be choked with millions of feet of logs headed to the mill in Bellows Falls and to those downstream.

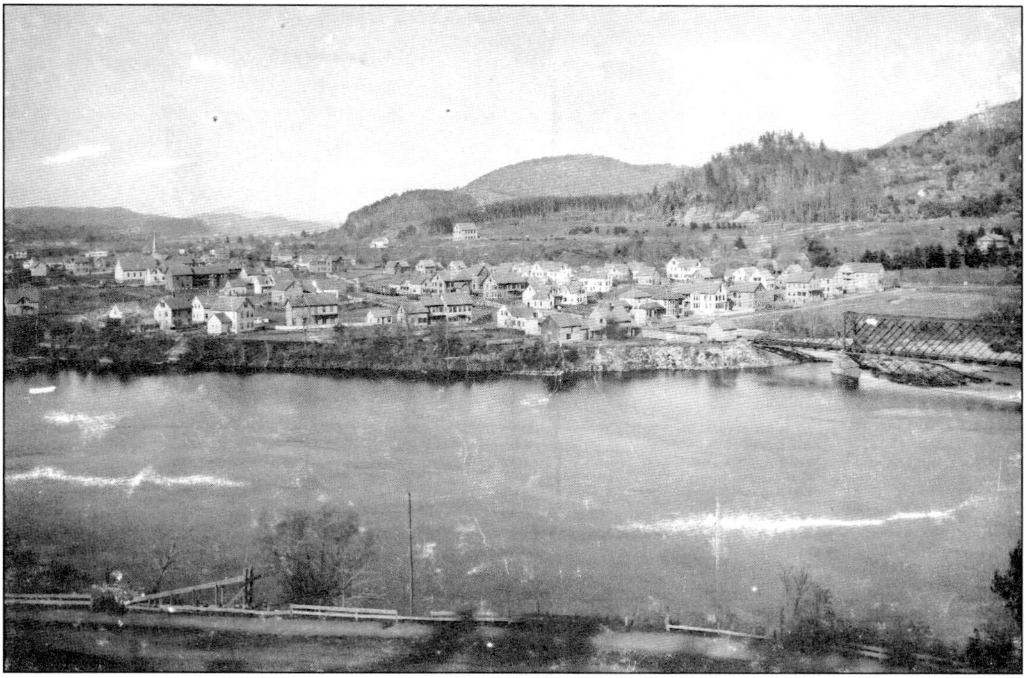

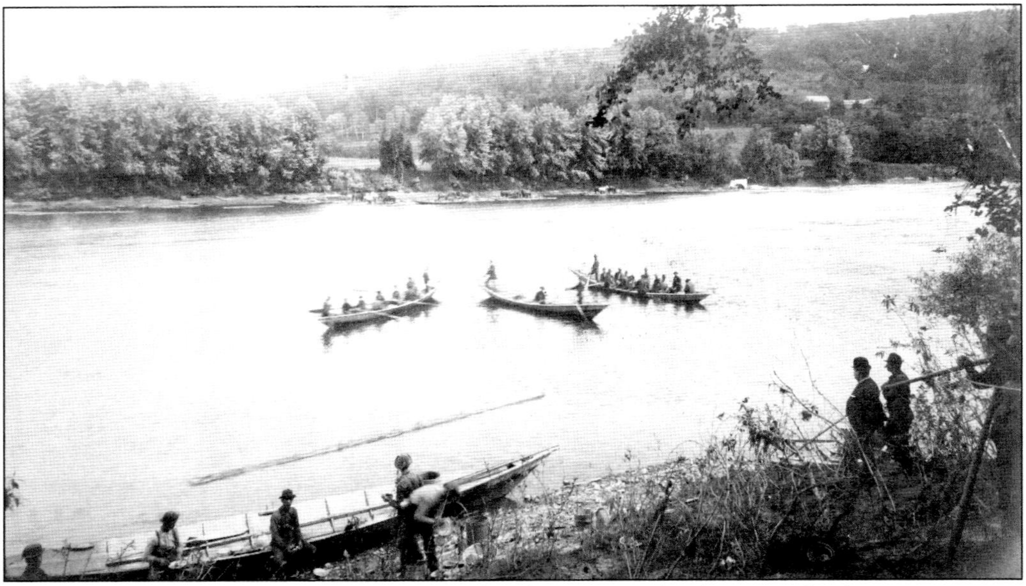

LOGGING ON THE CONNECTICUT RIVER. After the process of making wood pulp into paper was perfected in the 1870s, many million feet of logs came down the river from the northern woods in drives. In 1883, booms were constructed to control the flow of logs. In 1893, 70 million feet of lumber came through North Walpole, with up to 160 men and 40 horses working the river at a time. In the July 13, 1893, edition of the *Bellows Falls Times*, the article, "Among the Logmen," noted, "It will take until September to complete the drive, when the last of the men will be discharged, to wander back to camps up the river to go back to chopping, when their money is gone. This is the longest drive in New England—over 300 miles."

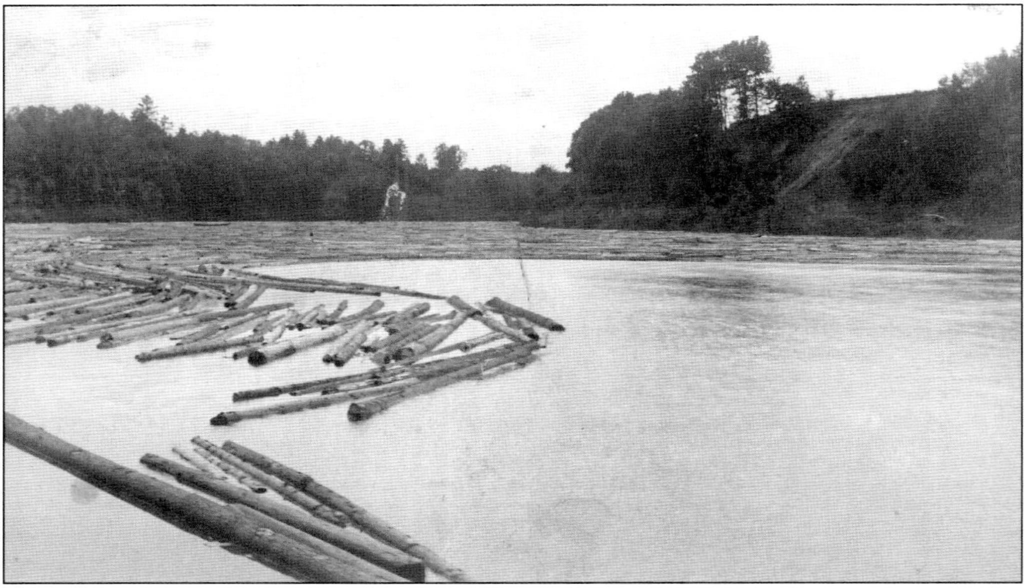

ST. PETER'S CHURCH, NORTH WALPOLE. Originally a mission church, St. Peter's was set up as a Roman Catholic parish in 1878. The church was built by volunteer labor (the foundation stone was hauled from Chester, Vermont, by horse and wagon) and was completed in time for midnight mass on December 25, 1877. The church cost $8,000 to build. (Courtesy of St. Peter's Parish.)

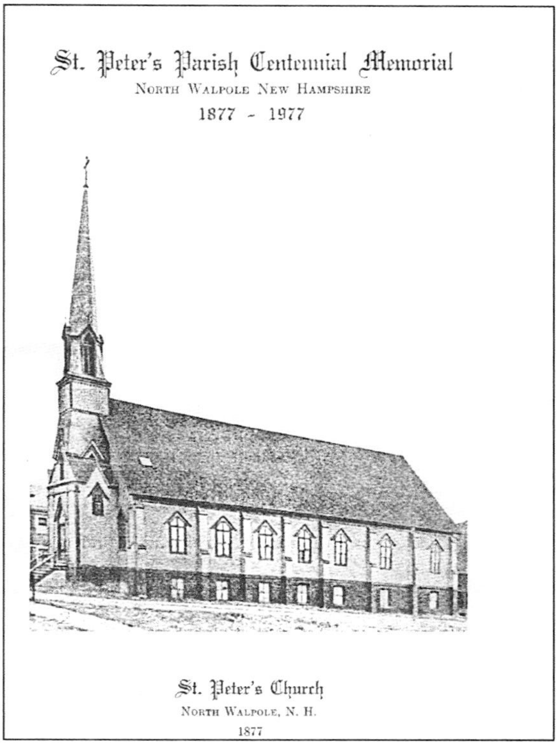

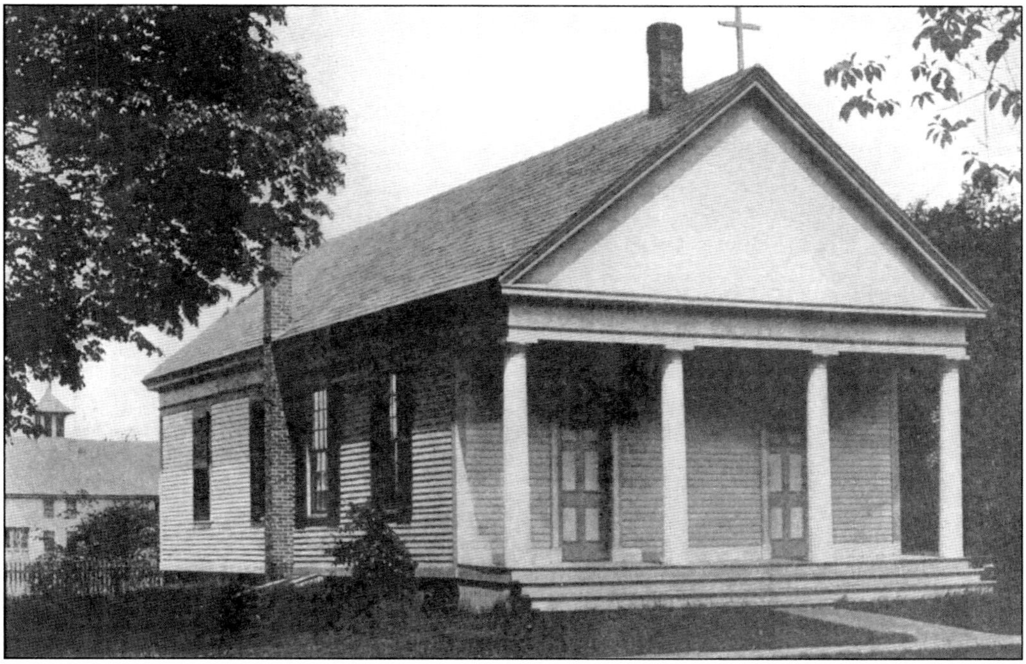

ST. JOSEPH'S CHURCH, WALPOLE. The building was built by the Methodists in 1845. The Reverend Daniel W. Murphy, who had occasionally celebrated mass in the town hall, purchased the chapel from the Episcopalians in 1869. When the parish of St. Peter's in North Walpole was established with Rev. Maurice Galvin as the first resident pastor, Walpole was attached as a mission, according to the St. Peter's 1919 Fifty Year Memorial Celebration pamphlet.

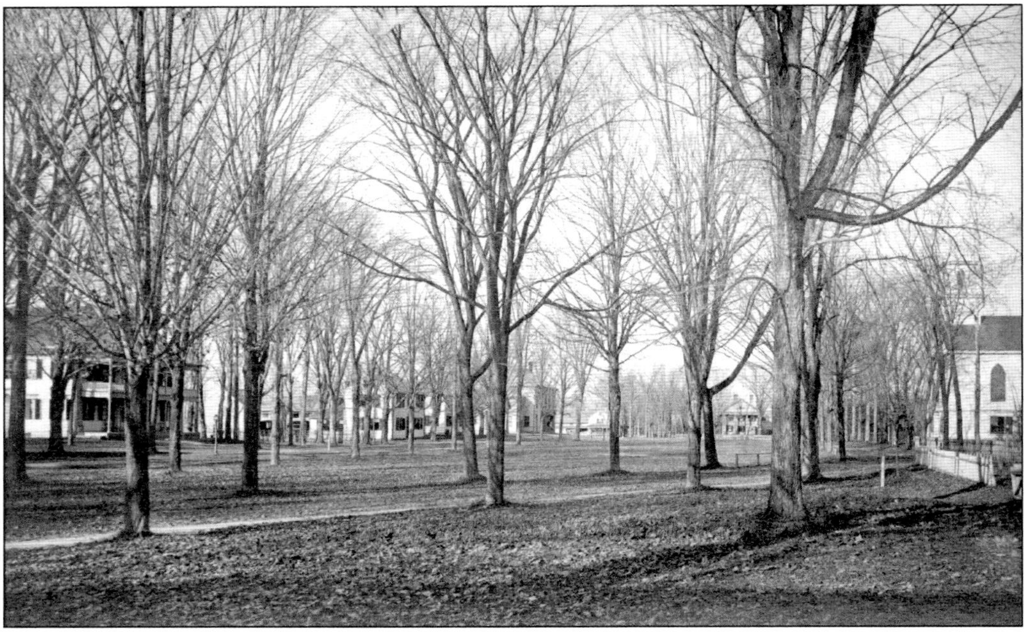

WALPOLE TOWN COMMON LOOKING NORTH. The common (also more formally known as Washington Square) has long been a location for play and gathering in the town. In 1883, there were tennis matches on the common, and in 1884, there were complaints that the baseball players were too noisy and profane. The town passed an article prohibiting cannon firing and circus exhibitions on the common.

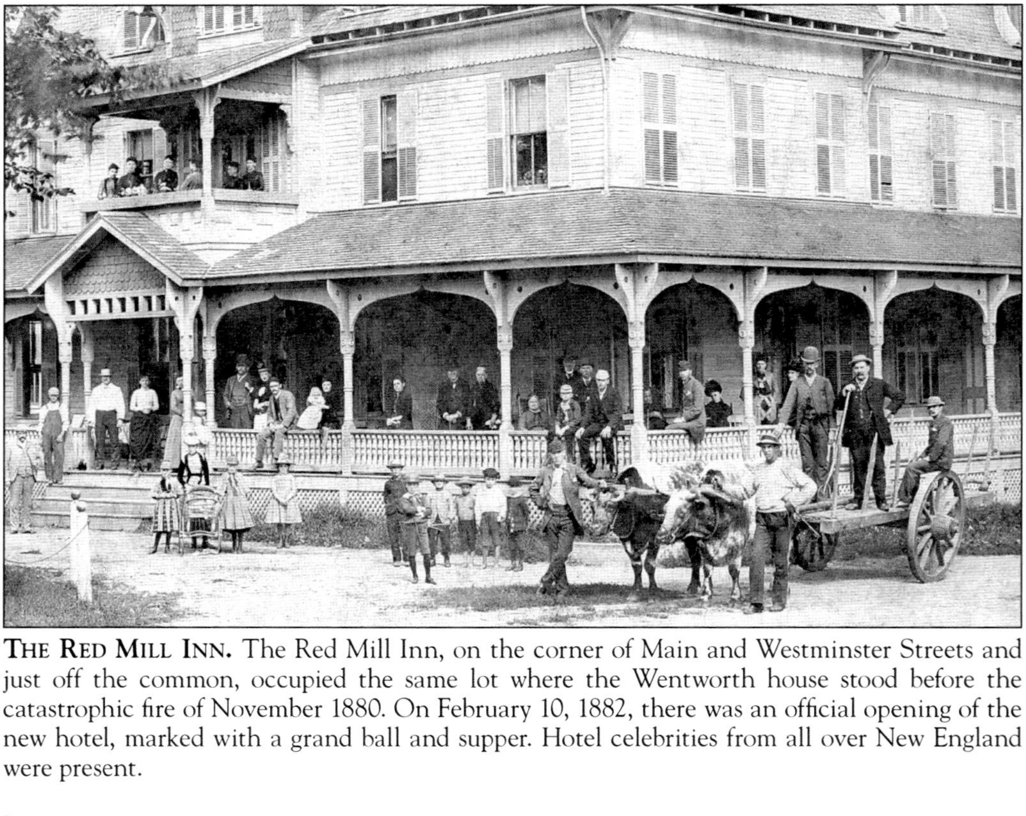

THE RED MILL INN. The Red Mill Inn, on the corner of Main and Westminster Streets and just off the common, occupied the same lot where the Wentworth house stood before the catastrophic fire of November 1880. On February 10, 1882, there was an official opening of the new hotel, marked with a grand ball and supper. Hotel celebrities from all over New England were present.

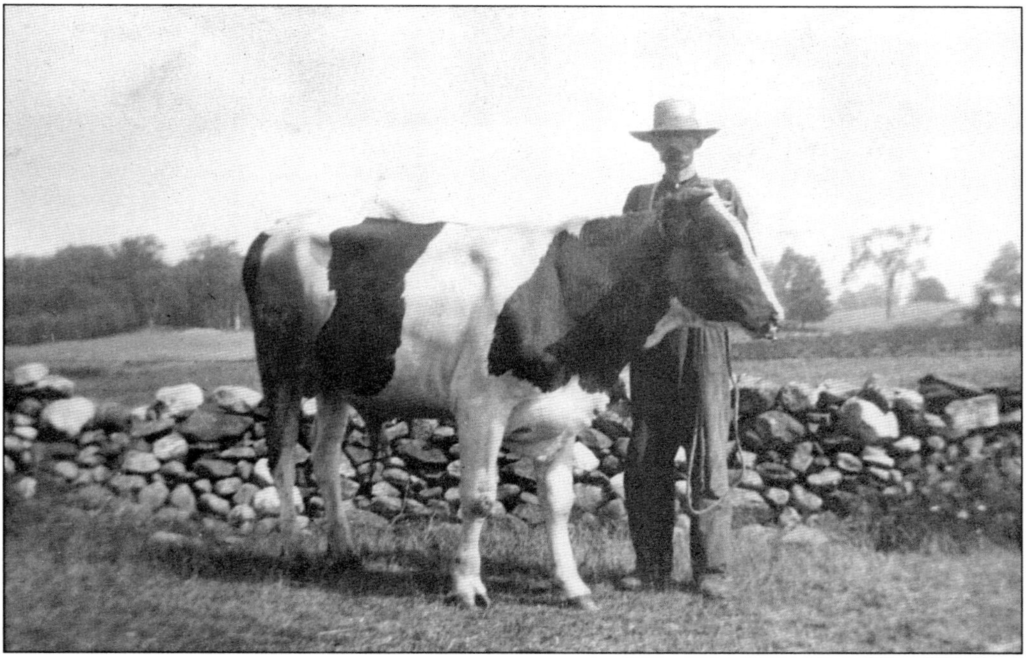

Norman Guild with Bull. This picture epitomizes the Walpole dairy farmer. The period around the Civil War was the heyday of New Hampshire agriculture and the turning point in the development of commercial agriculture, according to the University of New Hampshire's *The History and Economics of the New Hampshire Dairy Industry*. Norman Guild was the third generation in his family to farm on Ramsay Hill Road on lot No. 448. He was born in 1871 and lived until 1950. His grandfather William Guild first bought portions of lot No. 452 in 1808 and then lot No. 448 in 1821, where he settled. The land continued in the Guild family "for nearly 100 years." Elwin Guild's heirs sold the farm to Norman Guild in 1907, and the farm left the family in 1918. The Guild homestead (below) was typical of the farmhouses that dotted the Walpole countryside.

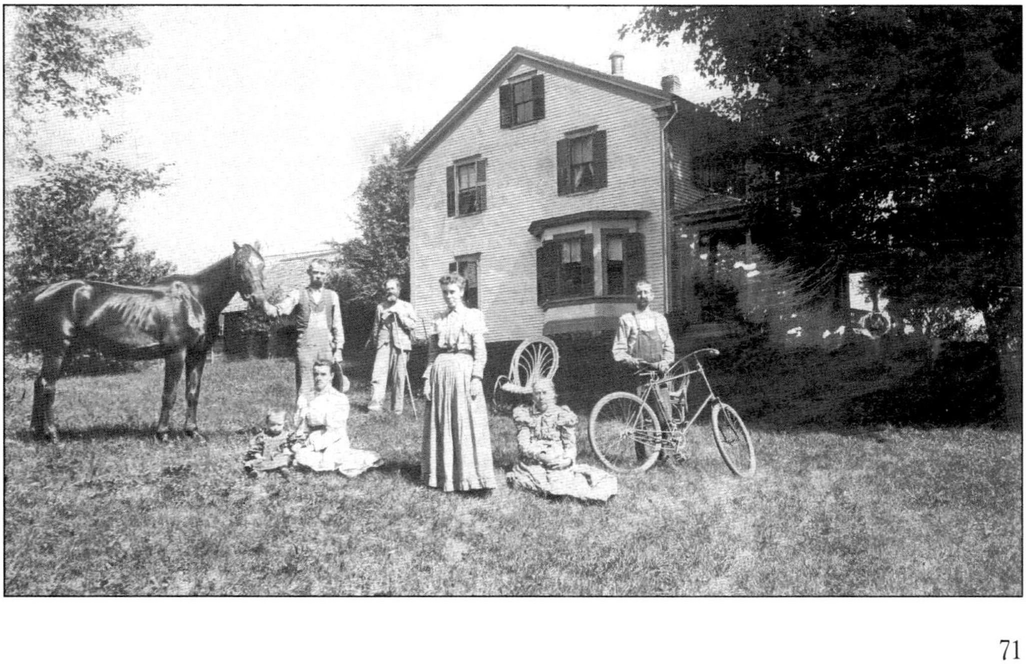

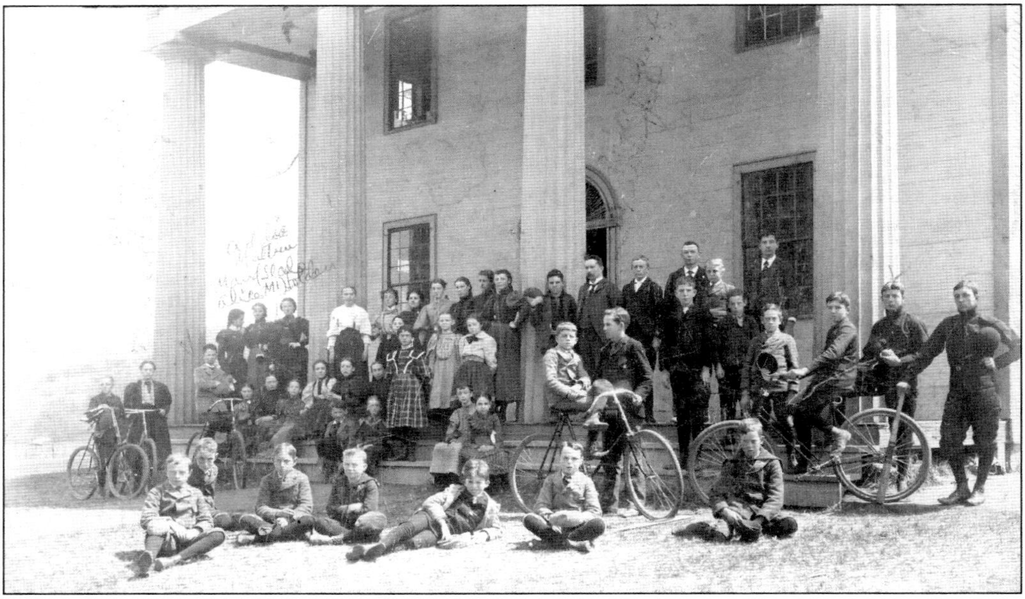

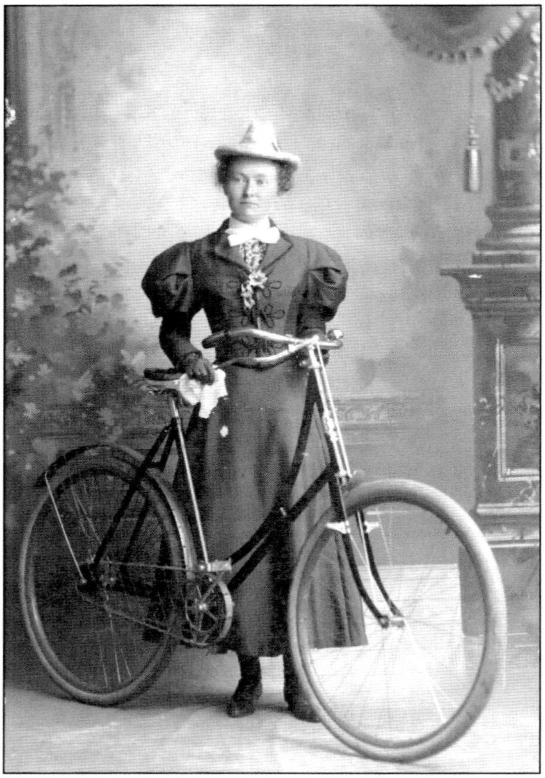

INTRODUCTION OF THE BICYCLE. In June 1878, the Honorable Thomas Nelson Hastings, a local "trendsetter and man-about-town," was astonishing the Walpole community with feats on his modern bicycle, which cost $150. His quickest time for one mile was 2.37 minutes. In 1879, bicycle racing on Main Street became a pastime, and bicycle riding on the sidewalks became a nuisance. In the above photograph of a group posing outside the Walpole Academy in the 1890s, there are five bicycles being proudly displayed by their owners, a vehicle that allowed students to ride to school rather than walk. Many students lived miles from the academy, and many of them walked the long and hilly distances each day, even in the harsh and blustery New Hampshire winters. At left, "Walpole cousin" Josie Kingsbury of Keene poses for an 1897 studio portrait in her cycling attire.

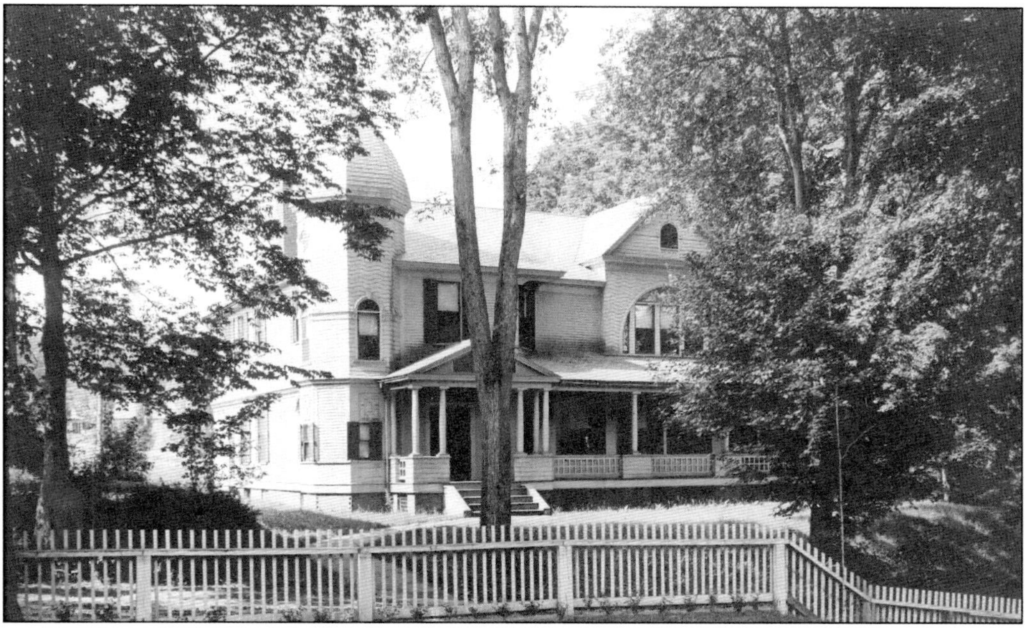

HASTINGS HOUSE. In 1895, Hastings, who moved to Walpole as a young boy, designed and gave this parish house (above) to the Unitarian church in memory of his wife, Amy Bridge Hastings. Built by Becwith of Claremont, it was dedicated on January 20, 1896. The Unitarian Ladies' Sewing Society is shown below, stitching in the front parlor of the parish house. The Hastings house continues to be an active part of the Walpole community today.

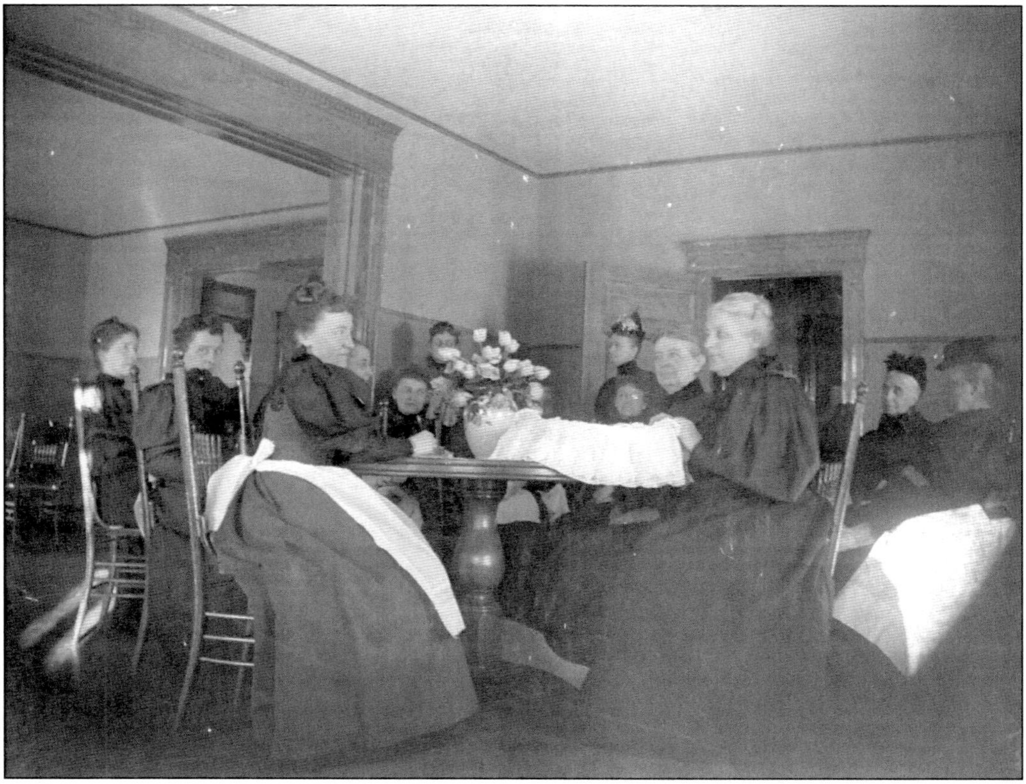

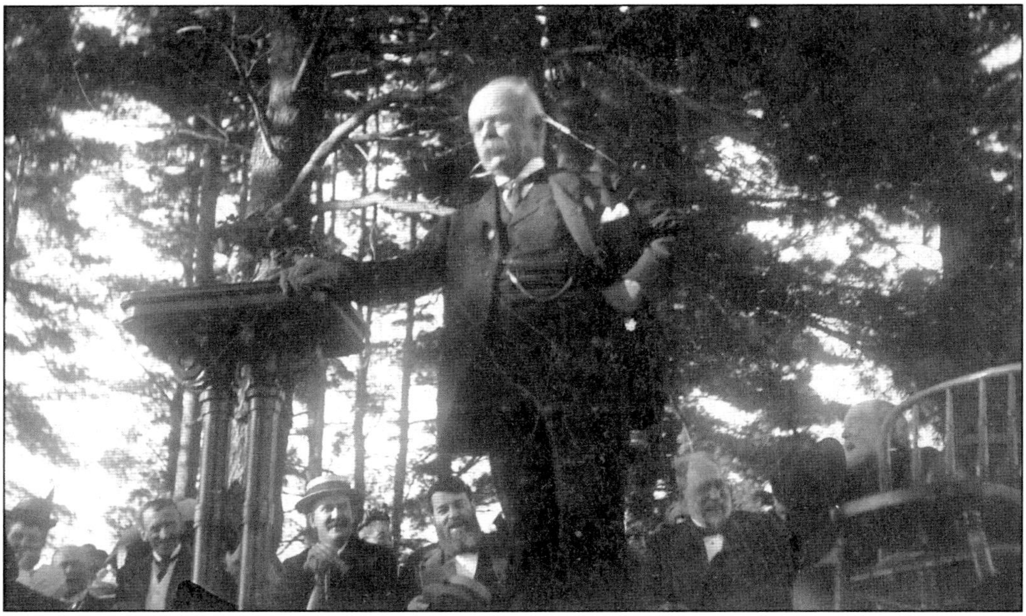

JUDGE HENRY HOWLAND AT WALPOLE'S FIRST OLD HOME DAYS, 1899. Over 1,200 people attended the first Old Home Day on August 30, 1899, held in Copley Amory's pasture on Old Drewsville Road near the site of the Flynt and Twitchell massacre. There was a picnic and program of music, singing, and speeches from nine of the town's leaders. Old Home Days continue in Walpole into the 21st century, currently being celebrated every third year.

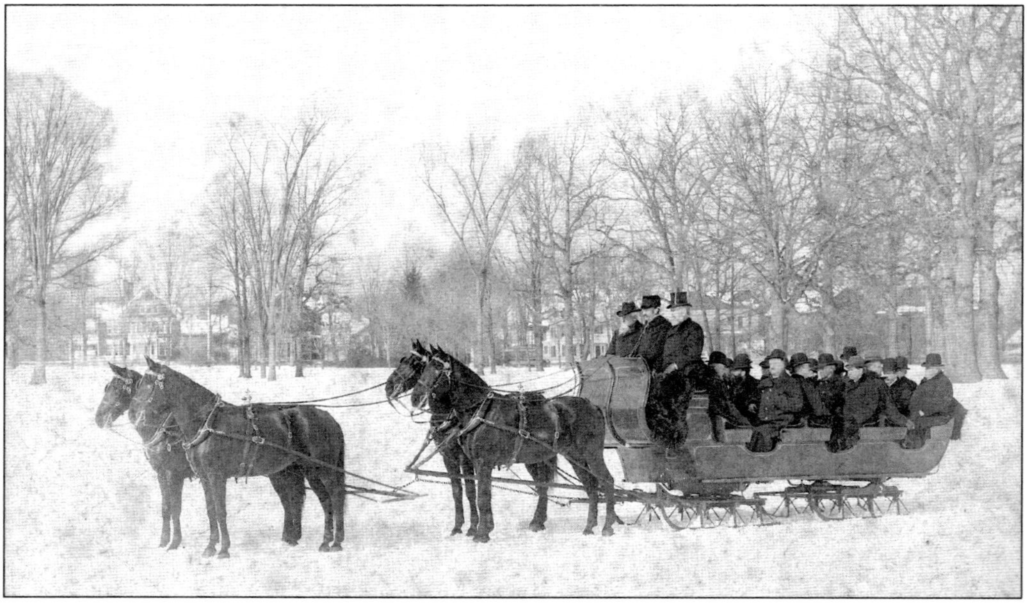

HOTEL SLEIGH. Sleigh rides were popular winter diversions, as evidenced by the large group of men in a horse-drawn hotel sleigh on the common. On a cold and windy night in 1884, 28 couples from Walpole went by sleigh to Westmoreland about seven miles away for supper. Returning, several sleighs were upset, and some men were obliged to walk home, leading the horses. This 1897 photograph is compliments of Thomas Nelson Hastings, an Old Home Days founder.

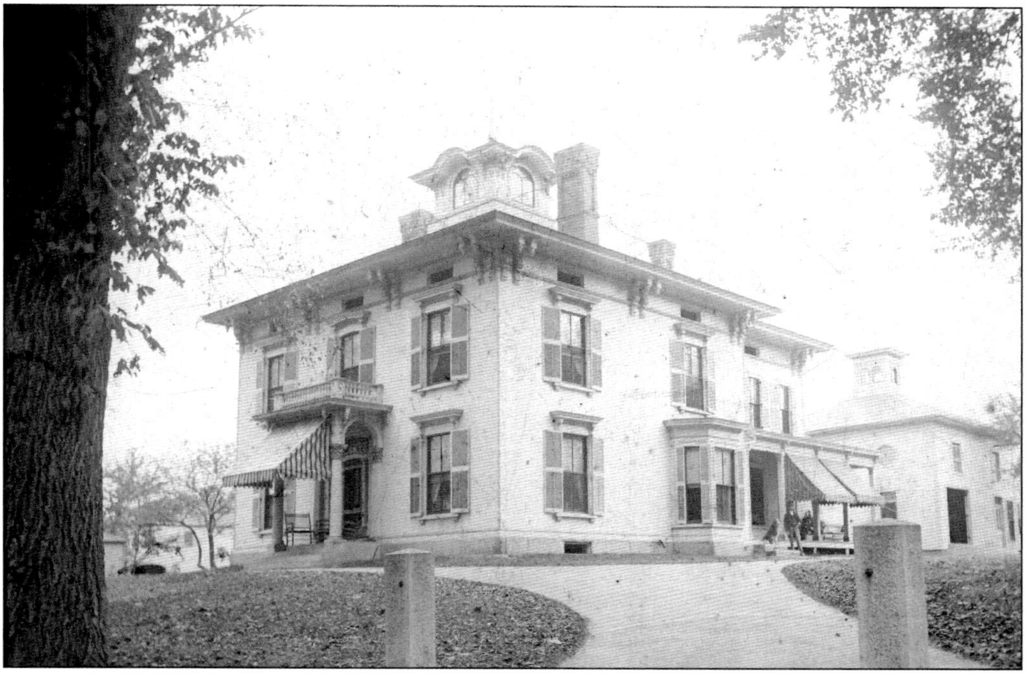

FRIENDLY COMPETITION. These two historic houses were constructed about the same time in the 1860s by two friendly Walpole entrepreneurs, ship owner Charles Hooper and local shirt manufacturer Silas Bates. They tried to outdo each other in the grandeur and height of their homes. When Hooper added a cupola to his Italianate villa (above), Bates tore off his roof and built one too. Hooper's extensive travels may have provided inspiration for the ornate style of his house, with its intricate scrollwork, rounded arches, and siding resembling shiplap. A sitting area in the cupola commanded a view of the comings and goings in town. The Bates house has indoor mahogany trim, silver doorknobs, marble and painted soapstone fireplaces, and a spiral staircase. Natural air-conditioning is provided by the central well that reaches up to the cupola.

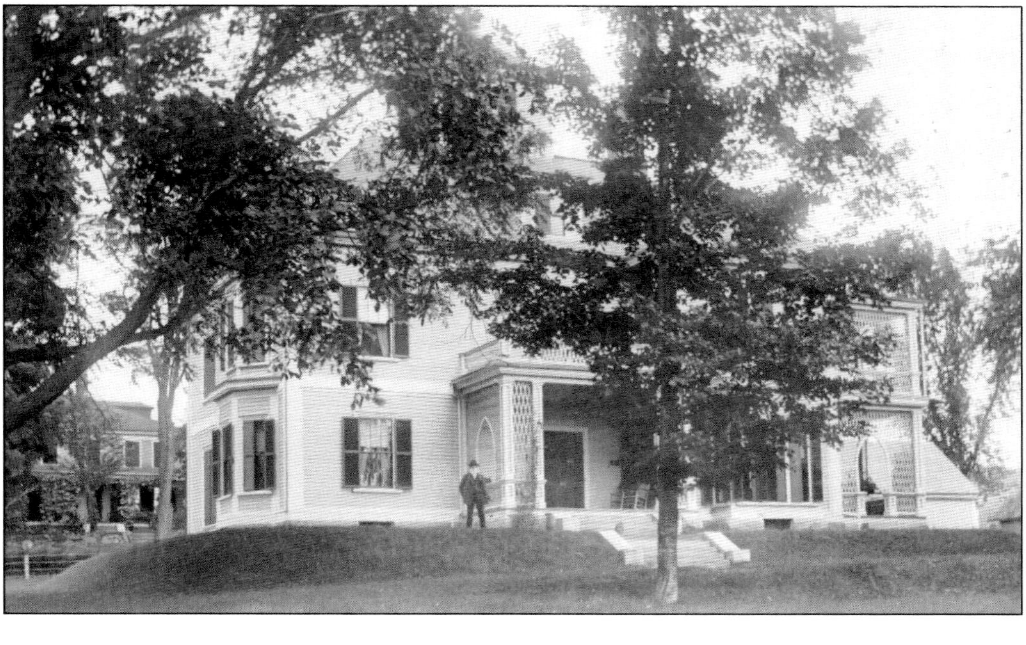

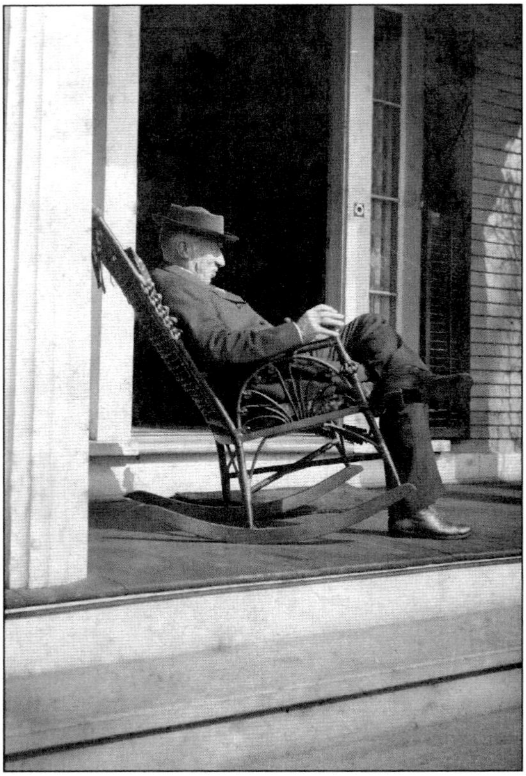

The Honorable J. G. Bellows. A lawyer and probate judge, Josiah G. Bellows (1841–1906) was the great-grandson of the town's founding father, Col. Benjamin Bellows. He was active in the community, a founder of the Savings Bank of Walpole, and an Old Home Days board member. The Bellows family figured prominently in the history of Walpole as politicians, ministers, lawyers, merchants, and farmers. Many of the town's historic homes were built by them.

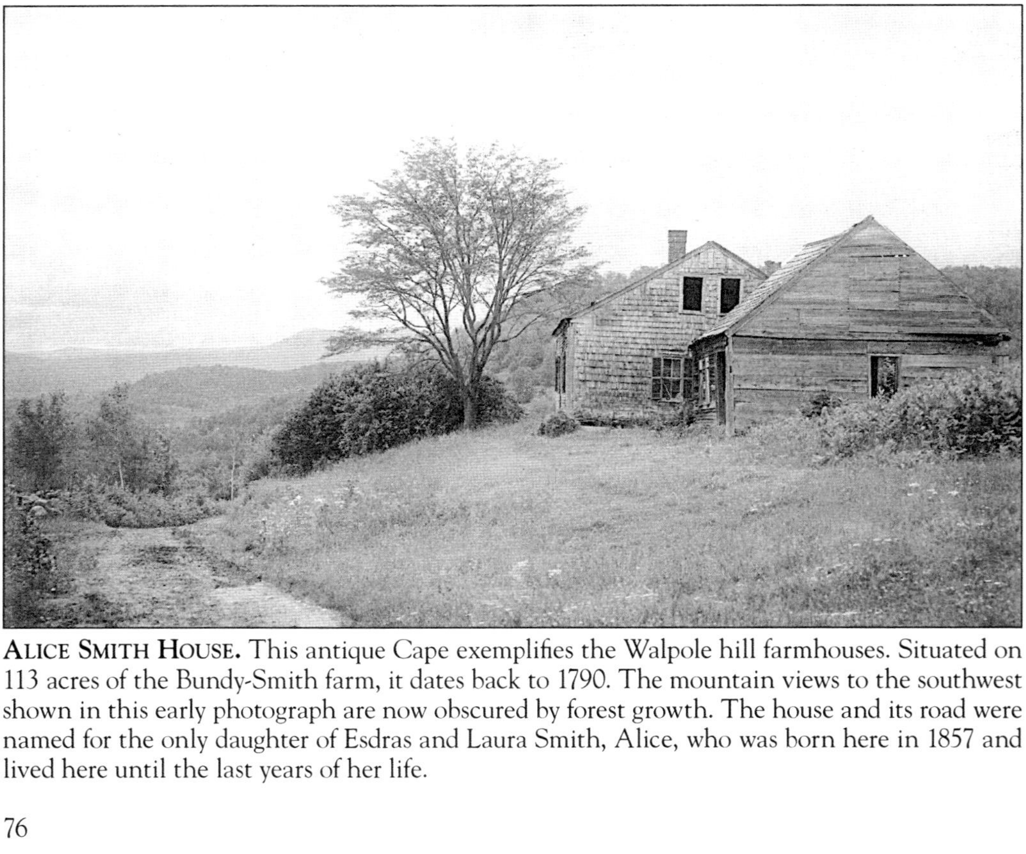

Alice Smith House. This antique Cape exemplifies the Walpole hill farmhouses. Situated on 113 acres of the Bundy-Smith farm, it dates back to 1790. The mountain views to the southwest shown in this early photograph are now obscured by forest growth. The house and its road were named for the only daughter of Esdras and Laura Smith, Alice, who was born here in 1857 and lived here until the last years of her life.

Five

Celebration and Catastrophe 1900–1950

Two world wars, the Great Depression, fires, and fierce storms marked the first half of the 20th century. The same period was also noted for its athletic events, parades, plays, and performances. The three business enterprises that dominated the Walpole economy for nearly a century were started during this time.

The 1900s began with the celebration of Walpole's 150th anniversary in 1903. About 700 people turned out for the speaking program in the town hall, and 1,000 spectators attended the afternoon athletic contests. A new drinking fountain was erected in the square in 1905, and in 1909, *The Canterbury Pilgrims* was presented on the common. The first town fair in 40 years was held in 1920, and a few years later, the town meeting authorized the leasing of land for a golf course. In May 1937, Nims Field, an athletic facility, was opened in North Walpole.

Blizzards, floods, fires, and hurricanes took their toll on Walpole. Under the weight of snow, the Unitarian church collapsed in 1920. The April 1933 blizzard blocked roads with eight-foot drifts, delayed trains for hours, and made milk shipment impossible for a week. In November 1927, the Connecticut River rose 20 feet above the dam and came over the bank in North Walpole. It took everything with it northeast of the arch bridge, including two houses.

The hurricane of 1938 was the defining storm of the first half of the 20th century. It struck on September 21 after five days of heavy rain. It left the village with no passable roads and few undamaged roofs and chimneys. Groves of pine and hardwood were destroyed. Fires were another defining aspect of this period. Nearby Fall Mountain burned twice, once in 1937 and again in 1948. The town hall was destroyed by fire in 1917, and North Walpole's Russell Hall burned in 1949.

Founded in 1921 by Oliver Hubbard, Hubbard Farms became an international, multimillion-dollar poultry producer. Ralph N. "Jack" Johnson became one of the largest John Deere distributors in New England, and Woodward Florist, a major seasonal employer, supplied a wreath to the White House every year.

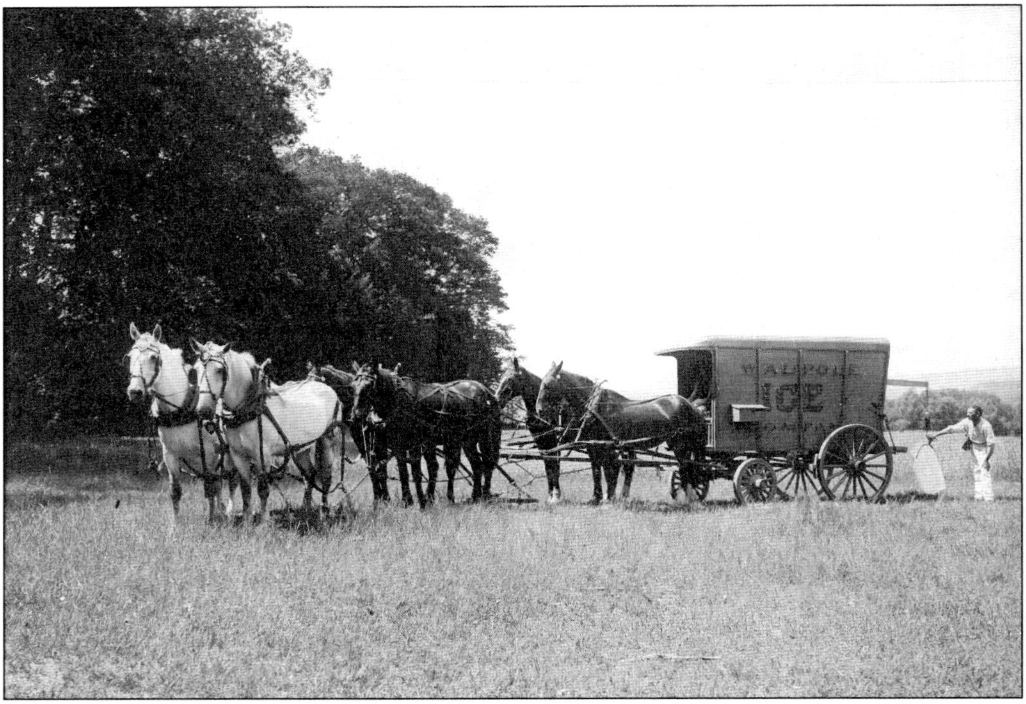

ICE AGE. The six-horse hitch and wagon above was a state-of-the-art conveyance for delivery of ice for food preservation at the dawn of the 20th century. Will Stowell is pictured weighing a block of ice for home delivery. Charlie Slade, owner of Walpole Ice Company, ran his operation at the town millpond, seen below. Slade, in the banded hat, assists his crew in cutting ice for the conveyor to the icehouse in the background about 1915. Walpole Ice Company delivered to Walpole on Tuesdays, Thursdays, and Saturdays, and to Westminster, Vermont, on Mondays, Wednesdays, and Fridays.

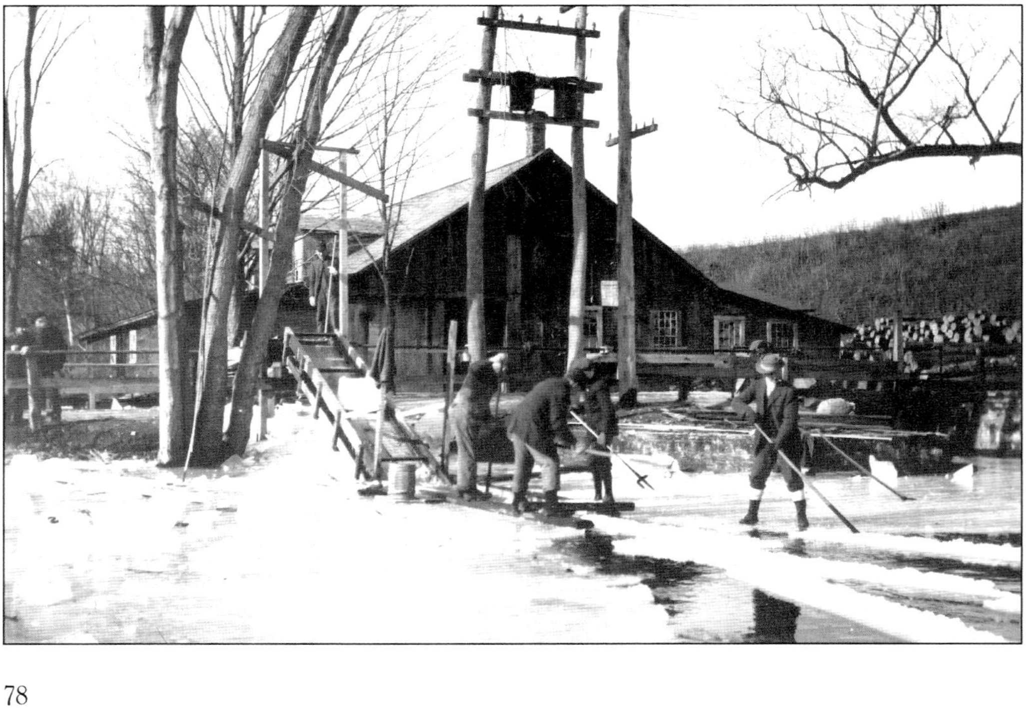

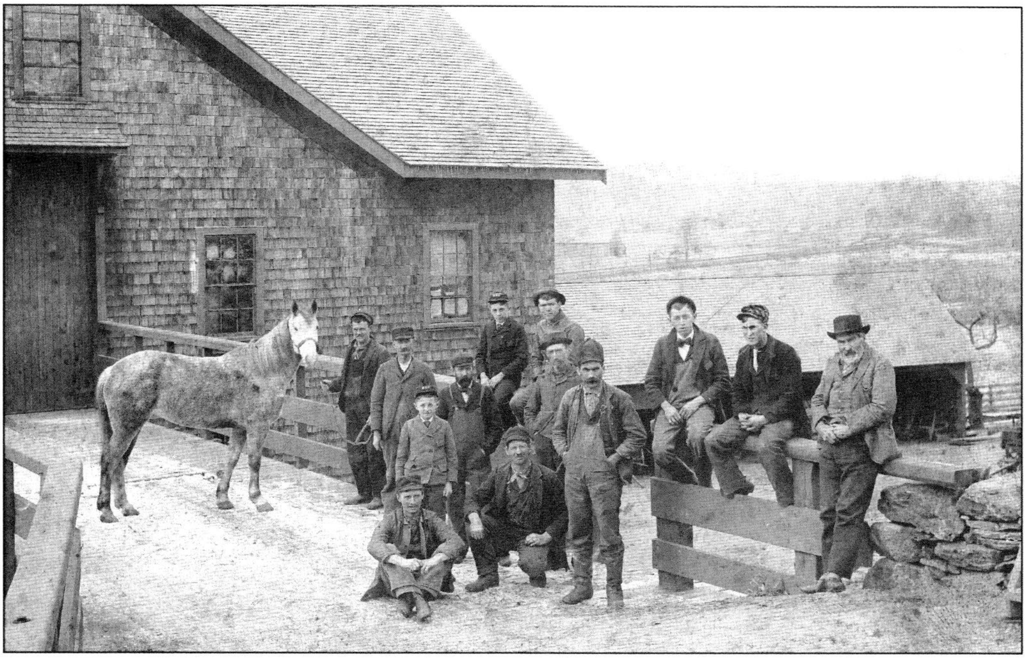

THE OLD HOMESTEAD. Homestead farm is site of the original homestead of grantee Benjamin Bellows for the town of Walpole. The 350-acre farm remained with the Bellows family until the 1890 death of bachelor the Reverend Thomas Bellows. Subsequent owner Copley Amory vastly improved waterworks and orchards, laid out a golf course on the Hubbard Road, and replaced several dilapidated barns. Here, workers stand before some of the new barns about 1900.

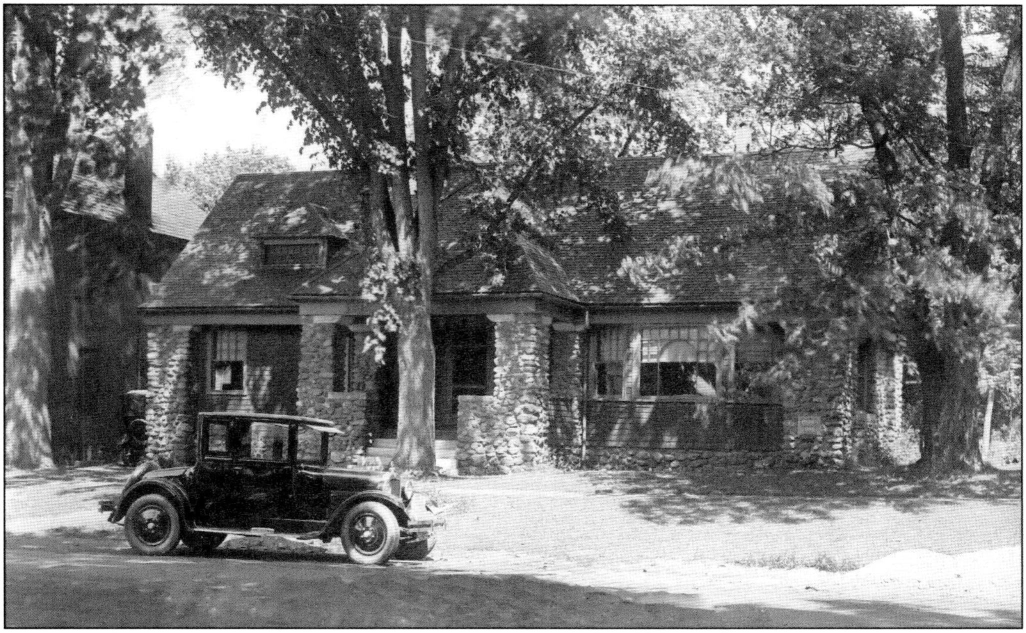

BRIDGE MEMORIAL LIBRARY. The native stone building was the gift of Hudson E. Bridge to the town of Walpole in memory of his father in 1891. The library, seen in this picture from the early 1930s, is situated at the village four corners on Main Street just east of the Howland Memorial fountain and provides an active window on the comings and goings of the village.

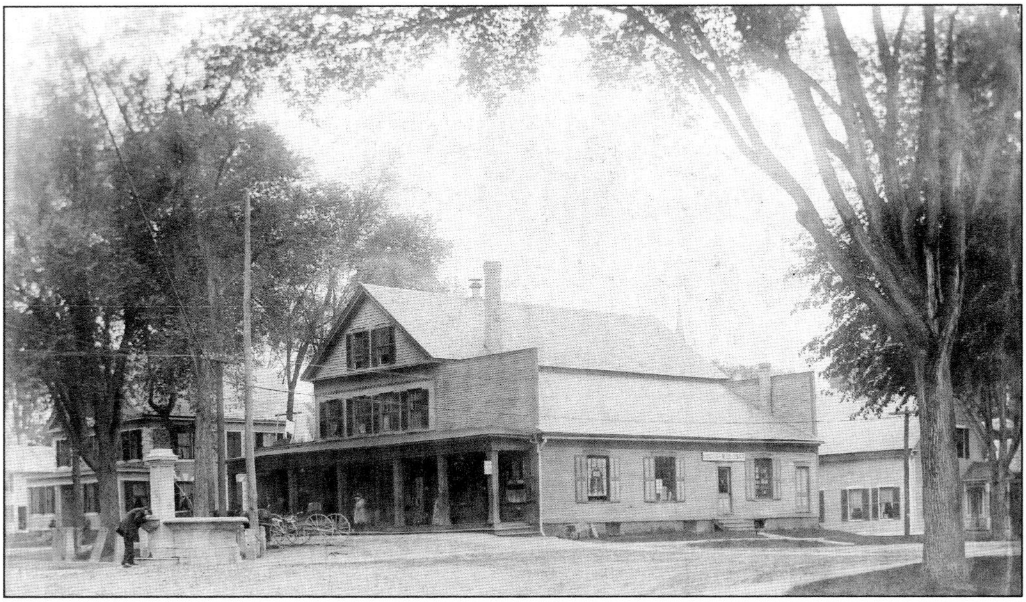

WALPOLE SQUARE FOUNTAIN. A new drinking fountain at the intersection of Westminster and Main Streets was erected in 1905. It was a gift of Charles P. Howland in memory of Henry E. Howland, "for man, horse, and dog." In later years, the catamount pillar was removed, and the basin used as a planter. In the early 1980s, an effort, spearheaded by Peggy Graves and Betty Prentiss, resulted in the catamount pillar being restored and the fountain brought back into working order and connected to the municipal water system. During the growing season, the base is bedecked with flowering plants.

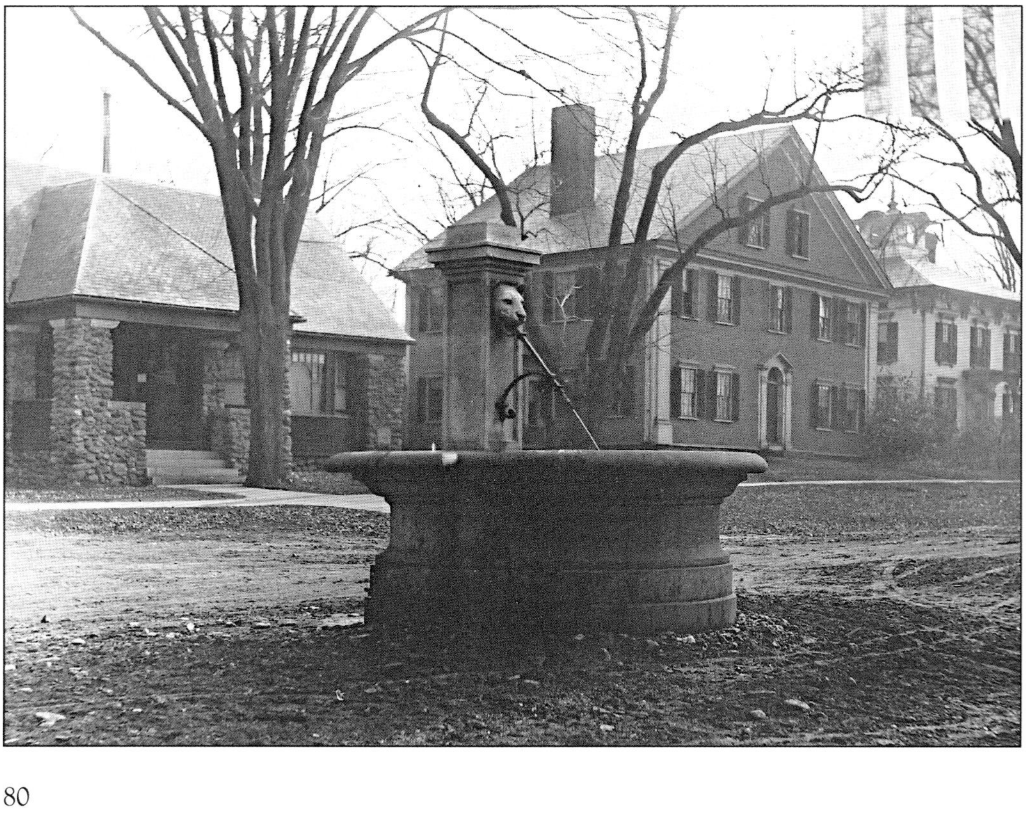

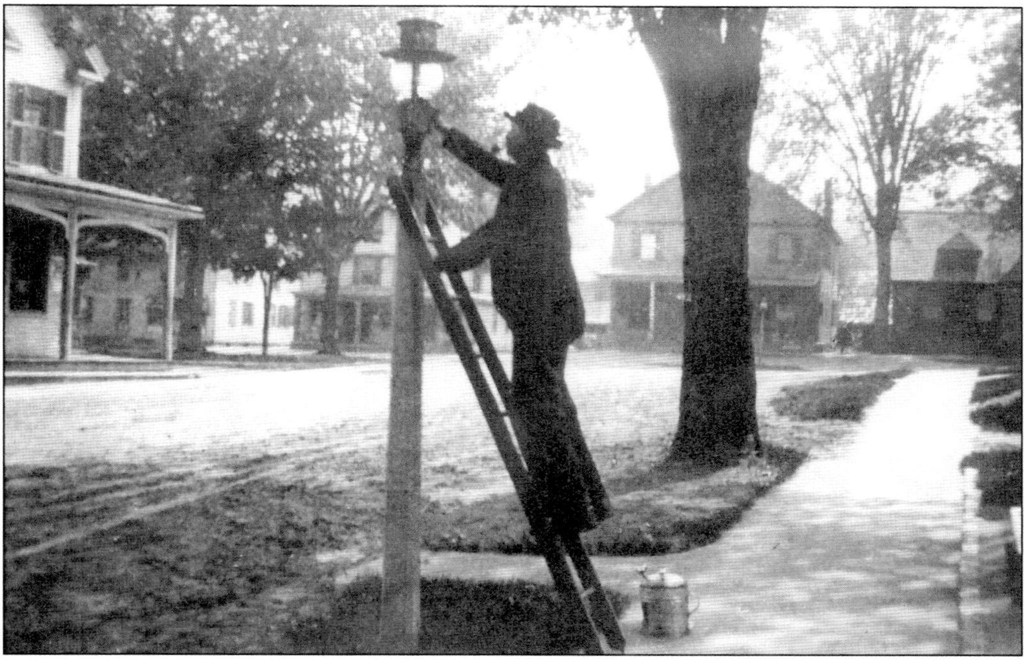

LAMPLIGHTER. This 1903 photograph depicts Charles Chickering, Walpole's lamplighter, refueling a lantern on Westminster Street. As a town employee, he served as a "bringer of light from the darkness" for decades and was known to everyone in town. About the time of this photograph, electrical utilities were arriving in Walpole.

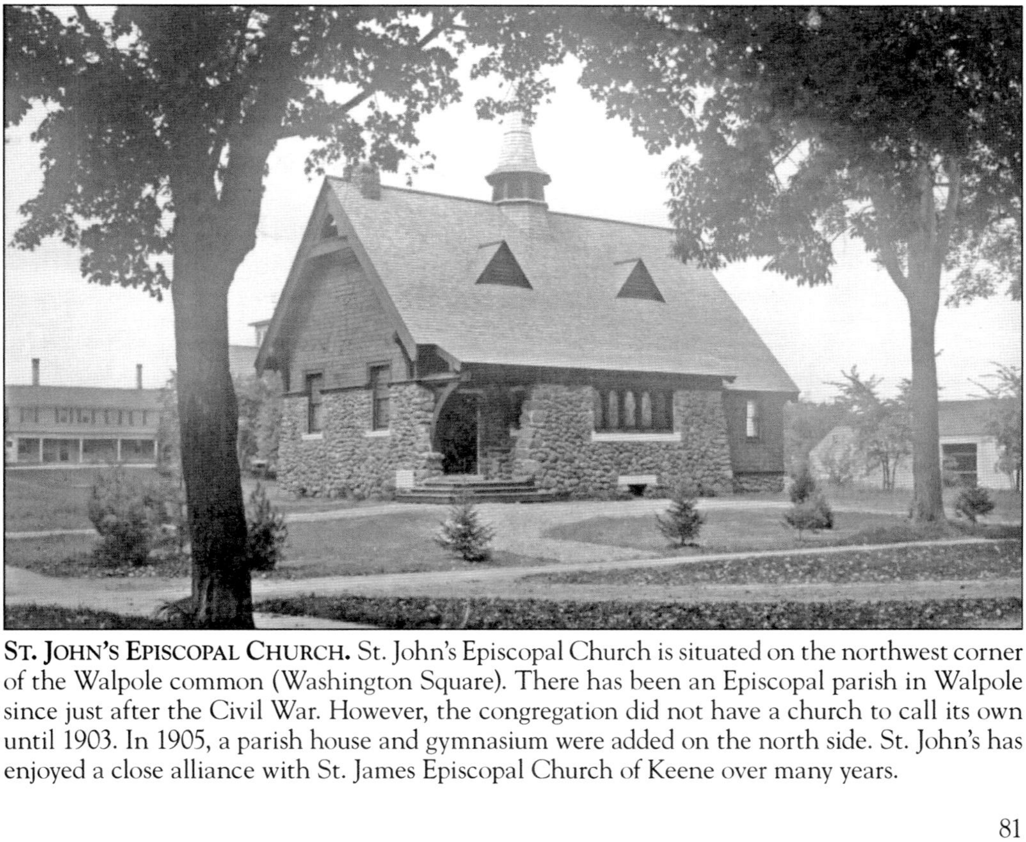

ST. JOHN'S EPISCOPAL CHURCH. St. John's Episcopal Church is situated on the northwest corner of the Walpole common (Washington Square). There has been an Episcopal parish in Walpole since just after the Civil War. However, the congregation did not have a church to call its own until 1903. In 1905, a parish house and gymnasium were added on the north side. St. John's has enjoyed a close alliance with St. James Episcopal Church of Keene over many years.

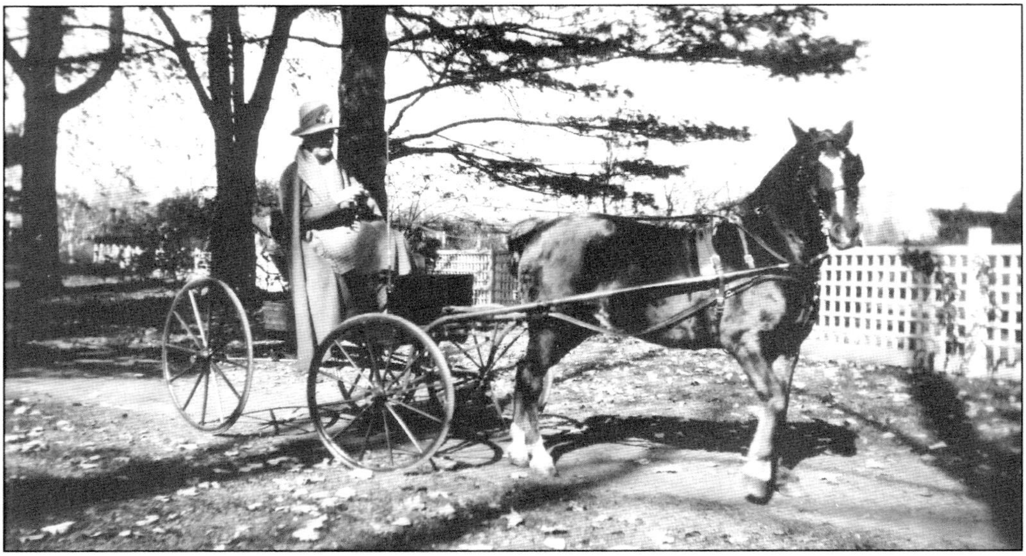

FANNY PEABODY MASON. Born in Massachusetts in 1865, Fanny Peabody Mason was the only daughter of William Powell Mason, a banker and manufacturer. As his surviving heir, she inherited a fortune and his estate on the Boggy Meadow Farm in 1901. She was a woman of many interests, who had an important role in supporting the arts, especially music. She often invited Boston musicians to River Road and held formal recitals there. She was active in Walpole community affairs and was a founding member of the first Walpole Historical Society board in 1930. She liberally supported the district nurse services; at her death in 1948, a bequest of $20,000 earned income for its support over many years. Her will included an estate of $4 million for charitable distribution. She left much of the Boggy Meadow woodlands to the Town of Walpole for conservation.

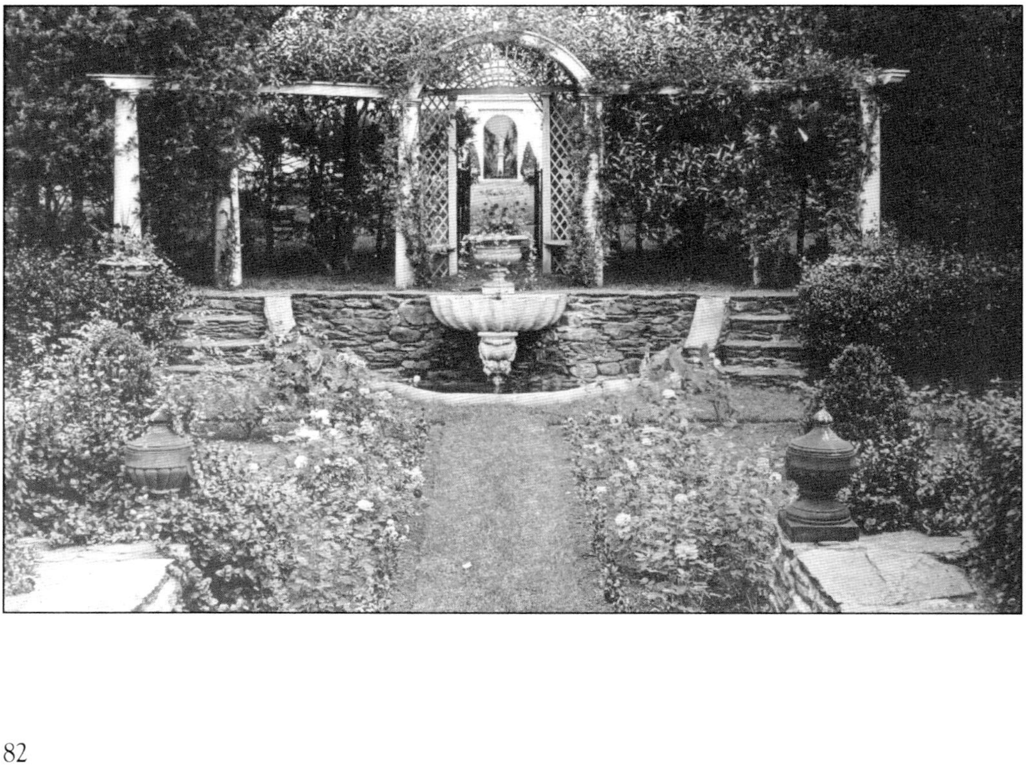

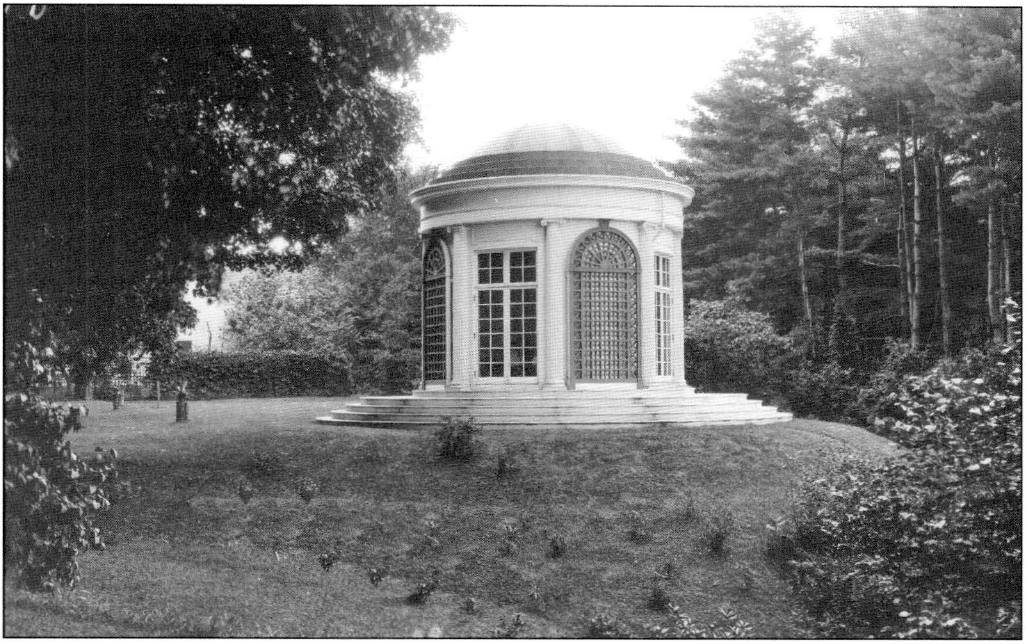

Fanny Mason Gardens at Boggy Meadow Farm. Gardening was among Mason's many interests, as can be seen in these photographs from the early 20th century. Above is her summerhouse, which provided guests with protected seating while enjoying the views from the mansion's bluff above the Connecticut River. Below, an enclosed arbor or pergola stands out among the garden features. The previous page shows her sunken rose garden. After years of neglect, the gardens were rebuilt in the late 20th century by her cousin and current owner, Powell Cabot.

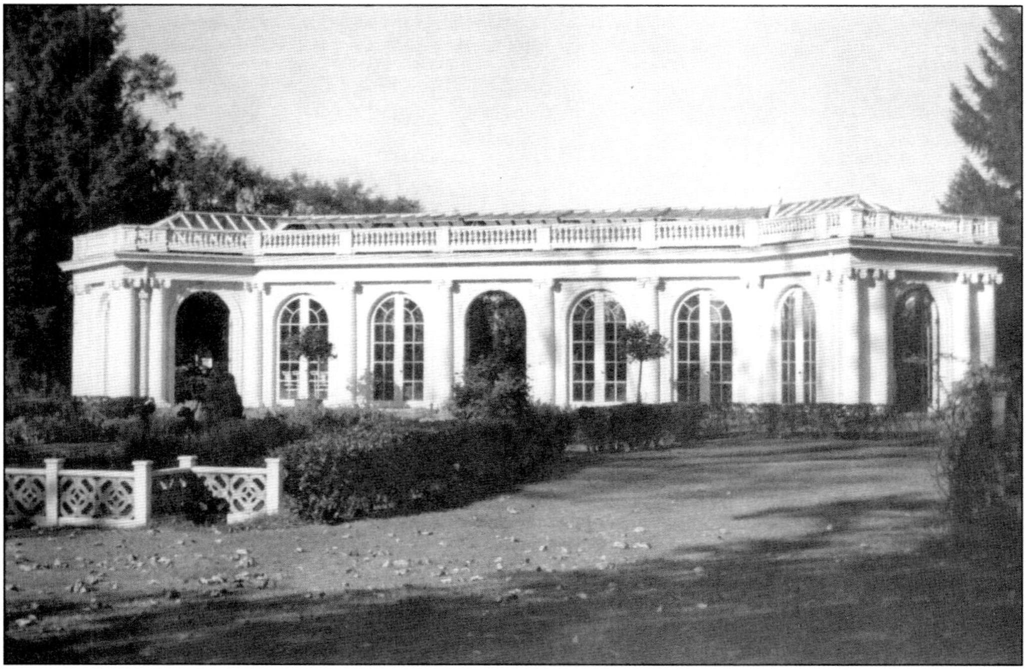

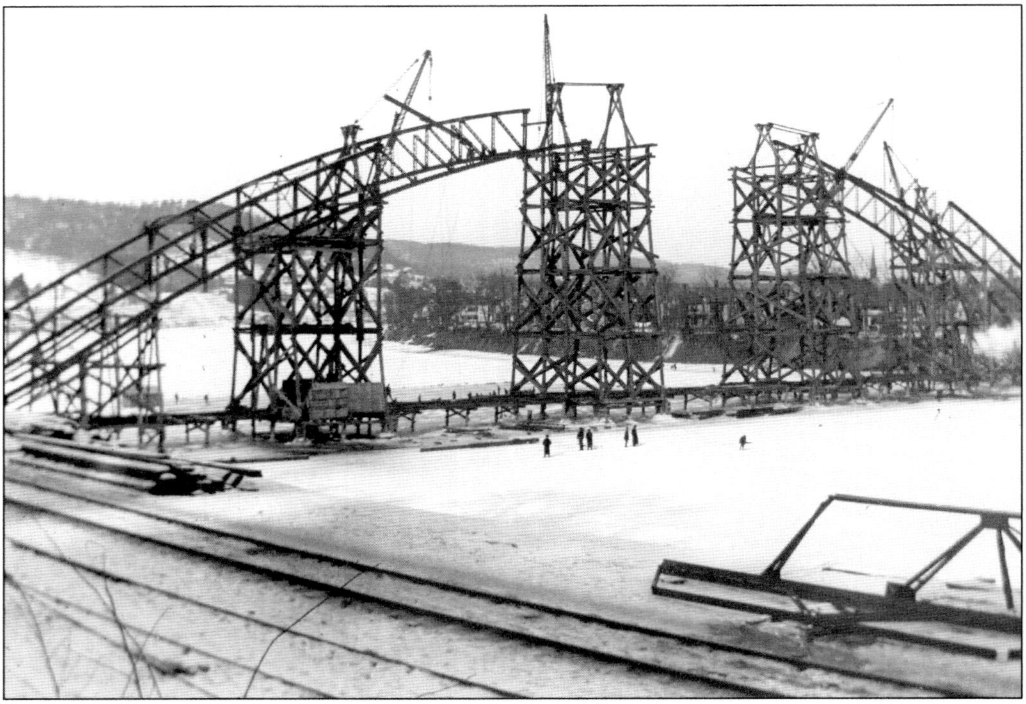

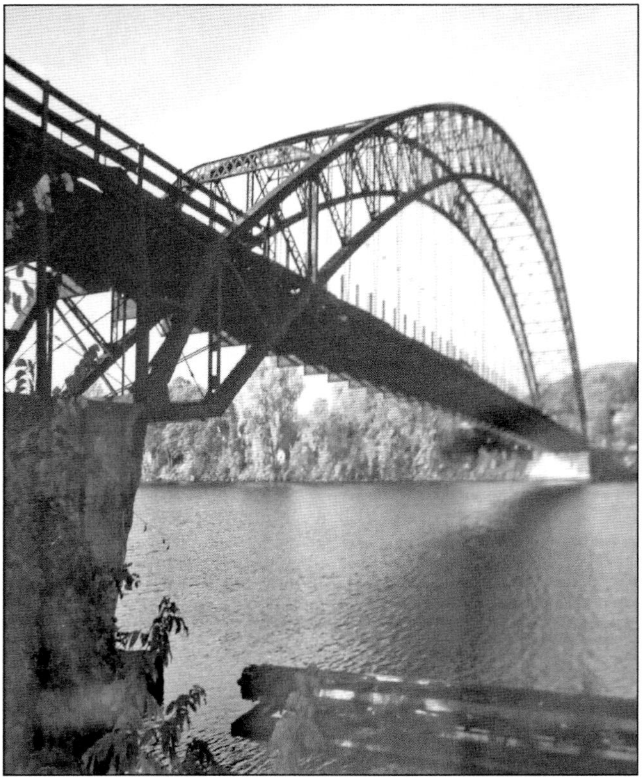

THE ARCH BRIDGE AT NORTH WALPOLE. At a cost of $44,939 and a weight of 450 tons, the arch bridge was located just north of the dam. Construction started in the summer of 1904 with firm, immovable abutments to resist the horizontal thrust of the spring of the arch. The roadway was suspended from the arch and at the time was the only bridge of that construction in the United States. The arch itself was 70 feet above the roadway, and the bridge span was 540 feet. "No money was spent to ornament this bridge"; the beauty it had was due to its structural lines. At left, with fireworks and the citizens band playing, the arch bridge was opened to traffic on March 20, 1905. No longer did the people of North Walpole have to cross the river by way of the old toll or railroad bridges.

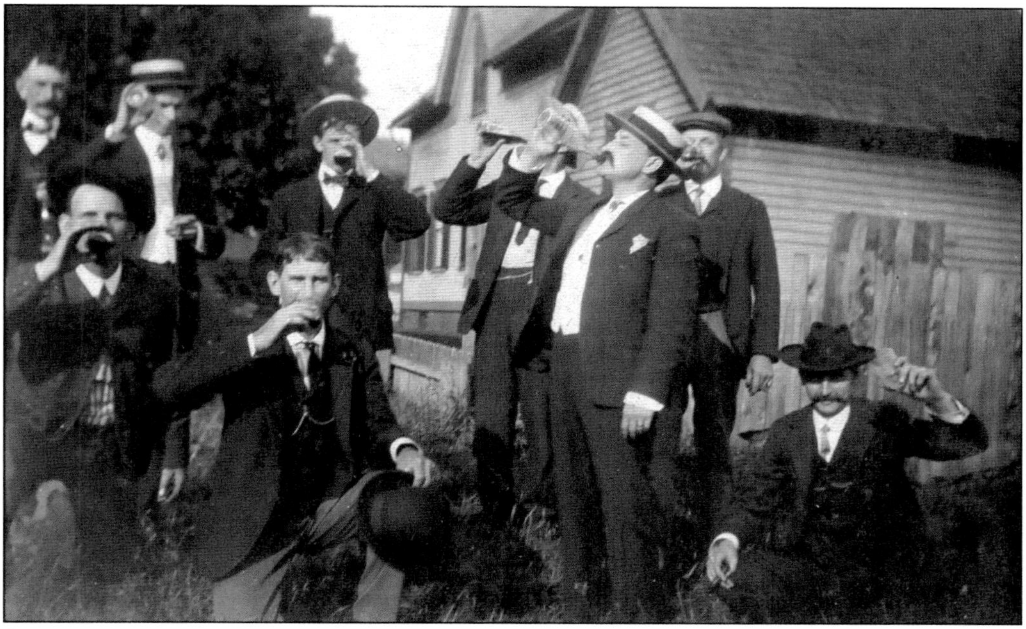

CONVIVIALITY VERSUS TEMPERANCE. Convivial drinking was a town tradition from the beginning. In one year, 4,800 barrels of cider were consumed in Walpole. This scene was a clambake in North Walpole. In the 1840s, a riot almost ensued when the legislature passed a restrictive law and storekeepers stopped the sale of rum. In November 1916, there was a huge temperance rally at the town hall preceded by a torchlight parade.

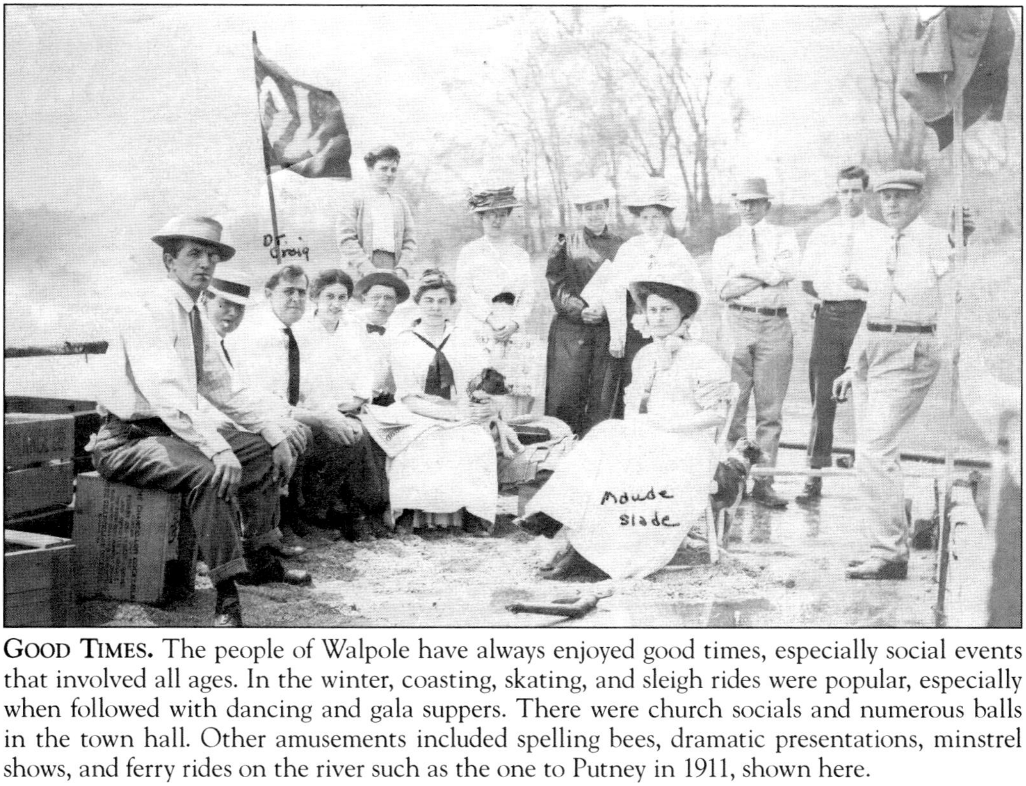

GOOD TIMES. The people of Walpole have always enjoyed good times, especially social events that involved all ages. In the winter, coasting, skating, and sleigh rides were popular, especially when followed with dancing and gala suppers. There were church socials and numerous balls in the town hall. Other amusements included spelling bees, dramatic presentations, minstrel shows, and ferry rides on the river such as the one to Putney in 1911, shown here.

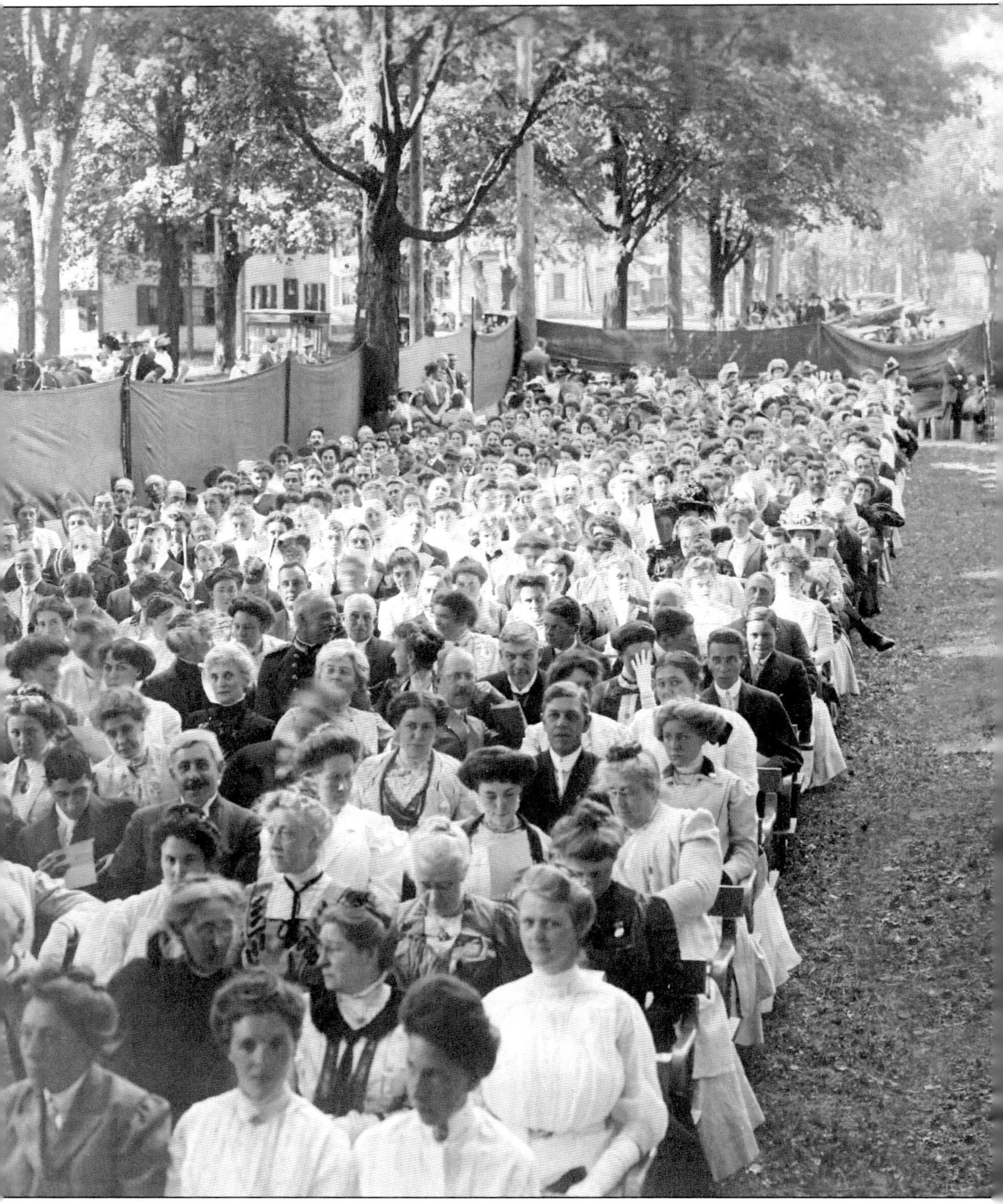

THE CANTERBURY PILGRIMS. In 1909, a performance of the comedy *The Canterbury Pilgrims* was performed on the common with 1,000 people in attendance, including Gov. Henry B. Quimby. The author, Percy MacKaye, was spending the summer in Cornish with his wife, a descendant of an old Walpole family. The son of famous actor Steele MacKaye, Percy MacKaye was a leading poet and playwright, with 10 of his works produced on Broadway. Prof. Franklin

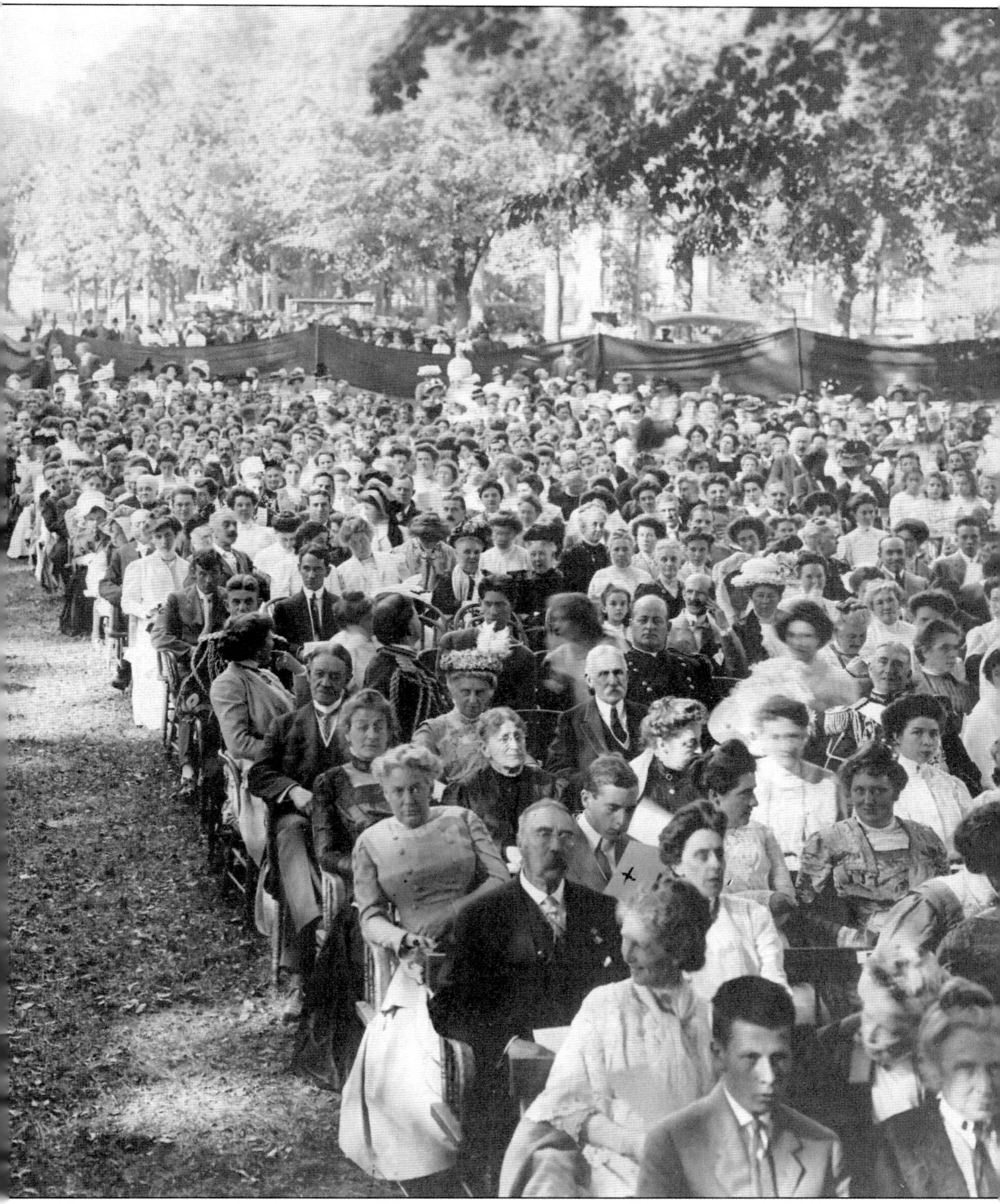

Hooper presented the play as part of the summer lecture series. The cast included 30 people from out of town and at least as many from Walpole. The stage was set up at the south end of the common. While everyone could see the performance, only about half could hear. The attendees arrived by special train and 100 automobiles. The production grossed $880, and expenses totaled $690.79.

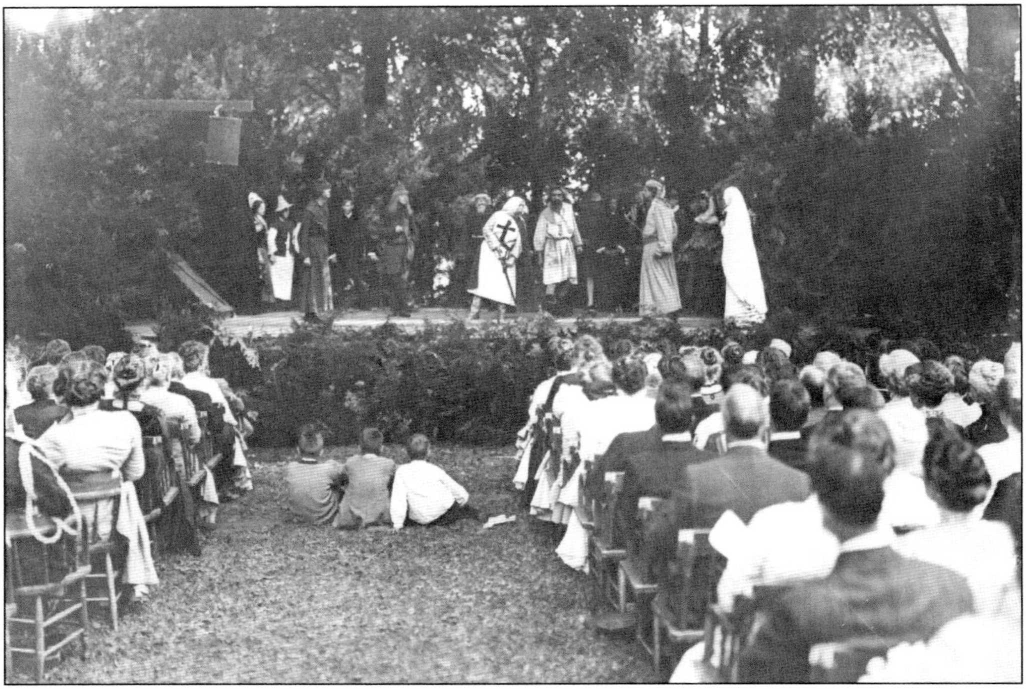

THE CANTERBURY PILGRIMS CONTINUED. Percy MacKaye's comedy, based upon Geoffrey Chaucer's *Canterbury Tales* (but including Chaucer in the cast), provided a rare opportunity for the community to witness a live performance of a contemporary comedy. Walpole had become a town enamored with theater, and the crowd may have been one of the largest to assemble on the common, then or since. While MacKaye's play lives on in American dramatic history, so too does the story of the crowd that assembled for this performance on that summer day.

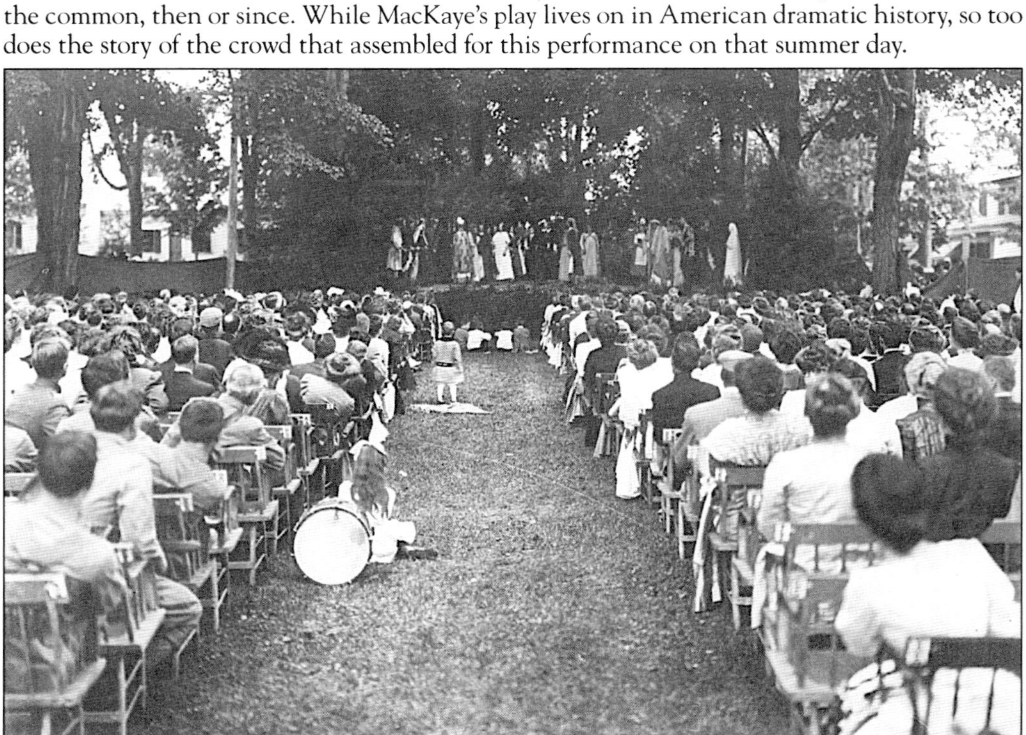

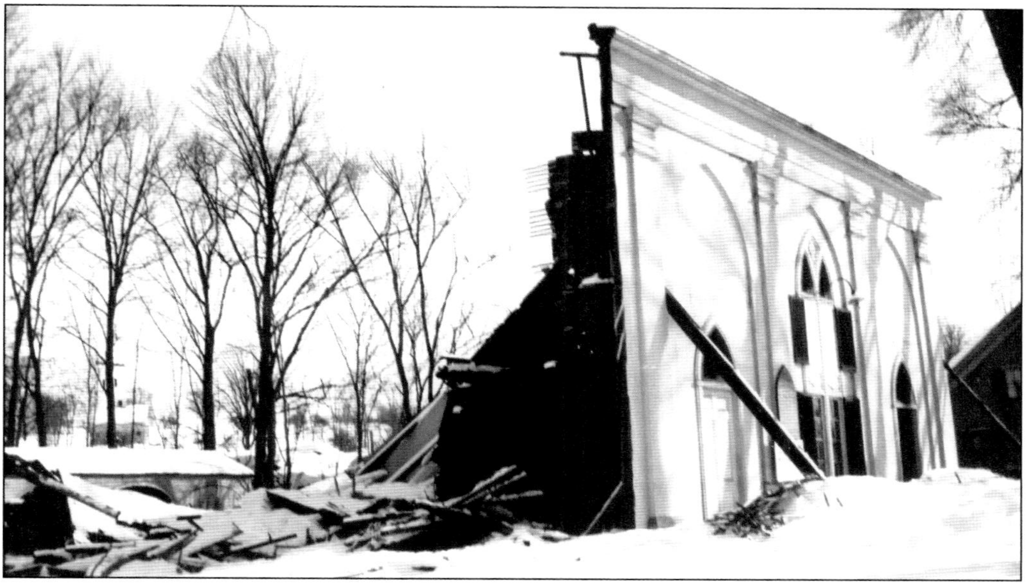

Unitarian Church Collapse. On the night of February 18, 1920, the Unitarian church on Main Street (see chapter 2) collapsed under the weight of wet snow. Only the front wall and organ gallery were left standing. The roof fell towards the rear, and the walls fell outward. The clock was destroyed, and the organ damaged. There was no insurance. Reconstruction was started in October of that year, and the new church was dedicated in September 1922. The organ and bell had been repaired, and furnishings for the new building (right) were donated by members of the congregation. The new church differs from the former in that the clock tower-entry stands outside the nave.

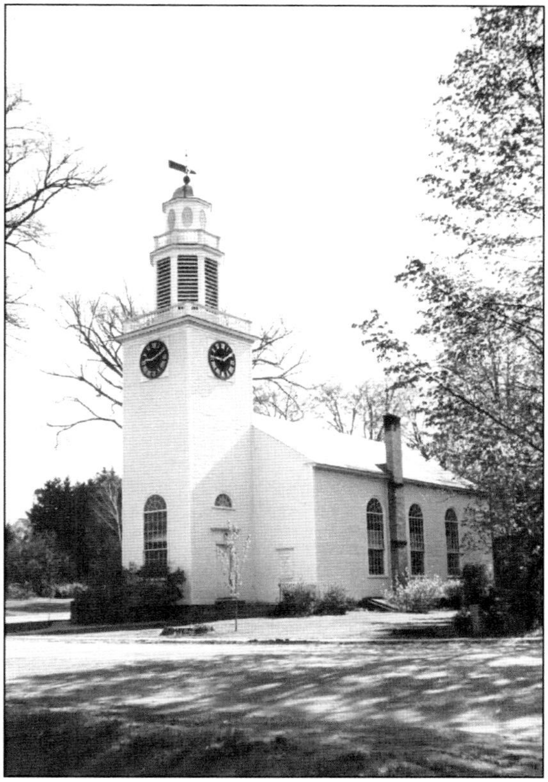

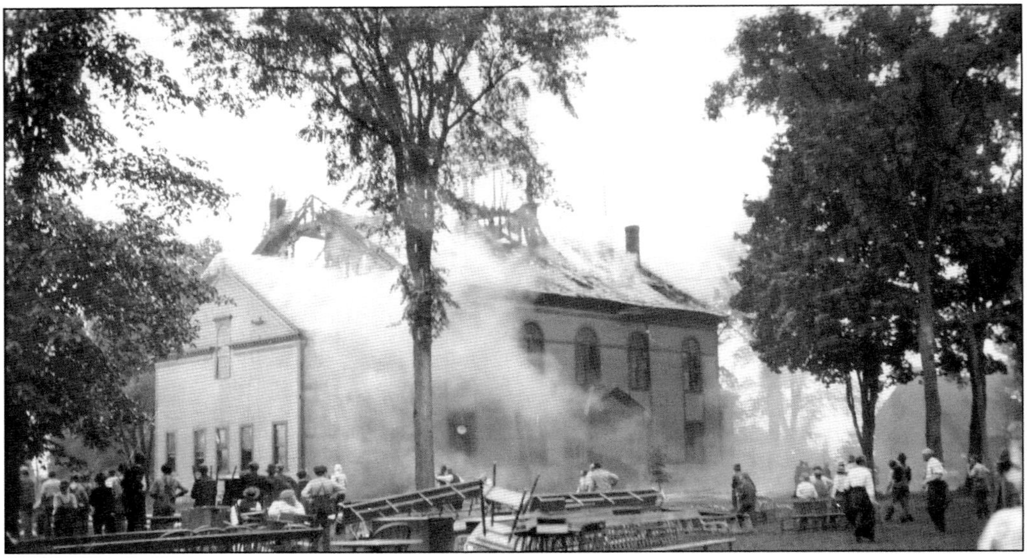

TOWN HALL FIRE. On Thursday, June 14, 1917, one of the most devastating events in the town's history occurred. Lightning struck the town hall. This was the historic building that had been so painstakingly moved from its original Prospect Hill location to the town common in the 1820s. The resulting fire completely destroyed the building. The Revere bell, which had been removed from the meetinghouse to be "in a safe place" in the relocation of the building from Prospect Hill and then rehung in the town hall, was damaged beyond repair. Full insurance of $9,000 on the building was allowed and $718 on the furniture.

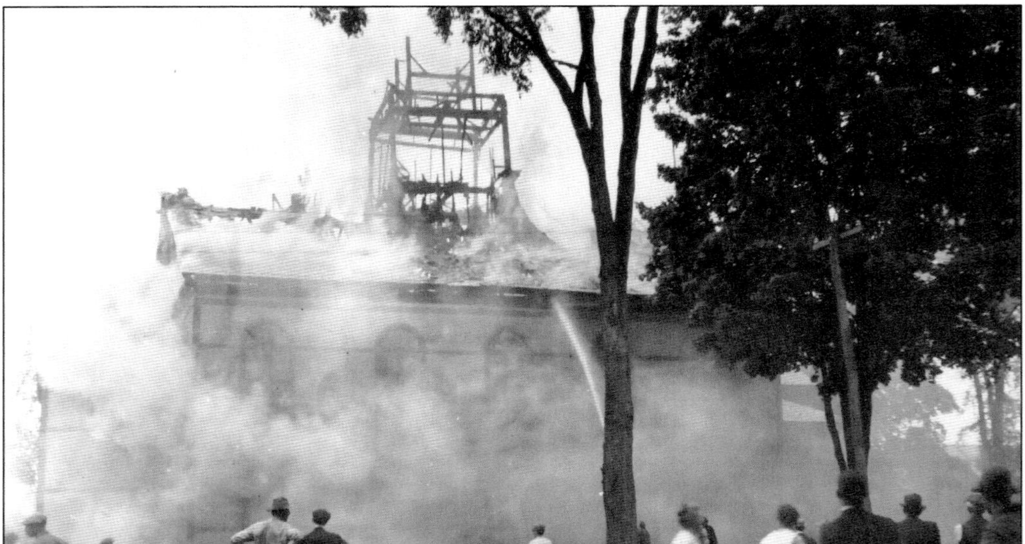

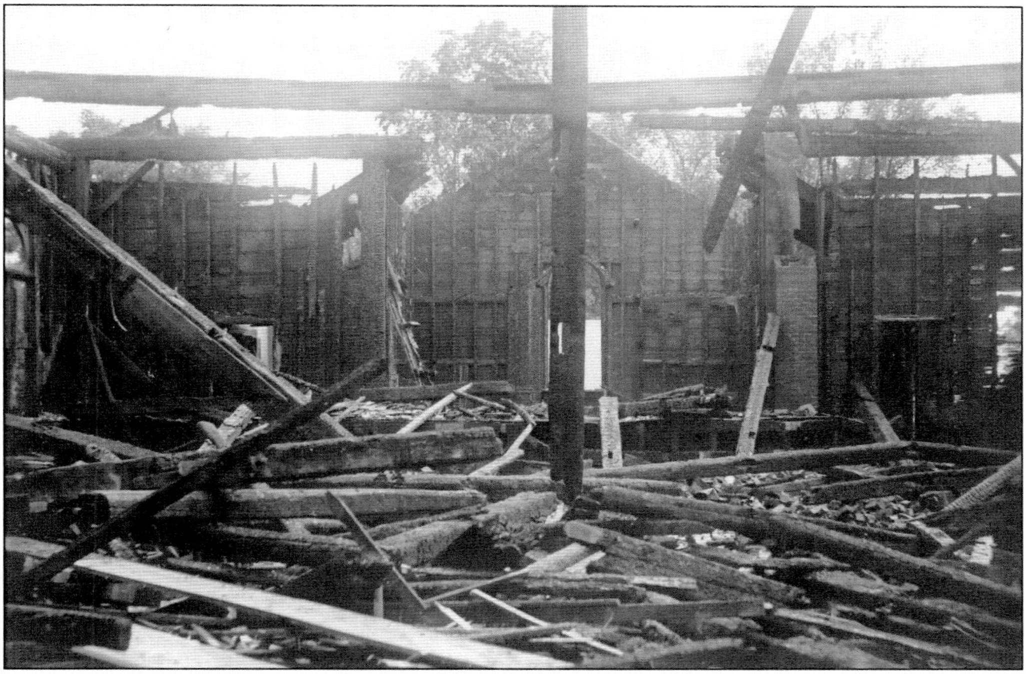

TOWN HALL REMAINS. The remains of the old town hall are shown above. At special town meetings in July and October 1917, a resolution was presented to appropriate the insurance money and an additional $15,000 to rebuild and refurnish the town hall. Balloting on the issue occurred from October 6 to 8 in the individual village districts and was ultimately approved on a town vote, 324 to 7. Plans for a new town hall were obtained through the "generosity of Miss Fanny Mason." The architect was James Purdon of Boston. A year later on June 21, 1918, the new town hall was dedicated with an orchestra, chorus, and speeches. It is said that there was "dancing until early morning." The new town hall, designed to reflect the architecture and function of the old, is seen below as it looks today.

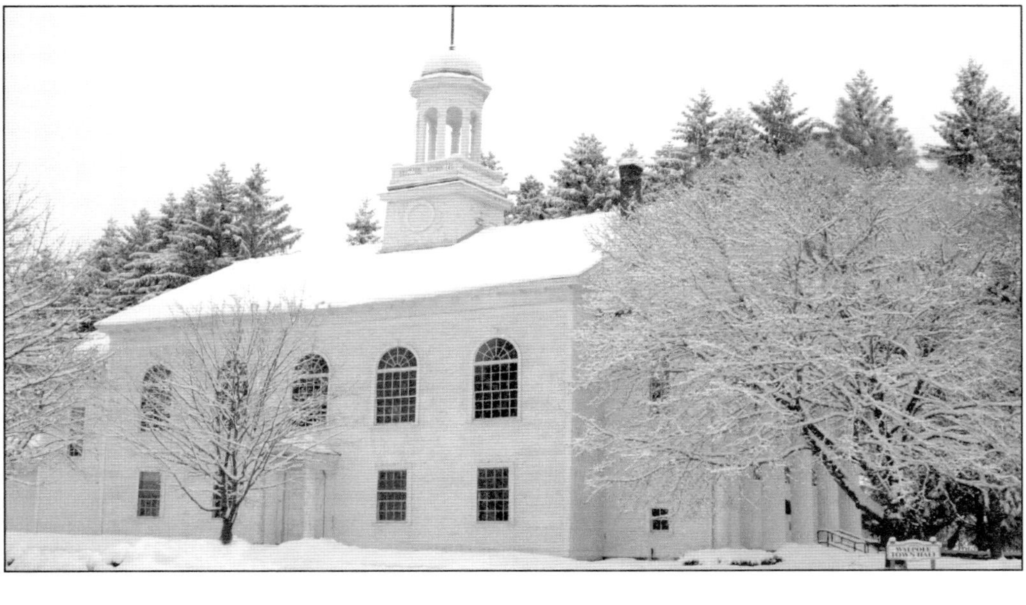

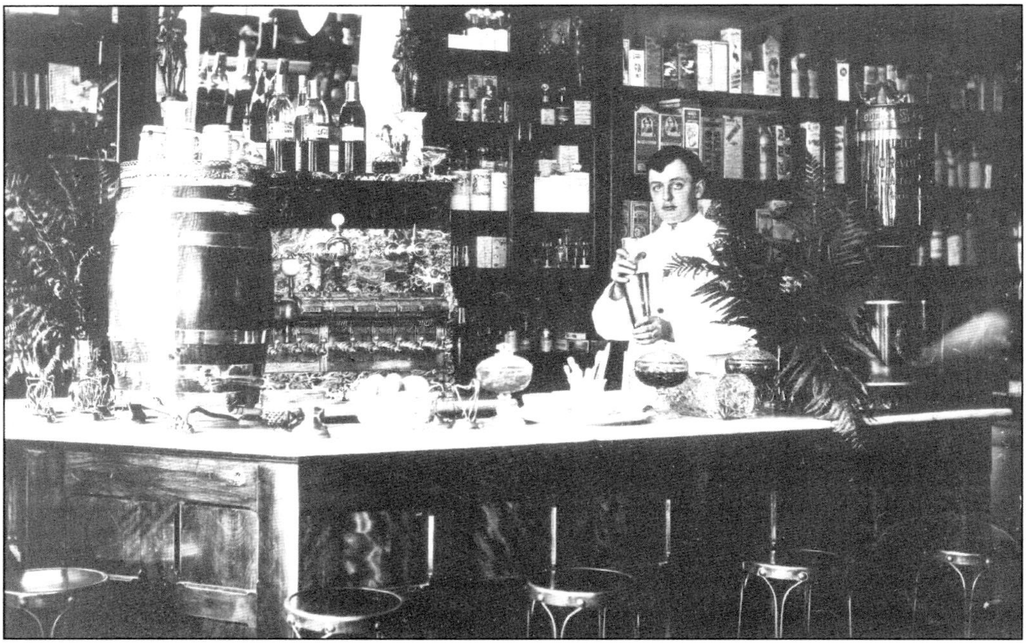

ARTHUR DAVIS DRUGSTORE. This picture of Raymond Galloway, taken about 1910, where he worked many years for Mr. Davis as his druggist assistant. Roy and Emma Peck arrived on Westminster Street in the 1920s, opening the facility as their drugstore.

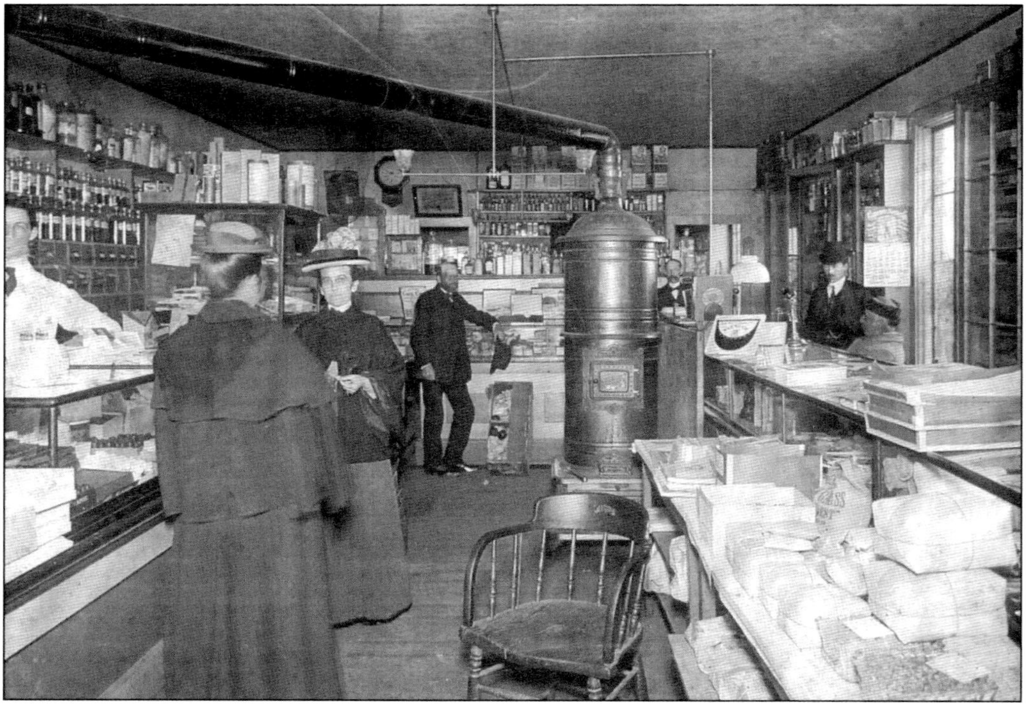

C. C. DAVIS. In the north part of the Wells Block on Main Street, the C. C. Davis drugstore carried on business from 1866 until 1946. It was advertised as "C. C. Davis Registered Pharmacist: Books, Stationery, Periodicals, Jewelry, Fancy Goods, Picture Frames, and Job Printing." The store contained the phone exchange for a time and they also printed the town reports.

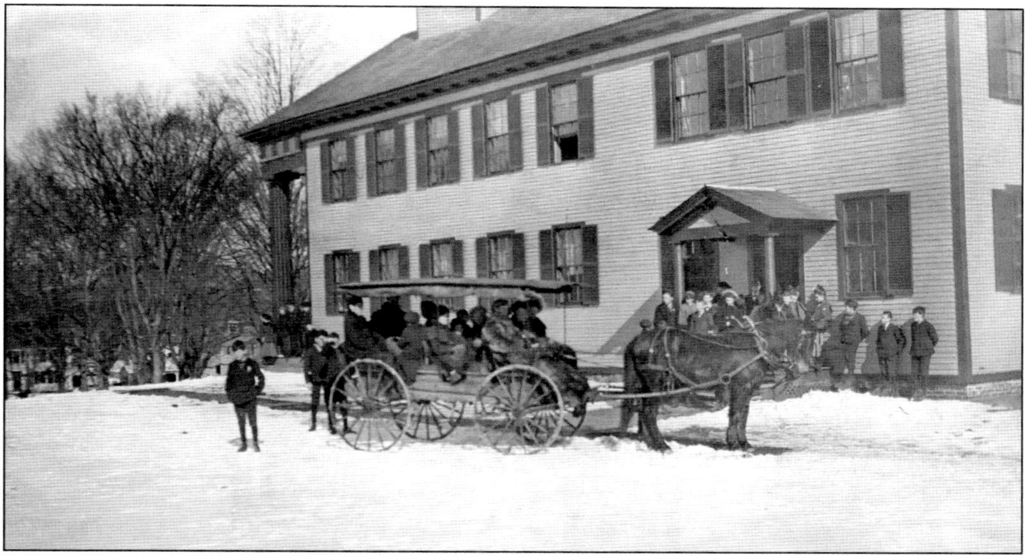

SCHOOL BUSES. In the early 1920s, severe snowstorms made getting to school at the academy difficult, especially from the hill districts. In January 1922 after a bad storm, "the school [horse] teams practically having to break the roads and all were late . . . one not arriving until 11:00 am." Later on in the same month, after another severe storm, the "school barge went through the street at an angle of 45 degrees with the children clinging to the top side to keep from falling out." Note the lunch pail in the bottom photograph, at right.

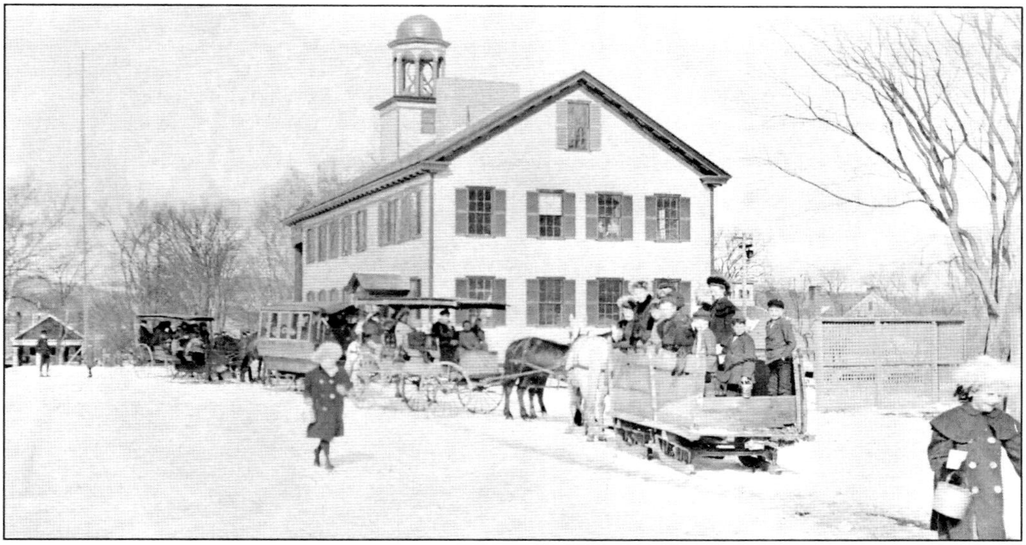

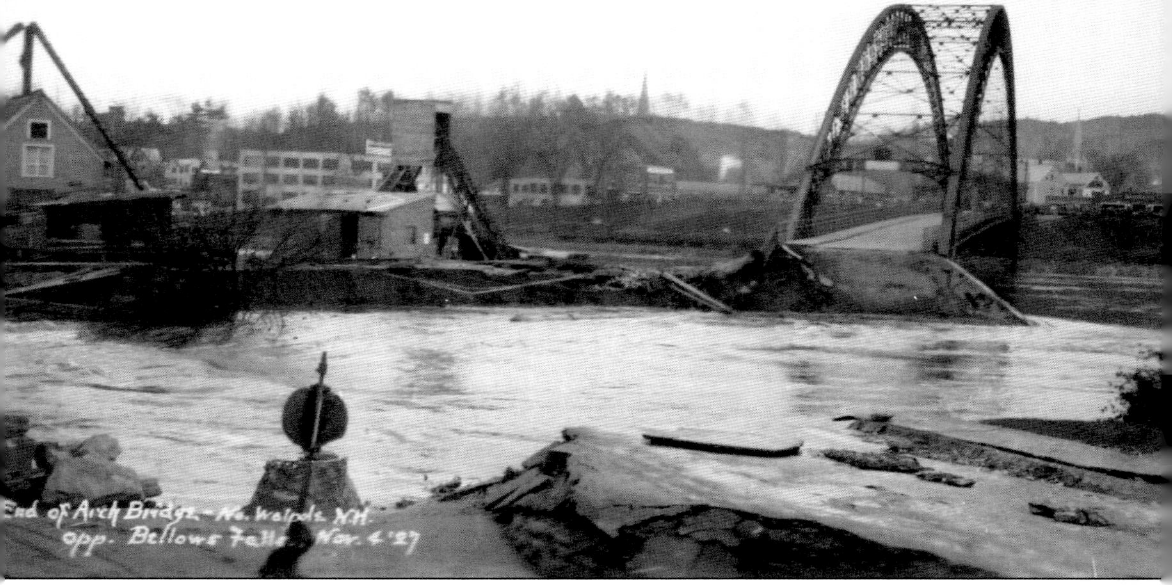

FLOOD OF 1927. At 5:50 p.m. on Thursday, November 3, 1927, the water began rising on the Connecticut River at North Walpole and Bellows Falls. By 10:30 a.m. the next morning, the river was 20 feet above the dam, six inches higher than the record of 1888. Prediction was that it would continue to rise for six hours; in preparation, the railroad bridge was weighted with loaded coal cars. Railroad service was suspended. On Saturday, the river came over the bank in North Walpole, cutting a new channel and taking everything with it northeast of the arch bridge as far as Vine Street. The two houses on the west side of Vine Street were carried away. National news media such as reporters and photographers from Pathe, Paramount, MGM, and National Geographic flocked to Walpole to cover this story, 150 of them staying at the Red Mill Inn. At the Westminster Bridge, the river was over the banks and into the meadows.

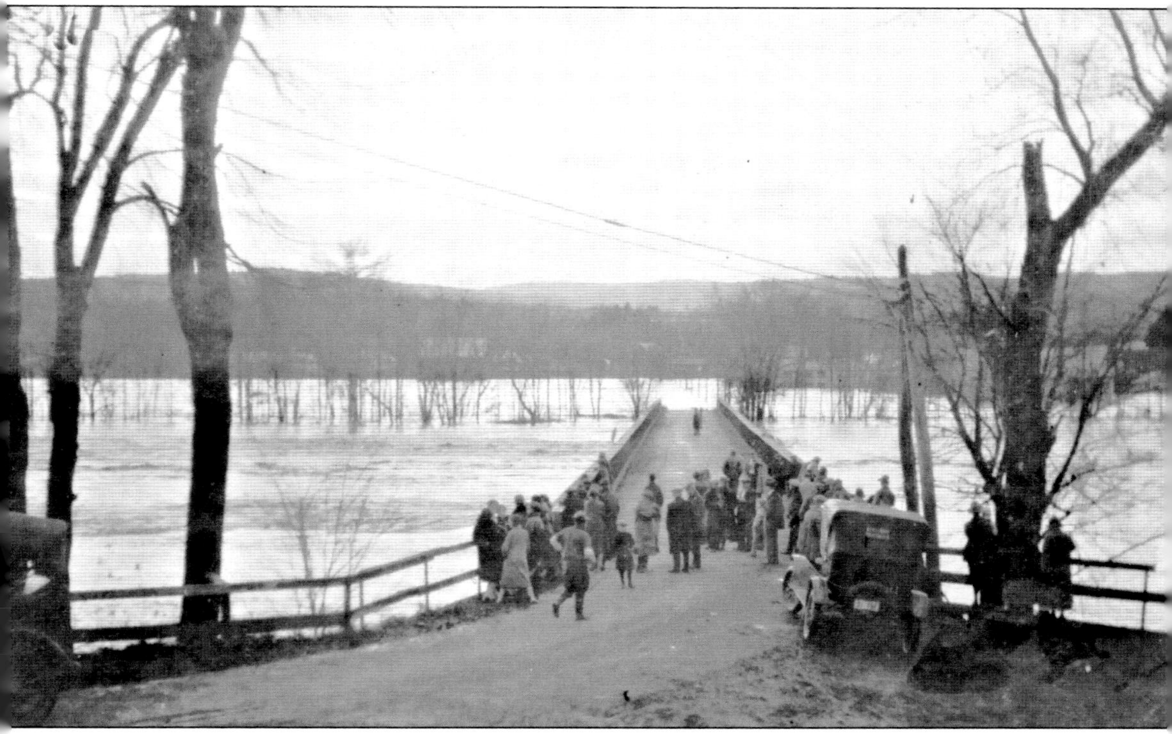

Flood of 1927 Continued. Downstream at the village bridge to Westminster, people thronged the riverbank all day on Friday, watching the awe-inspiring sight, with the river sweeping along great masses of debris and wreckage from the north. The waters flowed to the floor of the bridge, and the Westminster end was inundated. Everyone felt that the bridge was lost but cheered at news on Saturday morning that it had held. Power was out for a couple days, and train service was interrupted by a washout in Winchendon, Massachusetts. Herman Woodward's greens plant in Westminster, employing 50 people, was damaged by the flood, and some workers were removed to Walpole by truck and boat. Woodward ultimately moved his operations to Walpole. Power was out from Thursday night until Saturday night. Hubbard Farms had 25,000 chicks hatching in their electric incubators and had to transfer them to hot water heat. Barns and outbuildings on the Ward farm were washed off their foundations and floated in the fields. Meadows on both sides of the river were underwater.

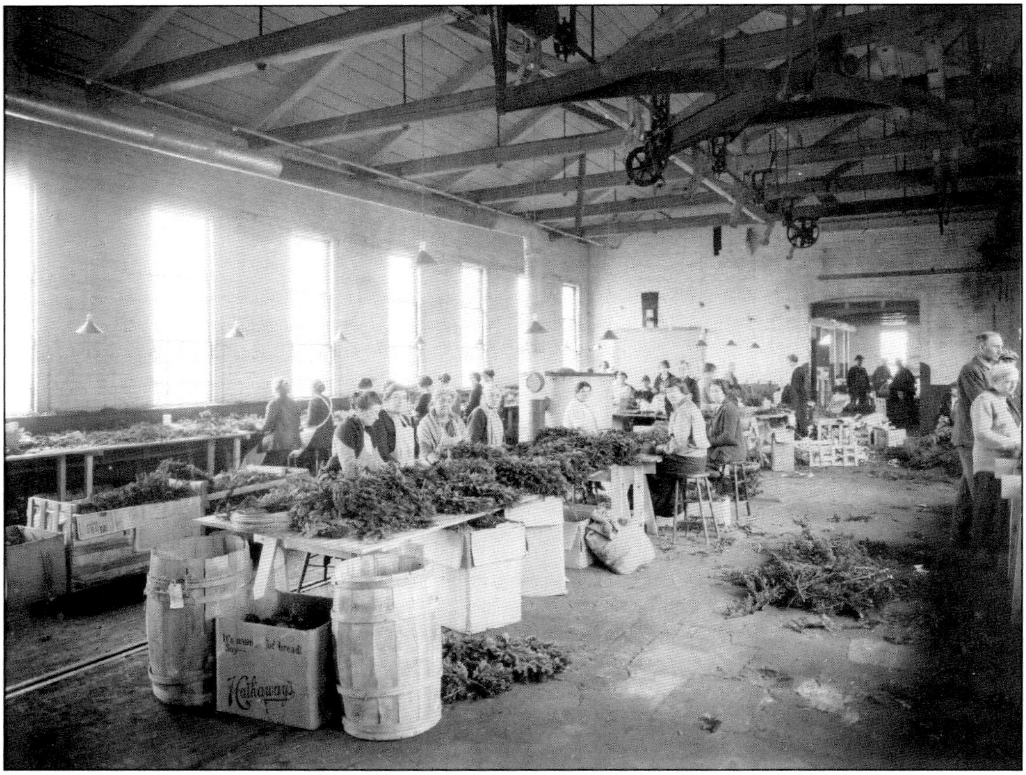

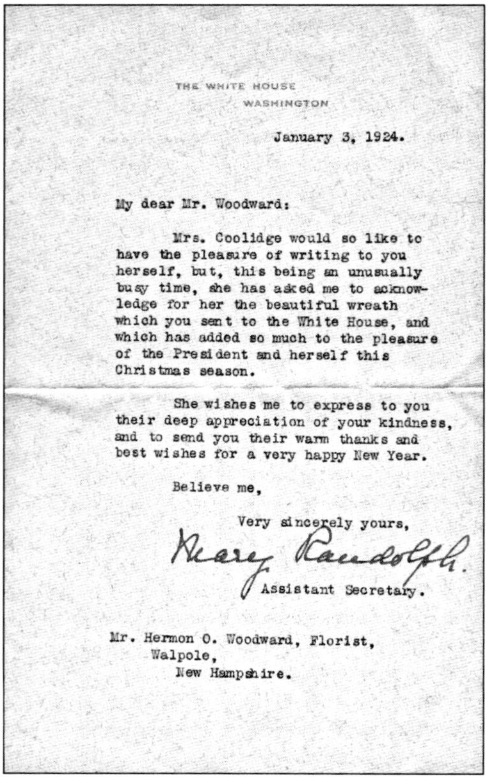

THE WHITE HOUSE
WASHINGTON

January 3, 1924.

My dear Mr. Woodward:

Mrs. Coolidge would so like to have the pleasure of writing to you herself, but, this being an unusually busy time, she has asked me to acknowledge for her the beautiful wreath which you sent to the White House, and which has added so much to the pleasure of the President and herself this Christmas season.

She wishes me to express to you their deep appreciation of your kindness, and to send you their warm thanks and best wishes for a very happy New Year.

Believe me,

Very sincerely yours,

Mary Randolph

Assistant Secretary.

Mr. Hermon O. Woodward, Florist,
Walpole,
New Hampshire.

WOODWARD'S. Woodward Florist was started as a Christmas greens business by Hermon Woodward in 1908 across the river in Westminster, Vermont. The business sustained thousands of dollars in damage during the flood of 1927 but was rebuilt and continued until the flood of 1936 destroyed the plant. He relocated his entire florist operation to Depot Hill in Walpole on property he bought from Fanny Mason. His sons Phillip and Elliot developed a wholesale business selling to gift shops and department stores ranging from New York to Philadelphia and the Midwest. For years, Woodward Florist sent Christmas wreaths to the White House. At left is a copy of a note of thanks from the Calvin Coolidge administration. (Courtesy of the Woodward family.)

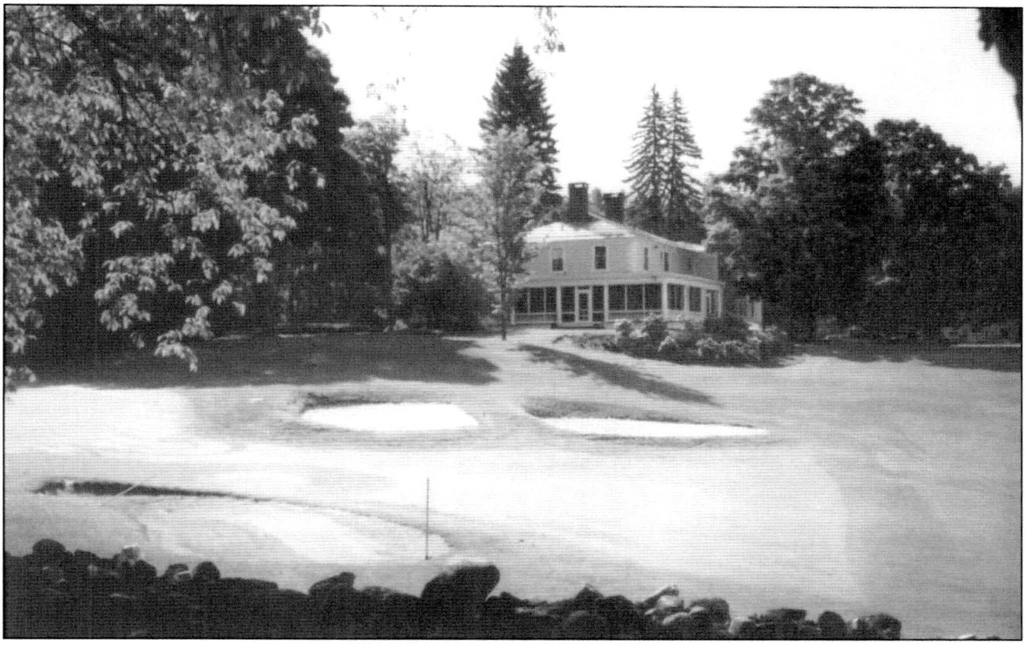

Hooper Farm and Golf Club. In early 1926, property known as the Meeting House Hill Farm was given to the town by the George L. Hooper estate. The town voted to lease the property to the newly formed Hooper Golf Club of Walpole. An architect was hired, and Italian workmen constructed the greens. Local labor was used to construct the fairways. The golf course was officially opened on July 2, 1927. The old Watkins Tavern at the top of Prospect Hill became the clubhouse. Below, golfers from the early days convene at the first tee for nine holes of sport and sun in traditional attire. Today golfers from far and near come to enjoy the fine features of this municipal club with its historic, Federal-style clubhouse. Lunch is served on the porch during summer months. (Below, courtesy of Ray Boas.)

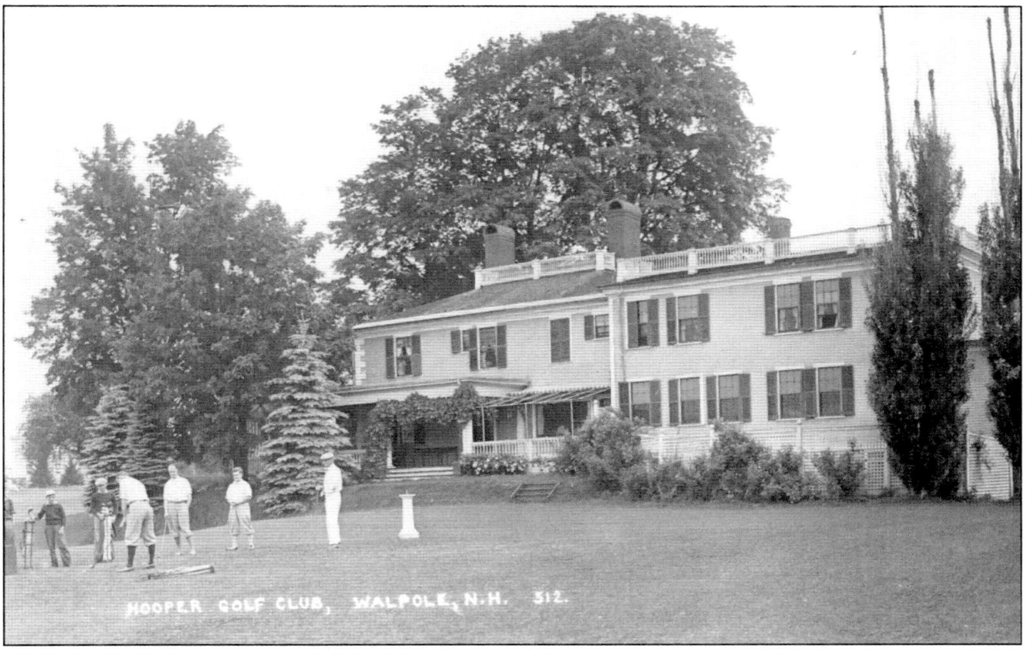

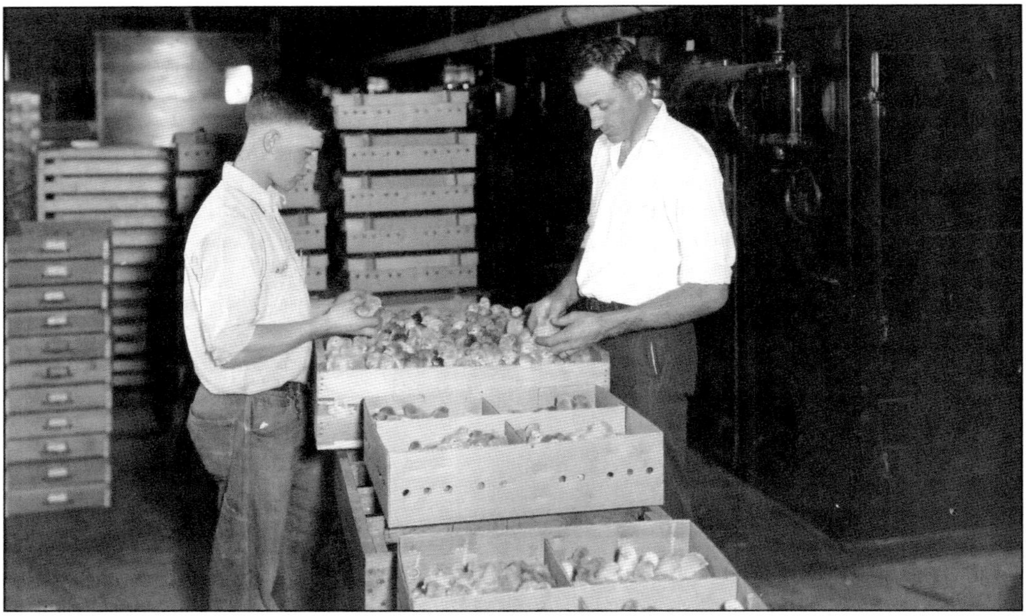

HUBBARD FARMS. After graduating from the New Hampshire Agricultural College (renamed the University of New Hampshire) in 1921, Oliver Hubbard, along with his father, Ira, started in the poultry business under the name Maple Hill Farm. They were able to produce a breed of birds free of destructive salmonellosis bacteria called pullorum and therefore increase the viability of the poultry they sold. Also at this time, changes in postal regulations allowed the use of the mail to deliver their chicks. This made it possible for a wide geographical distribution and market for their poultry. In the above 1933 photograph, Hubbard (right) is inspecting new chicks. Below, workers Mark Howard (left) and Frank Mitchell pose on one of the growing fleet of trucks for transporting Hubbard chicks to market about 1933 (Courtesy of Hubbard Farms.)

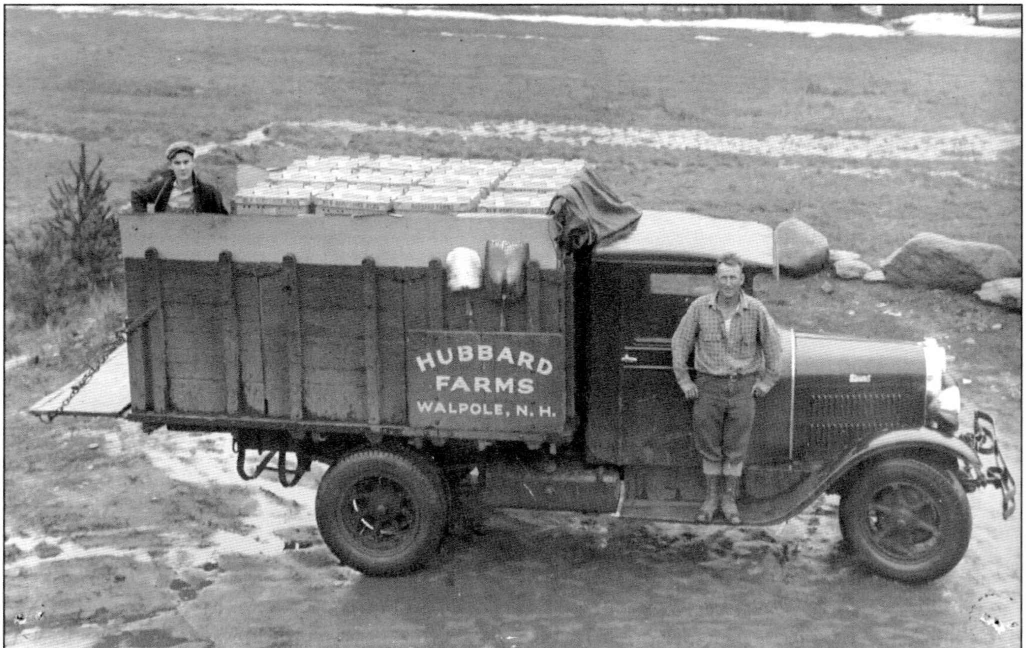

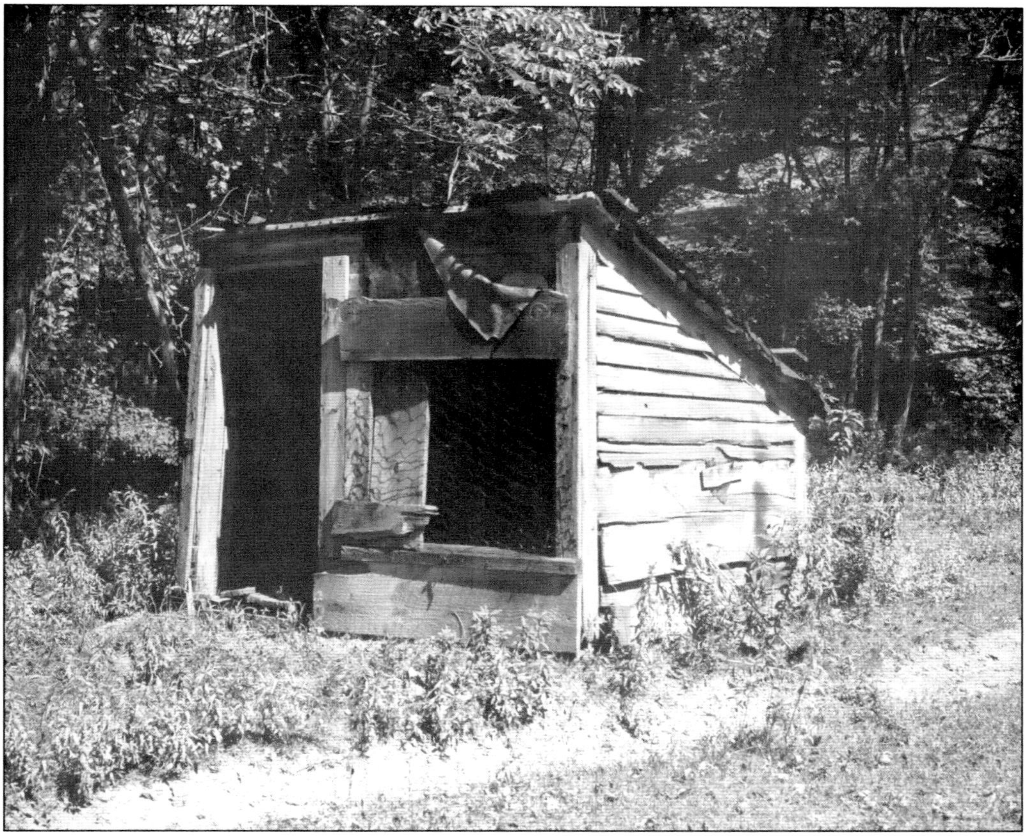

HUBBARD EXPANSION. During the first year, they produced between 5,000 and 10,000 pullets. In 1925, they were hatching and selling 100,000 chicks and renamed the business Hubbard Farms. Three years later, they hatched and sold 320,000 chicks. By the end of the decade, Hubbard Farms had expanded into New York and in 1933 established a hatchery in Ephrata, Pennsylvania, which proved to be a critical step in the company's expansion. The small structure, above, is reported to be the first chicken coop of the Hubbard operation. Below, the Hubbard Farms operation is shown about 1935. (Courtesy of Hubbard Farms.)

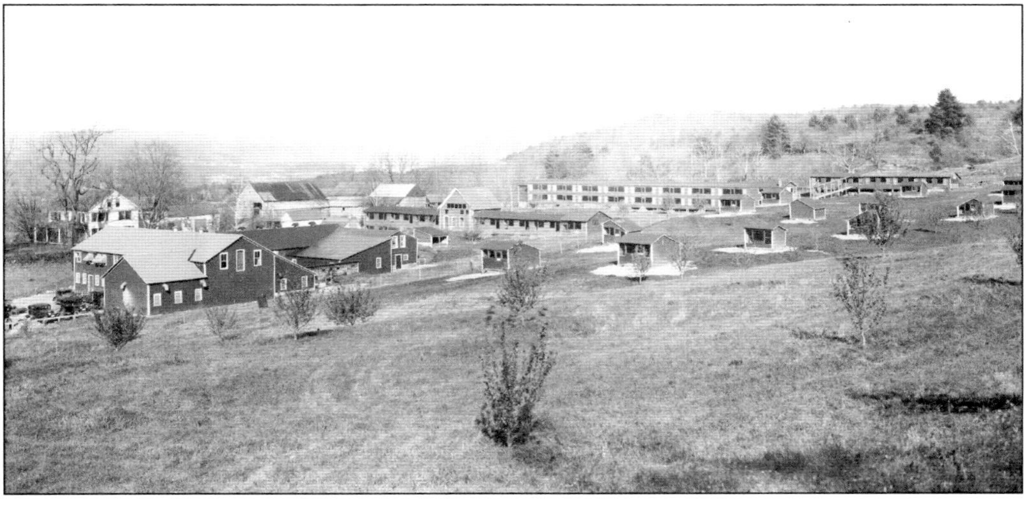

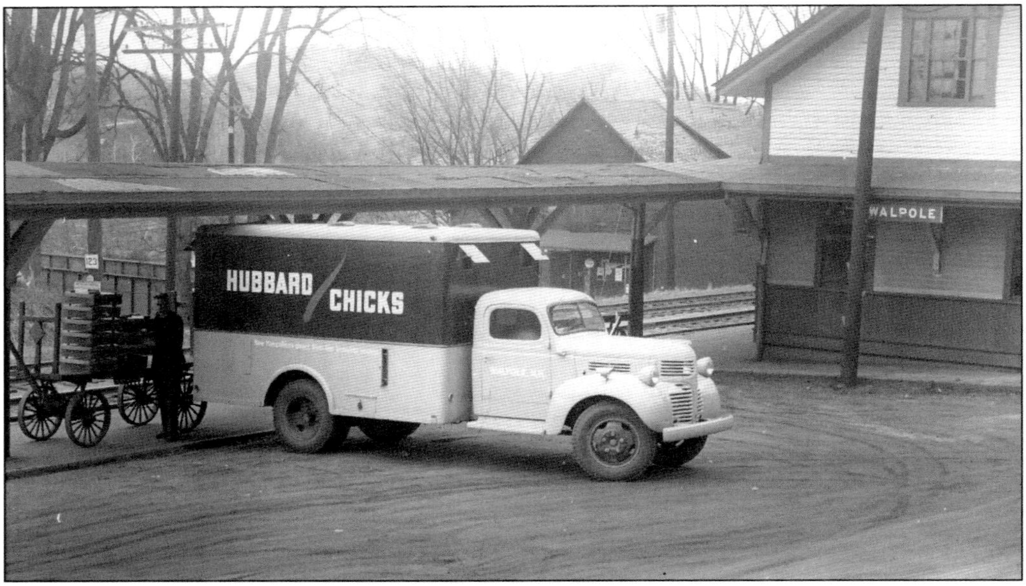

HUBBARD FAMILY BUSINESS GROWS. Oliver Hubbard's brothers Austin, Leslie, and Donald joined the family business. Eventually Hubbard Farms became one of the largest and most detailed genetic poultry breeding research operations in the United States. The foundation breeding stock developed in Walpole was sent to multiplication farms in Pennsylvania, North Carolina, and Belgium. Above, an early truck sits at the railroad depot preparing to deliver chicks. Below, the 1950s Hubbard office complex on Turnpike Street and the truck fleet appear with several members of the family and staff. By the 1960s, Hubbard Farms was an international corporation with operations in Belgium, Italy, and Japan. In 1996, Hubbard Farms celebrated its 75th anniversary. Today it is a wholly owned subsidiary of the Grimaud Group of France, the second-largest group worldwide in the multispecies genetic selection industry. It operates under the name Hubbard LLC, with home offices continuing in Walpole. (Below, courtesy of Hubbard Farms.)

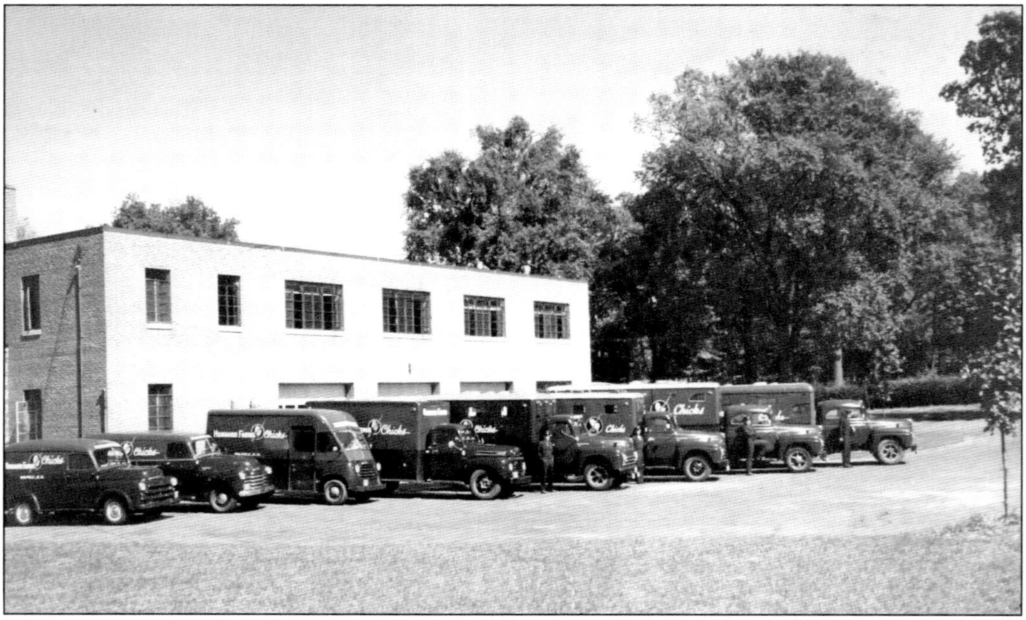

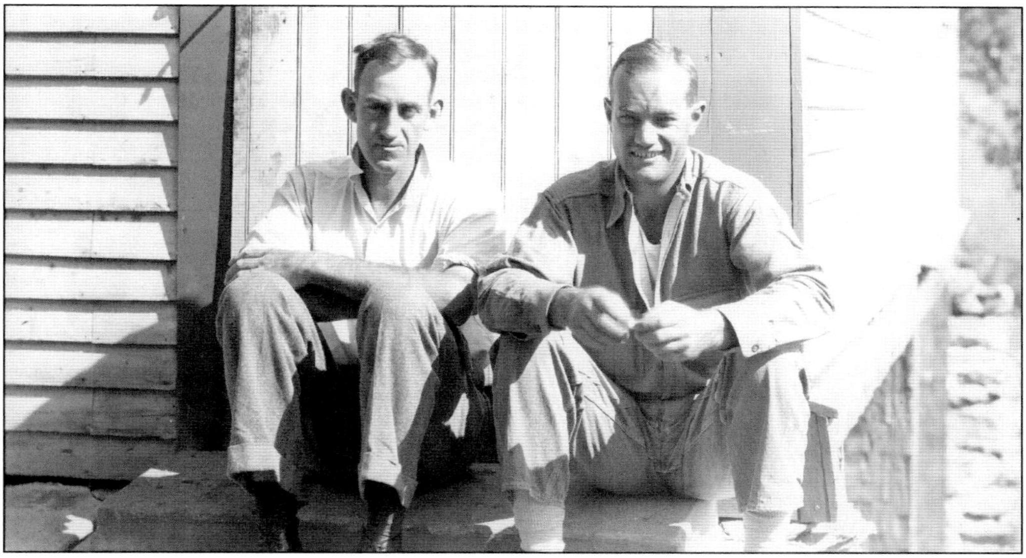

RALPH N. "JACK" JOHNSON AND OLIVER HUBBARD. Young farmer-businessmen Ralph N. "Jack" Johnson (right) and Oliver Hubbard enjoy a moment's relaxation together from their busy lives in this photograph taken about 1935. Both men went on to develop large businesses, one becoming a multinational company. (Courtesy of Hubbard Farms.)

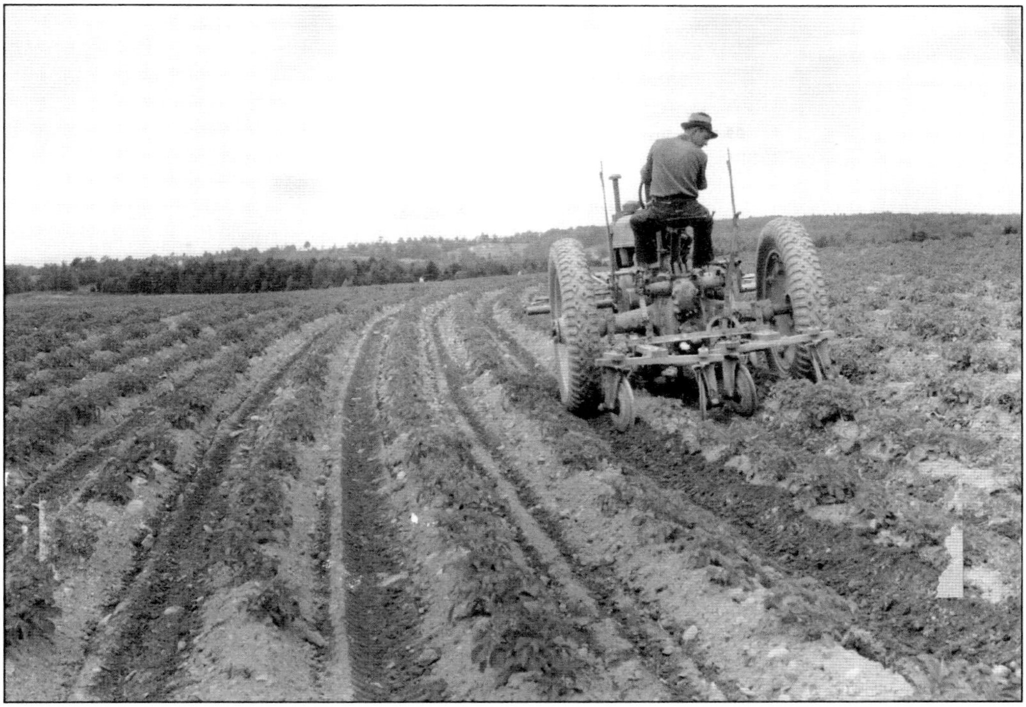

RALPH N. "JACK" JOHNSON. Johnson started raising potatoes in Walpole in 1929 on Fay Hill. At the same time, he took an agency for John Deere farm equipment. By 1941, he was the largest potato grower in the state with 115 acres under cultivation. As his potato farming grew, so did his farm equipment dealership, and he moved the business to various locations in the village. In 1943, he bought a building and land from the Bellows homestead to house his vast amounts of new and used farm machinery. The business remains in the same location today.

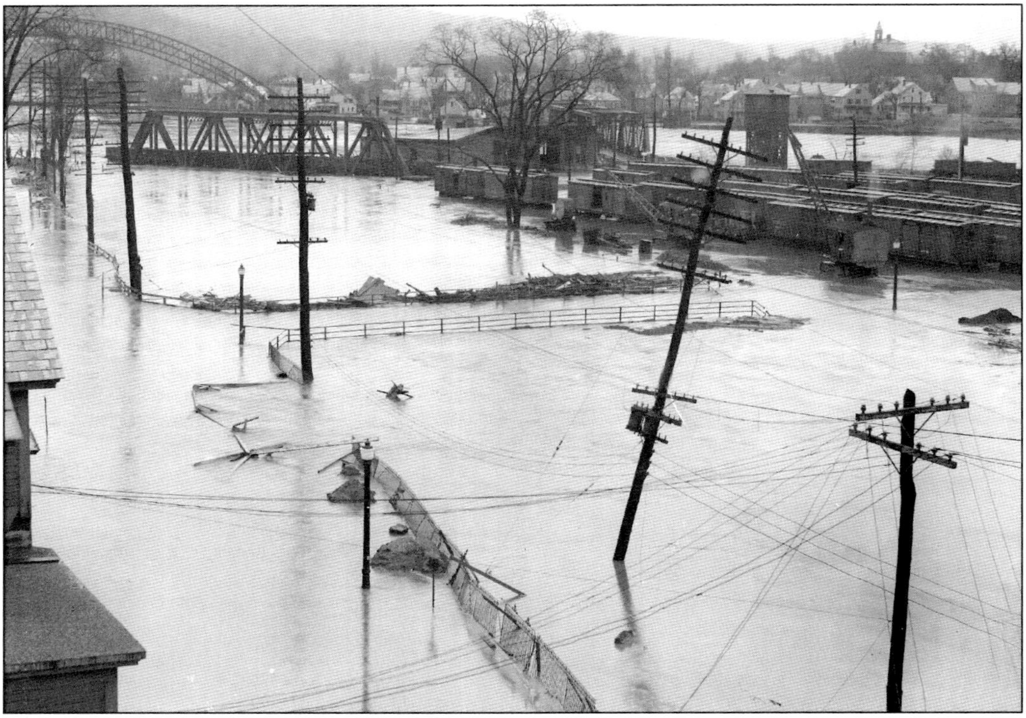

FLOOD OF 1936. In March 1936, heavy rains and the breakup of an ice dam brought more flooding to Walpole. At one point, more than 100,000 cubic feet of water per second were going over the dam at North Walpole. Some North Walpole families were evacuated; the east end of the arch bridge was underwater. The power company blew its cofferdam under the railroad bridge to save the town. At the southern boundary of North Walpole, access to the Vilas Bridge (site of the first bridge across the Connecticut River) was washed away. At the Westminster Bridge (below), the river covered the bridge, cutting a new course on the Vermont side. A crowd gathered at the bridge to see if this 1911 bridge would hold; again, it did.

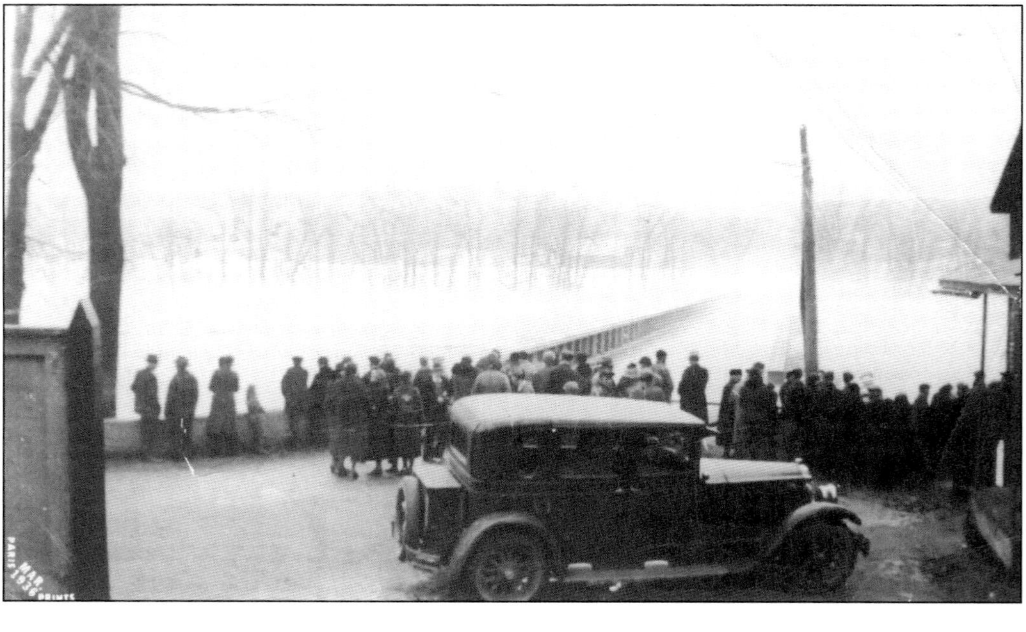

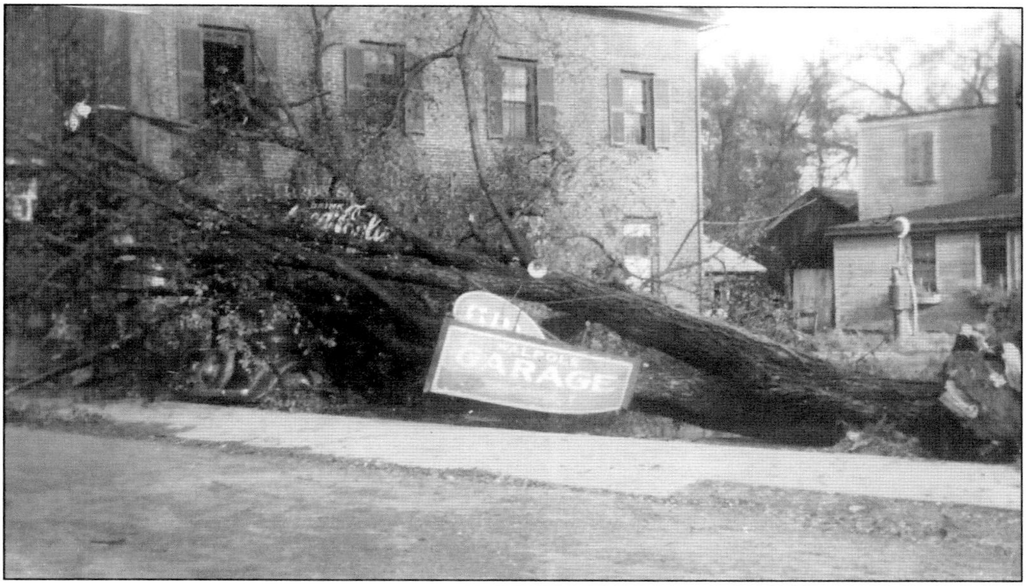

HURRICANE, 1938. On the afternoon of September 21, 1938, following five days of heavy rain, the worst natural disaster in the history of Walpole struck. The next morning saw roofs crushed or torn away and few chimneys left unharmed. Whole groves of pines and hardwoods were gone, and maple orchards were "fit only for working into firewood." Not a street in the village was passable. Trees uprooted on School Street fell on W. W. Shackley's house and barn (below). Many farm buildings and silos were moved off their foundations by the blasts of wind; a full tobacco barn collapsed north of town. At the same time, the river was steadily rising, threatening to add to the menace of the wind.

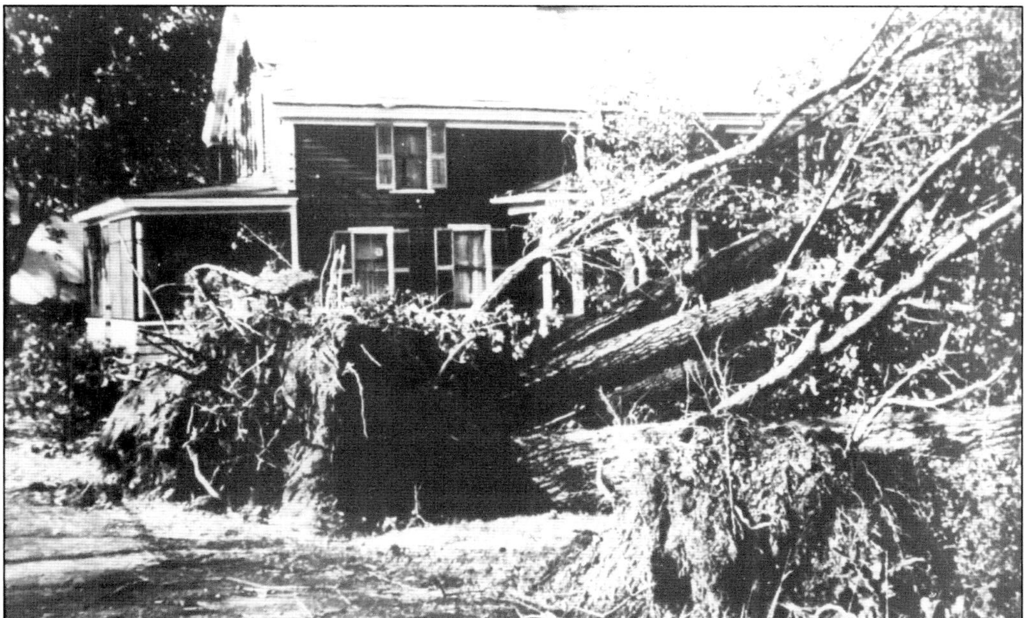

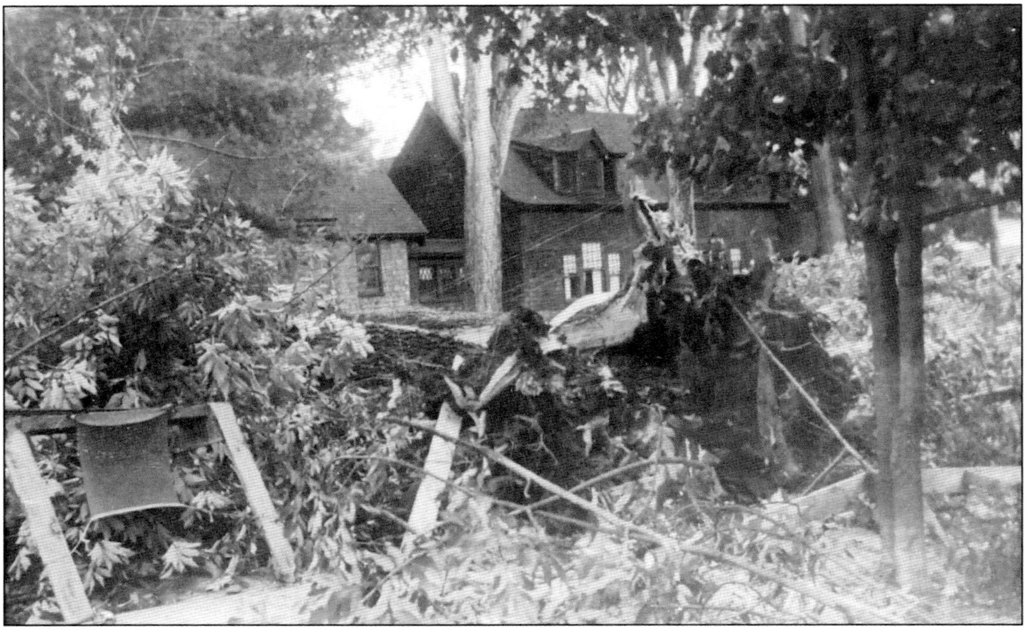

HURRICANE AFTERMATH, 1938. All transportation, electrical utilities, and communications were at a standstill. Housewives fortunate to have electric stoves were left to improvise ways of providing meals for their families. There was discussion in town hall of the federal plan for salvage of hurricane timber; plans made to store such timber in local ponds were not carried out. Instead, salvage timber was dry-stored on part of the Amory farm. Given the amount of downed timber in the woodlands, the forest fire hazard was especially great and resulted in a fire on May 6, 1939, on Fall Mountain. Telephone and power crews from around the country were sent to New England to help repair the damage, like the Northwest Bell Telephone crew from Nebraska (below), which worked in Walpole in October 1938.

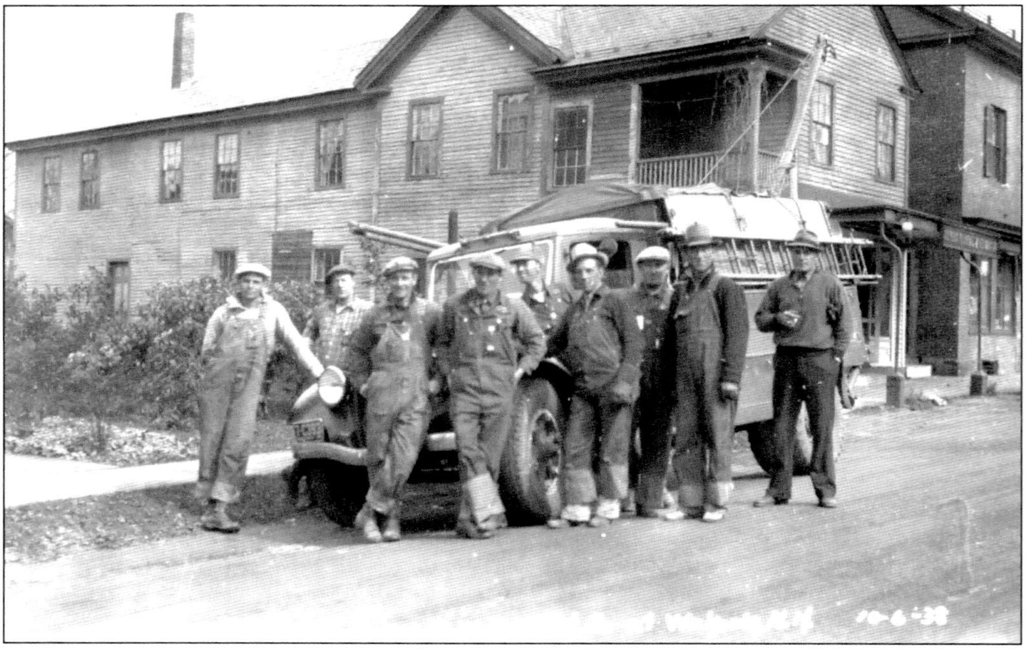

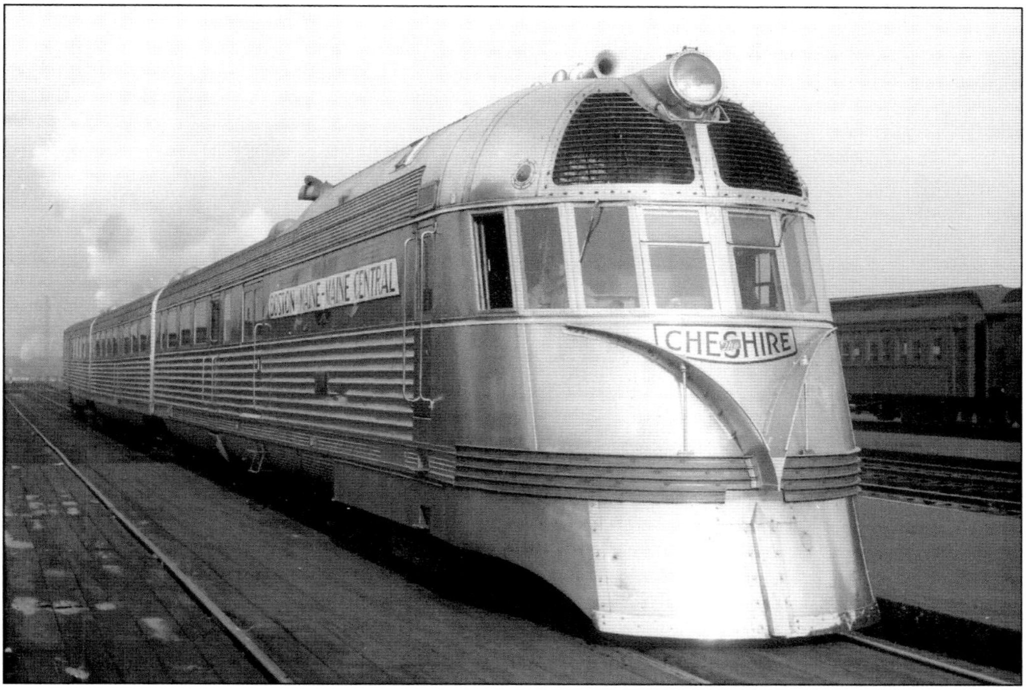

THE *CHESHIRE* AND ITS WRECK. The train was built by the Budd Company of Philadelphia and delivered to the Boston and Maine and Maine Central Railroads in 1935. Originally designated the *Flying Yankee*, it was renamed the *Cheshire* (for Cheshire County), and in November 1944, it began running between White River Junction, Vermont, and Boston. In January 1945, the *Cheshire* (below) was wrecked in Walpole with "slight injury to passengers." It seems a housing on the front of the train dropped, causing the train to split a switch, enter a short sidetrack, derail, and plow into a Hubbard Farms storehouse. The frozen Connecticut River is visible in the background. (Above, courtesy of Historical Society of Cheshire County; below, courtesy of Hubbard Farms.)

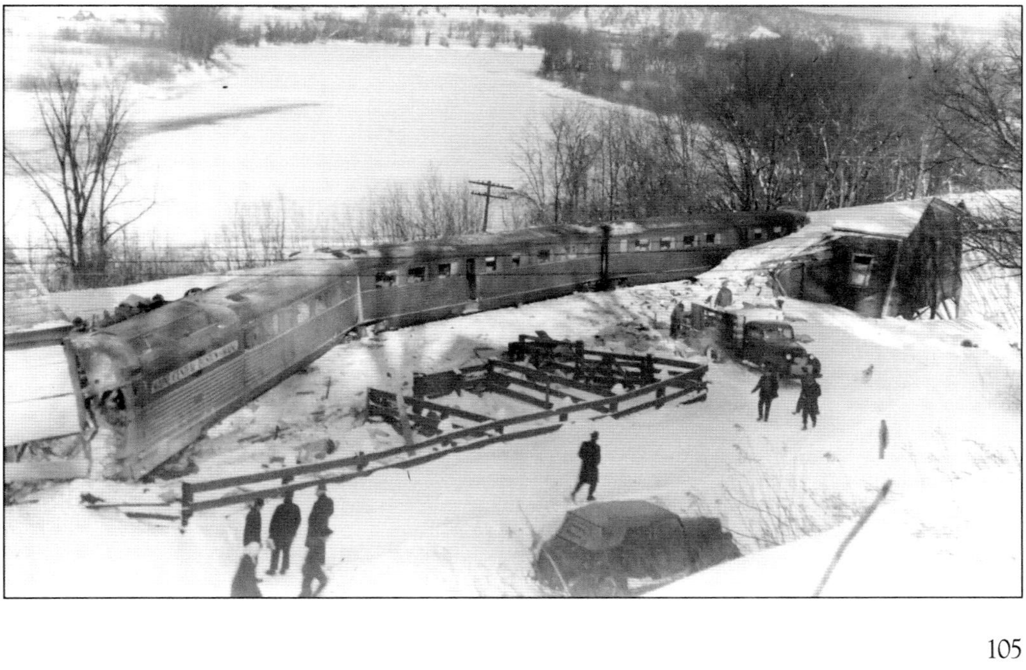

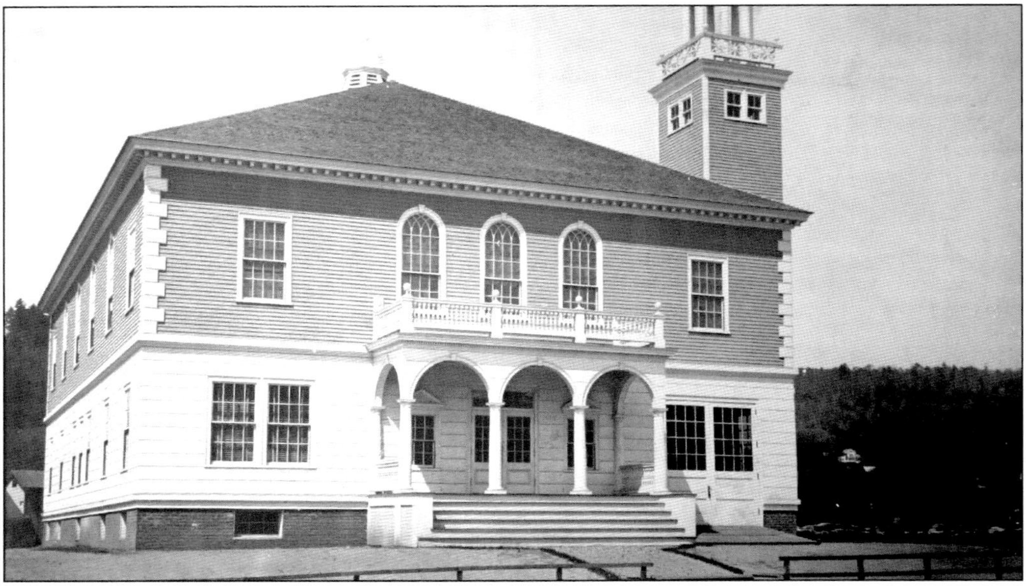

RUSSELL MEMORIAL HALL. Given to North Walpole in 1902 by William A. Russell, the hall housed the library, village offices, the fire department, a banquet room, a kitchen, and an assembly hall. As a social center, it was the scene of weekly dances, firemen's balls, dramatic presentations, and even prizefights. The building burned on the night of January 31, 1949. Hampered by zero degree weather, firemen still managed to save the fire truck parked in the basement. Lost were the 2,500-book library, precinct offices, jail, sports and social center, and costumes for an upcoming minstrel show.

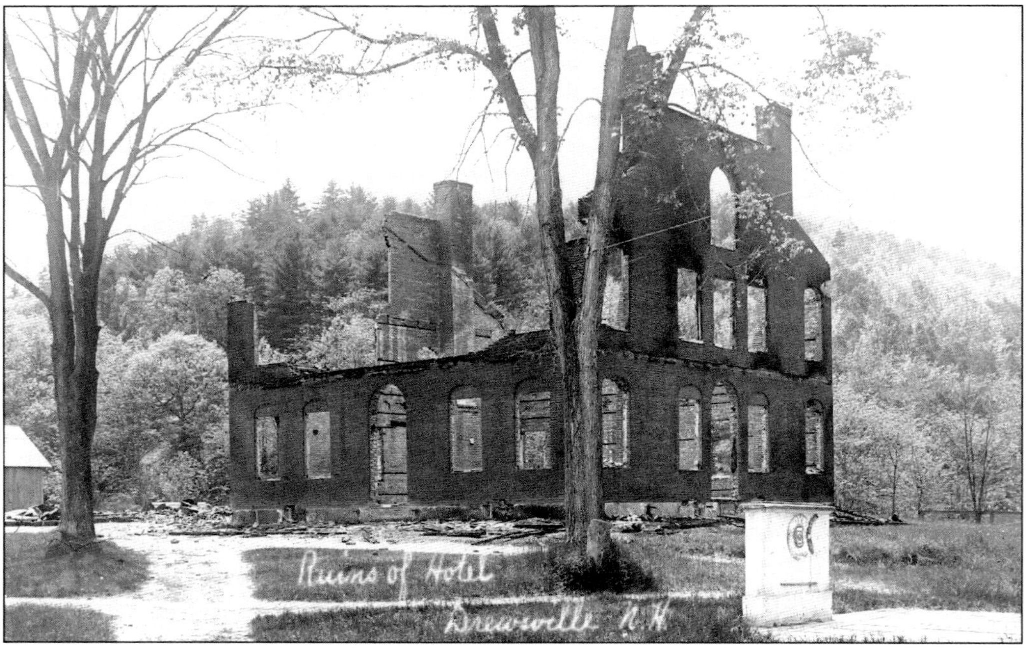

THE MOUNTAIN HOUSE FIRE. Another village center of activity was the Mountain House of Drewsville (see chapter 3). Built by village founder Thomas Drew in 1810, it passed through several owners to Dennis Brennan by 1907. Shortly thereafter, a fire broke out at two in the morning, and the entire building was quickly consumed by flames.

Six

Change and Preservation 1950–2000

By mid-1950, the United States was again engaged in international conflict—in Korea. In Walpole, the railroad era was ending, with the cessation of rail service coming in 1952. Despite local resistance, its historic depot was demolished in 1962, making way for the new Route 12 highway, bypassing the village.

The post-World War II baby boom was filling Walpole's schools, which to this point had been rural and multigraded in one or two rooms, with the academy housing the high school. In the 1950s, state-mandated school consolidation and the information age pressured schools to adjust.

In 1961, the town celebrated its first state Class S basketball championship for Walpole High School, which had occupied its new building on Turnpike Street just 11 years. Two years later, Walpole became part of the multitown Fall Mountain Regional School District, with a new high school opening in nearby Langdon in 1966.

The 1960s saw the formation of a planning board with subsequent creation of a master plan. In 1976, controversy arose over the selection of Walpole as the site for a pulp mill. As opposition grew, the proposal was ultimately defeated.

Walpole commemorated the nation's bicentennial with a weekend celebration in July 1976. Old Home Days were observed periodically, as they have been since 1899. The Walpole Players, founded during Old Home Days in 1985, has been performing regularly ever since.

The late 20th century saw growth, with housing and commercial expansion, especially north of the village. There were a number of empty buildings in the village after several businesses moved from there. Community members explored ways to renew the vigor and quality of life in the village. Renovation began on several historic buildings, resulting in reduced rental opportunities for small businesses and housing. Ultimately, members of the Hubbard family formed a nonprofit organization—the Walpole Foundation—to continue those efforts.

In 2000, several residents were asked for their views of Walpole's future. They felt the town must continue planning efforts to manage change, retaining its historic features and status as a real farming community. As one respondent put it, "There are New England towns that have the same sense about them as Walpole, but many have become too self-consciously quaint. I'd hope that wouldn't be the case here—that we'd always have the vibrant mix of new people, old people, the past, and new blood that makes it a dynamic community".

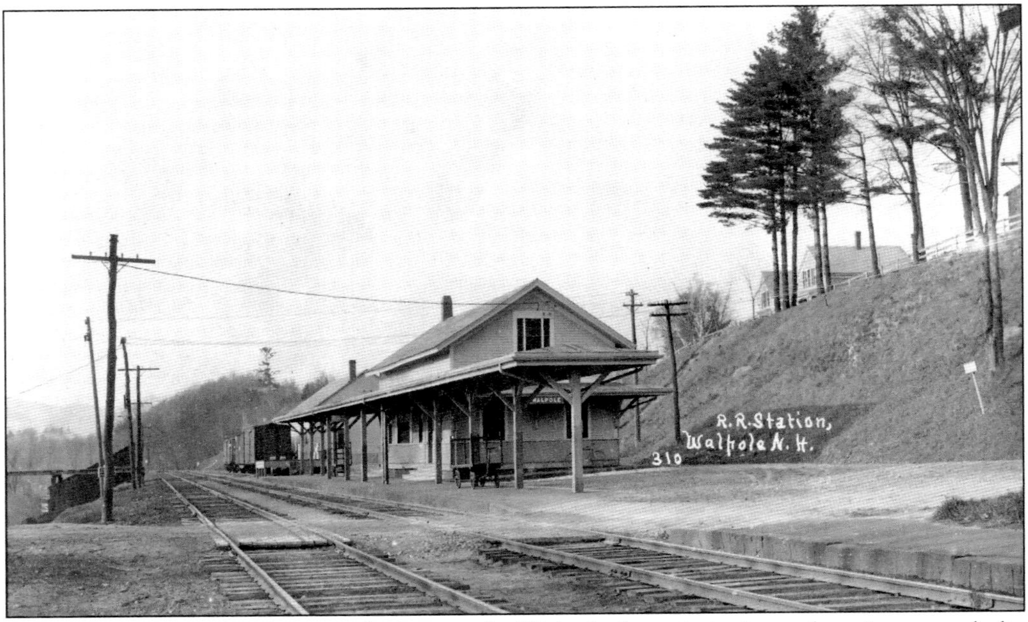

WALPOLE DEPOT. The photograph above is the Walpole depot in its latter days. It was symbolic of the railroad culture, linking local communities and distant destinations. Parents put their children on the Saturday afternoon train for a dime to attend the movies in Bellows Falls, returning for them a couple hours later. The depot was built in 1905 and, despite local opposition, was demolished in 1962, making way for the new Route 12 bypass.

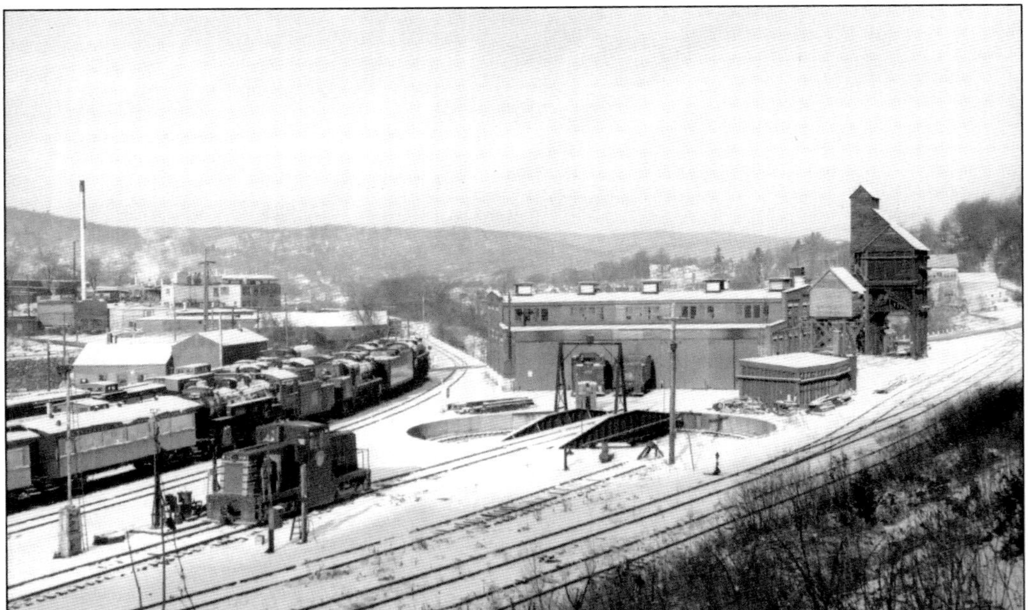

NORTH WALPOLE RAIL YARD. This railroad yard and roundhouse complex had served the industry for many years. At the time of this photograph in 1962, it was home to the Steamtown USA project of F. Nelson Blount of Dublin. Plans for using the site as a steam locomotive museum were abandoned due to conflicts with state plans for the new Route 12. Today the rail yard is base for Green Mountain Railroad's excursion and freight operations.

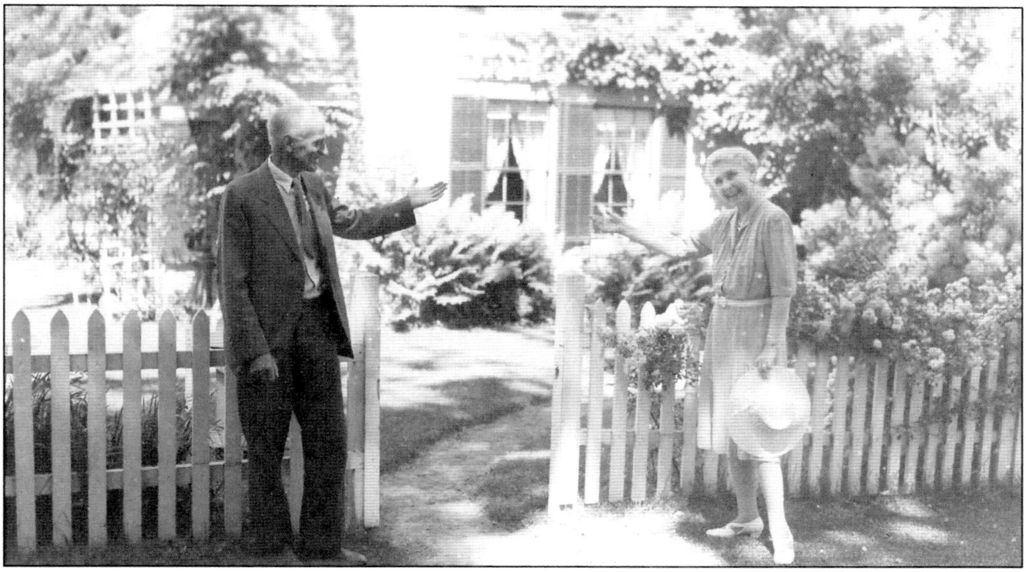

Thorndike H. and Ellen Bellows Robinson Endicott. Thorndike H. Endicott and his wife, Ellen Bellows Robinson Endicott, are shown in their garden on Wentworth Road. She was the daughter of Dr. Henry Whitney Bellows. She helped raise the initial funds that allowed the Walpole Historical Society to purchase the village's oldest house as its first home in 1930. She was a founding member of the society's board and active for many years.

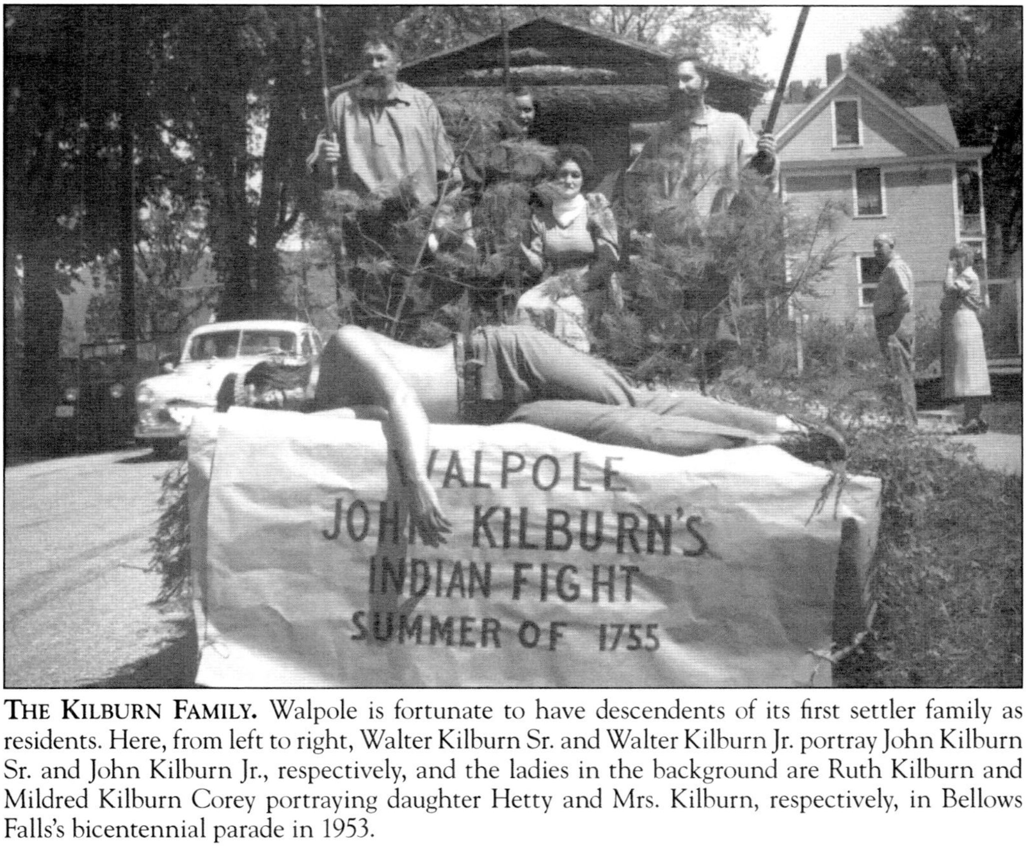

The Kilburn Family. Walpole is fortunate to have descendents of its first settler family as residents. Here, from left to right, Walter Kilburn Sr. and Walter Kilburn Jr. portray John Kilburn Sr. and John Kilburn Jr., respectively, and the ladies in the background are Ruth Kilburn and Mildred Kilburn Corey portraying daughter Hetty and Mrs. Kilburn, respectively, in Bellows Falls's bicentennial parade in 1953.

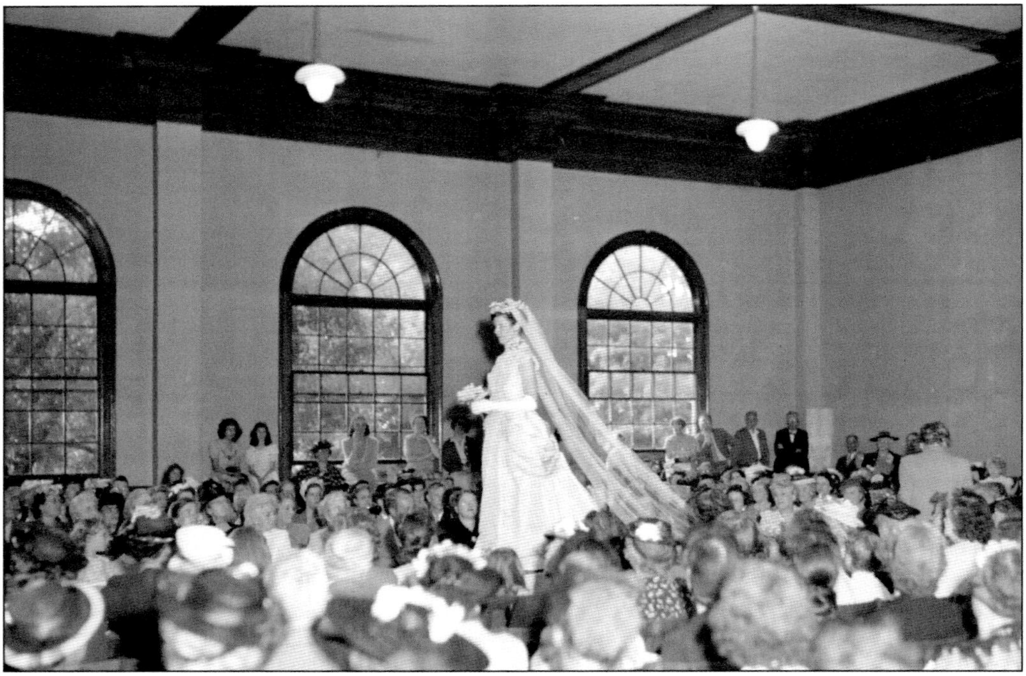

Walpole Bicentennial, 1952. At the bicentennial celebration of the settling of Walpole, a fashion show was held at the town hall, featuring the historical society's collection of antique costumes. Lida Hubbard Rathbone (above) wore a bridal ensemble. Ann Rogers (below, left) wore the dress of Molly Bellows from the 19th century. The dress was a gift to Bellows from her uncle's trip to Paris. Rogers went on to a teaching career in Walpole and is now retired. Langdon Bellows (below, right) was an original board member of the Walpole Historical Society. As one can see, the event enjoyed standing room only. Fashion trends of the 1950s are also seen, including ladies' hats galore.

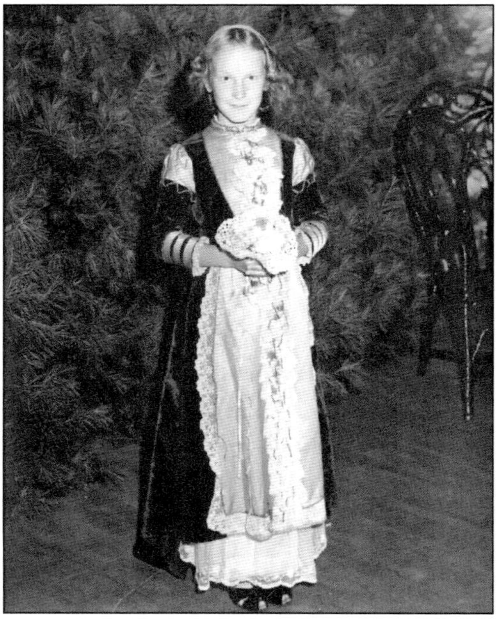

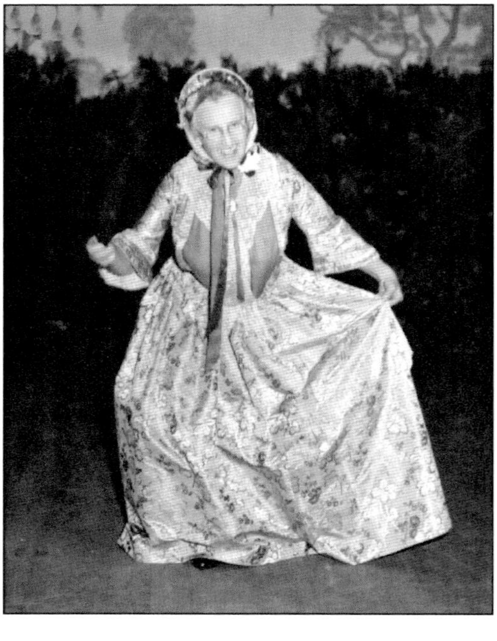

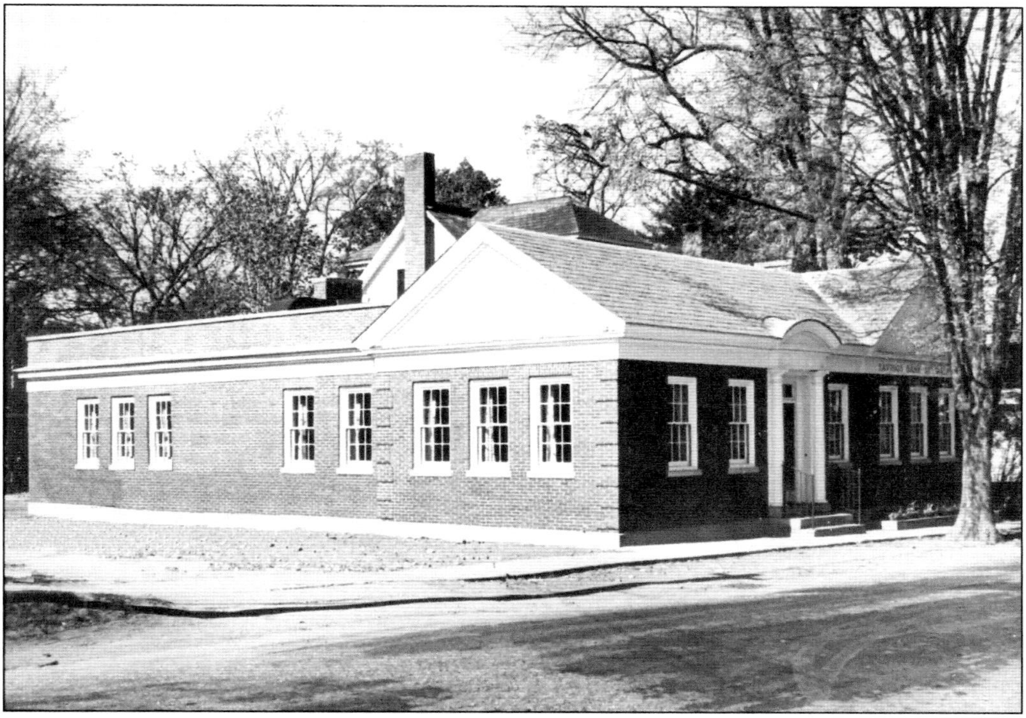

SAVINGS BANK OF WALPOLE. In 1962, a longtime landmark on Westminster Street, the Walpole Inn, was razed after years of decline. Built in its place was the Savings Bank of Walpole (above), a business that had been in Walpole providing banking services on a continuous basis since 1892. In 1990, the bank moved the majority of its operations to the North Meadow Plaza (below), maintaining the village location as a branch. The majority of the branch's office space is now home to Dartmouth-Hitchcock Clinic, an entity that has provided medical services in Walpole, at another location, since 1982.

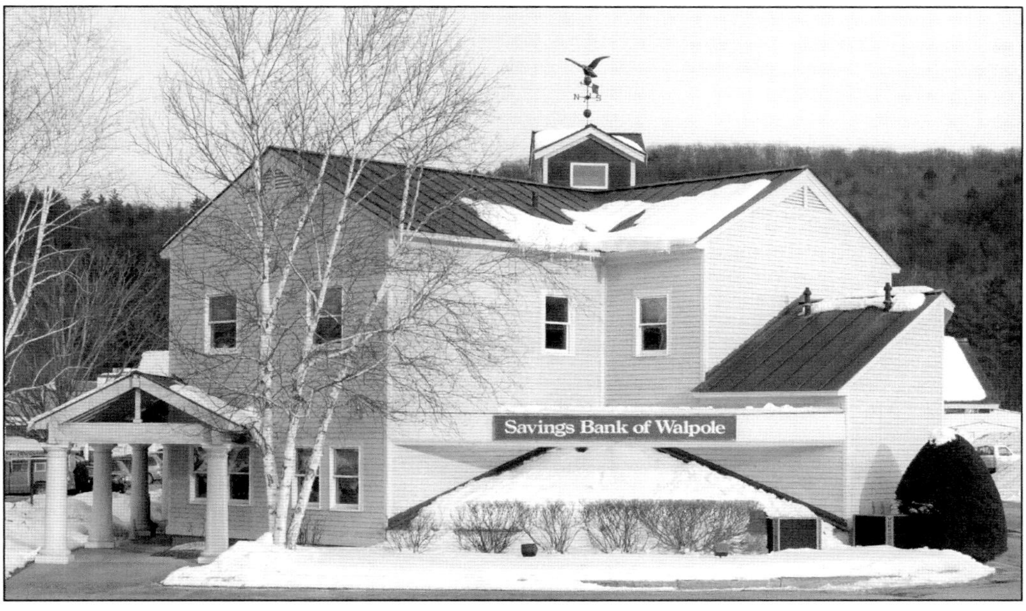

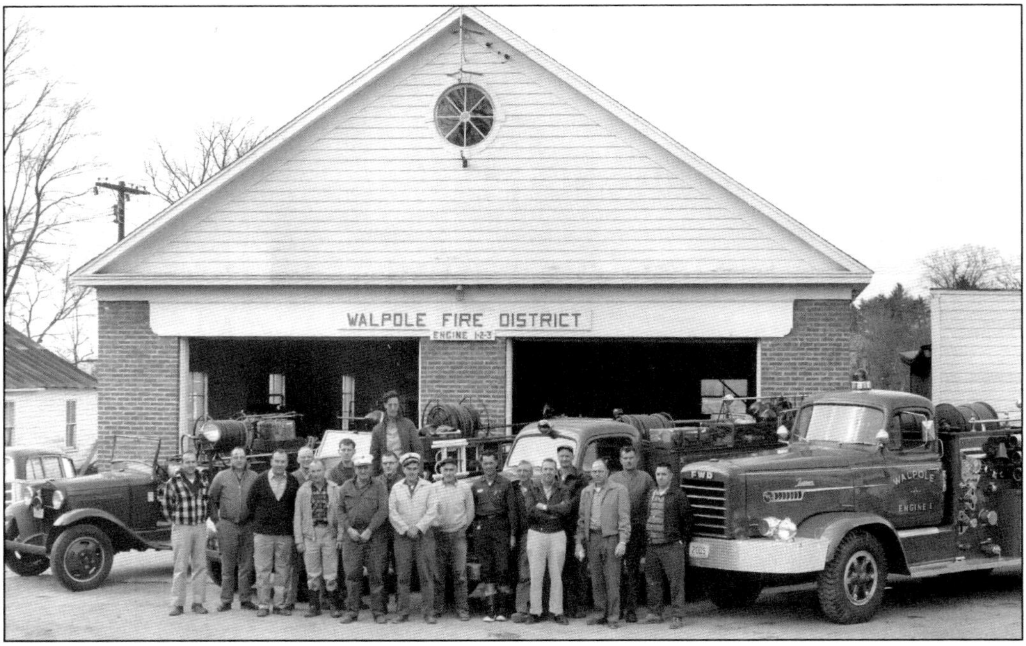

SAFETY MATTERS. Pictured here are the fire stations for Walpole Village (above) and North Walpole in 1952. The fire departments are separate entities with individual chiefs and deputies; members of both departments are volunteers. Identified in the photograph above of the village department are Tedd Murray, Felix Aldrich, Traf Hicks, Maurice Fairbank, Donald Sawyer, Neil Swift, Joe Kilburn, David Staples, Robert Aldrich, George Hurlburt, Thomas Baldwin, Richard Aldrich, Lyle Jeffrey, Harry Boudrieau, August Speckman, Floyd Paterson, Wayne Polley, and Loubert Brooks. The North Walpole Fire District was established in 1886 to "take action against fire" and is administered by the North Walpole District Commissioners. By 1902, the station occupied the basement of the new Russell Hall and did so until the 1949 fire. The new station (below) was its replacement. The Walpole Police Department works from an adjacent office.

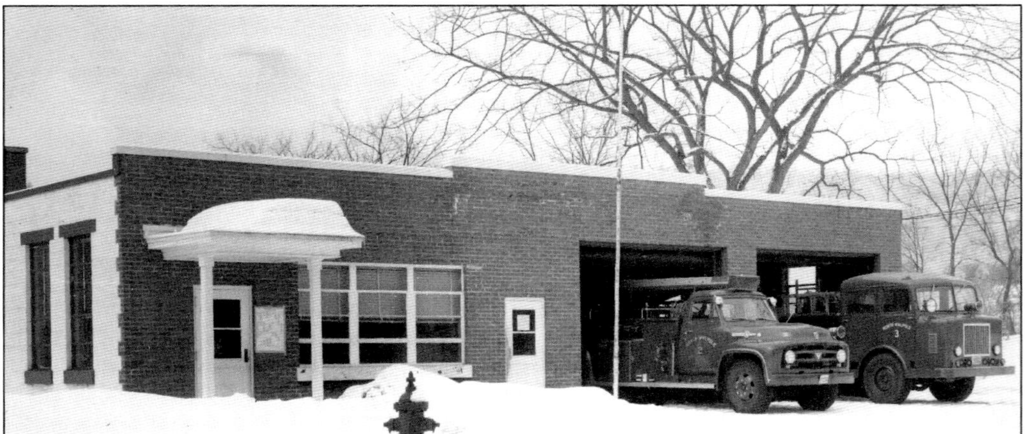

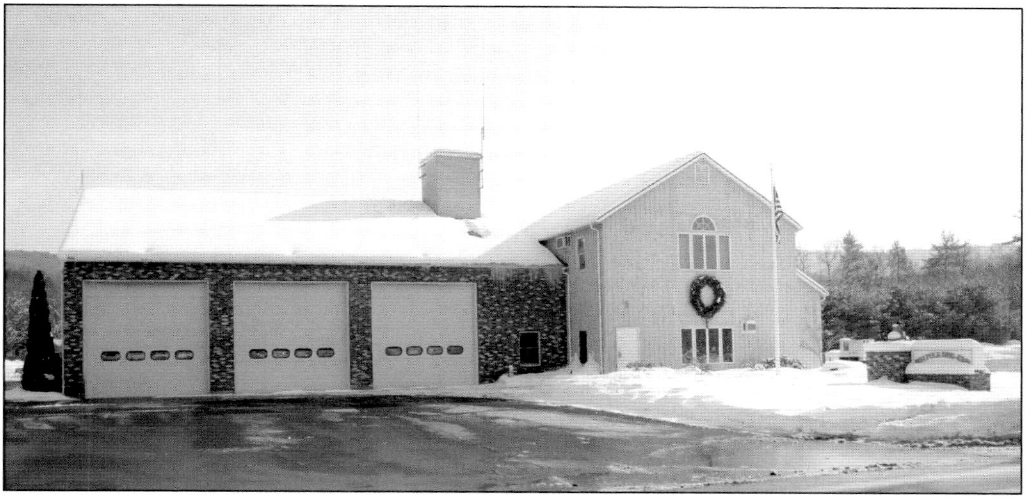

Safety Matters Continued. In 1990, given growth in the upper village and constricted traffic entry at the village fire station, a new station was constructed on Turnpike Street near the access to Route 12 north. Now the village department is staffed by 48 volunteer members, with Chief Dick Hurlbert and Deputy Chief Mark Houghton in charge. North Walpole has 20 volunteers with Chief Edward Hasselman and Deputy Chief Jay French directing operations. Recently, a private, nonprofit ambulance volunteer force was adopted by the village department; nearly two dozen firemen are certified emergency medical technicians for rescue service. In North Walpole, rescue services are contracted out to a private ambulance service. Below, village firemen, from left to right, Anthony Fry, James MacLean, Patrick Wright, Luke Joslin, Hurlbert, Houghton, Dennis Wright, and Jesse Moore, are attending a regular, Sunday check on trucks and equipment.

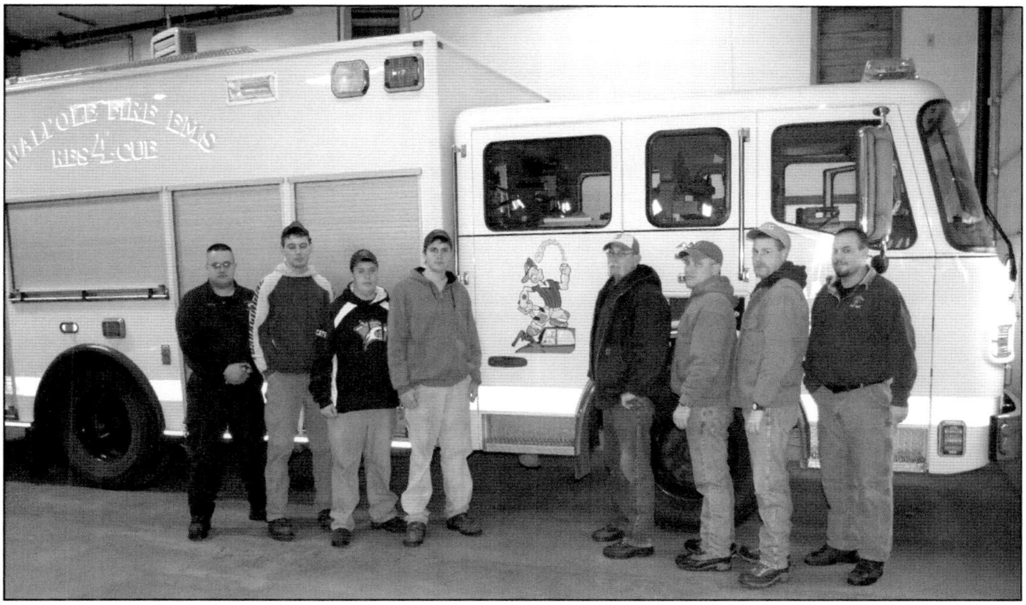

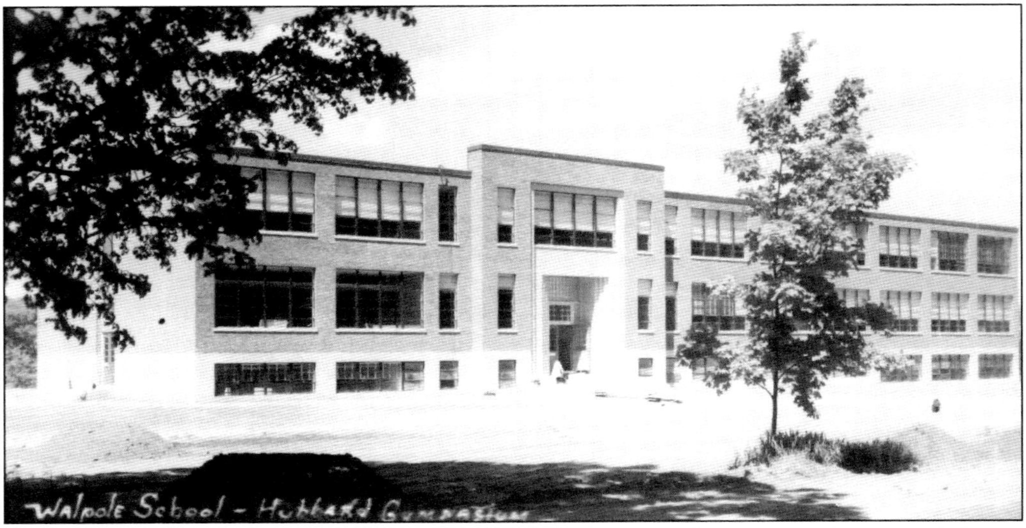

SCHOOL CONSOLIDATION AND EXPANSION. With the passage of a new state law, consolidation of Walpole's 14 schools had begun in the late 1880s; smaller schools were closed. In the 1950s, a new kindergarten through 12th-grade school in the village (above) and an elementary school in North Walpole were built. North Walpole high school students were tuitioned to Bellows Falls. In 1957, the little school at the village site was added for primary grades to accommodate a bulging school population. Today while all high school students attend Fall Mountain Regional High School, principal Sam Jacobs (below) directs all three schools for kindergarten through eighth grade. The secret to Jacobs's success in nearly 30 years in the Fall Mountain district is by knowing each of his students.

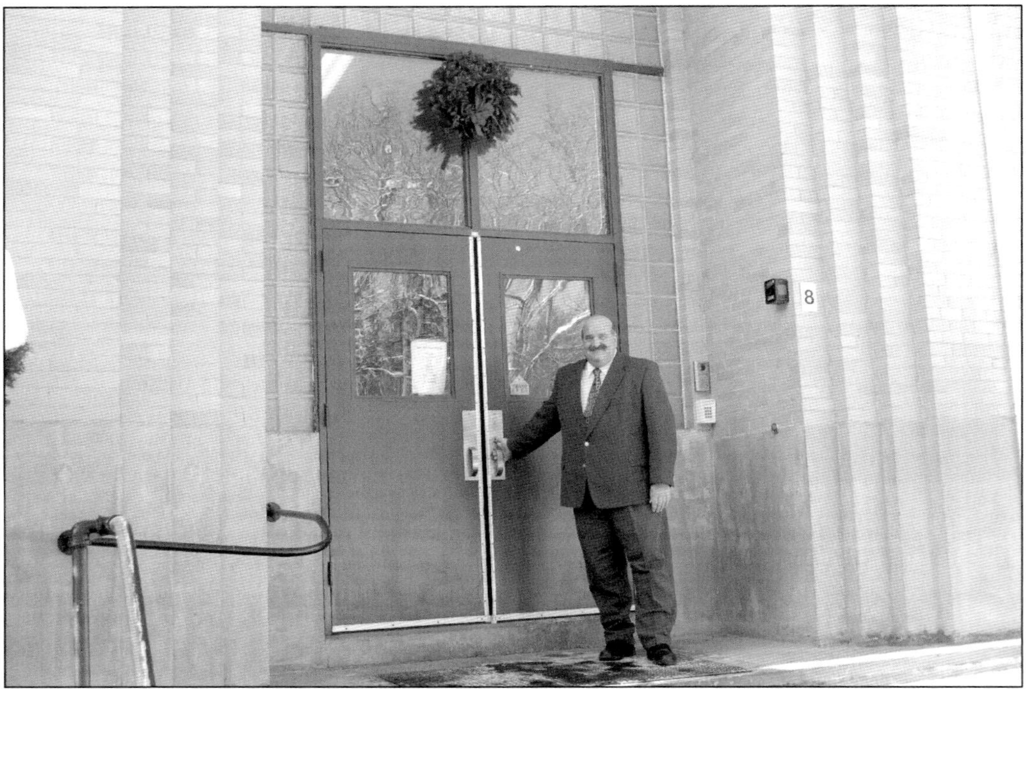

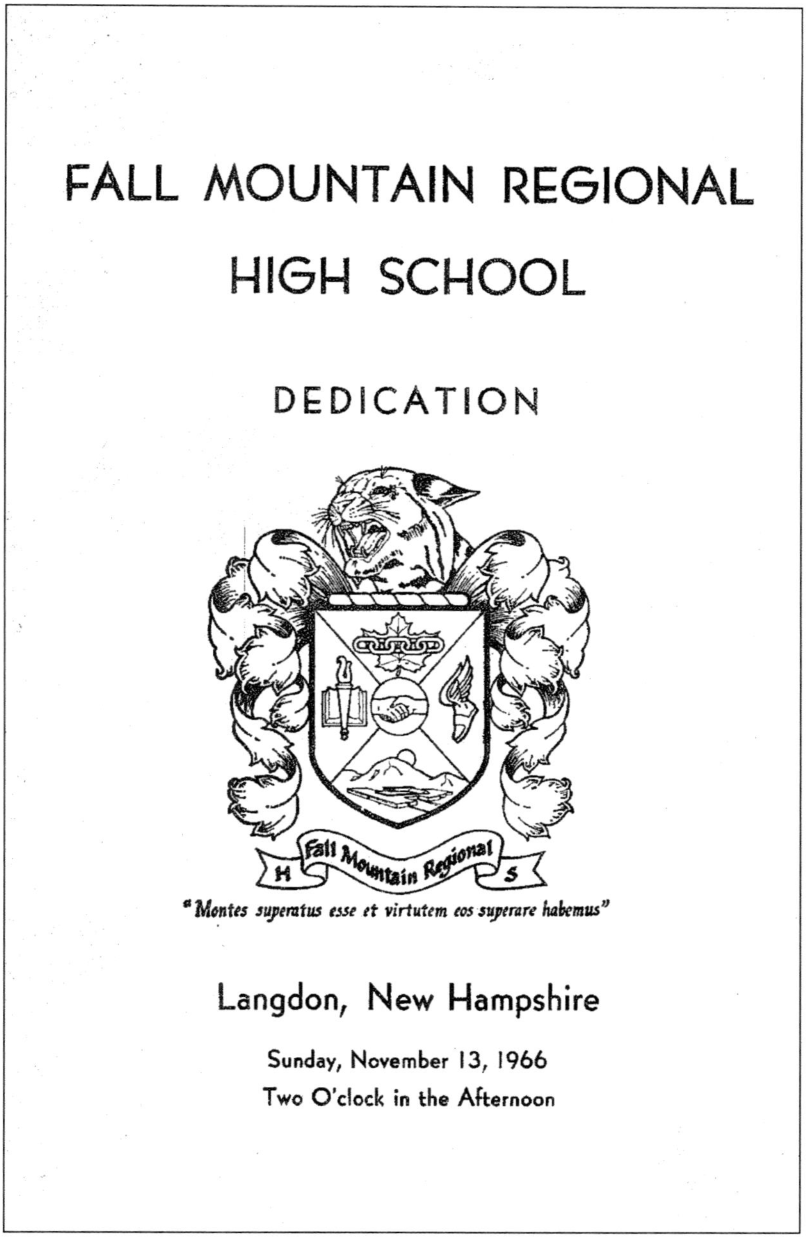

FALL MOUNTAIN REGIONAL

HIGH SCHOOL

DEDICATION

"*Montes superatus esse et virtutem eos superare habemus*"

Langdon, New Hampshire

Sunday, November 13, 1966

Two O'clock in the Afternoon

FALL MOUNTAIN REGIONAL SCHOOL DISTRICT AND HIGH SCHOOL. Towns in the Walpole area were all dealing with high student numbers and the increasing cost of educating them. Soon after the state legislation authorized the development of regional (rather than municipal) school districts in 1963, the towns of Acworth, Alstead, Charlestown, Langdon, and Walpole collaborated to form such a district and named it for its geographic center—Fall Mountain. All schools, including a new high school, were to be administered by the new New Hampshire Supervisory Union No. 60. By the summer of 1965, construction was underway, and Fall Mountain Regional High School opened in the fall of 1966. The dynamics of the new building, including staffing, transportation, supplies, equipment, and academic and athletic opportunities, made the high school a focal point of the region. (Above, courtesy of New Hampshire Supervisory Union No. 60.)

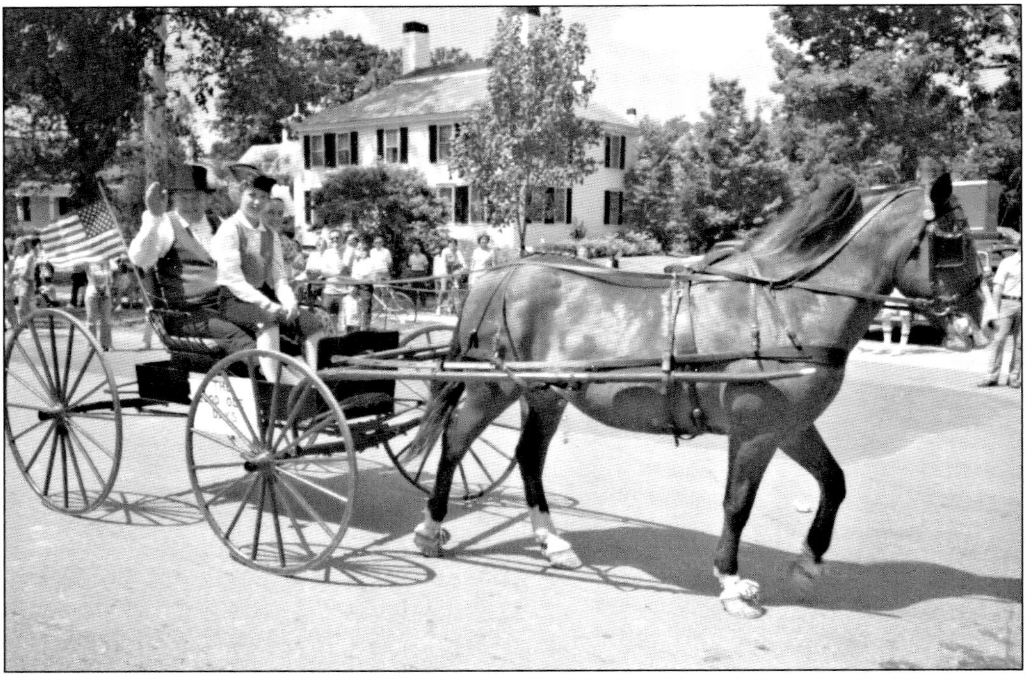

UNITED STATES BICENTENNIAL. Walpoleans of all ages paused to observe the nation's 200th anniversary on July 4, 1976. A huge parade, exhibitions, a Walpole Bicentennial Commission celebratory publication of reflections, and a gala ball at town hall were all part of the activities. Above is an unidentified family in a horse cart. Dutchie and William Perron (below, left) turn a reel in the evening's gala ball, with Joseph Stucker turning in the background, all in Revolutionary period costume. Other dancers are unidentified.

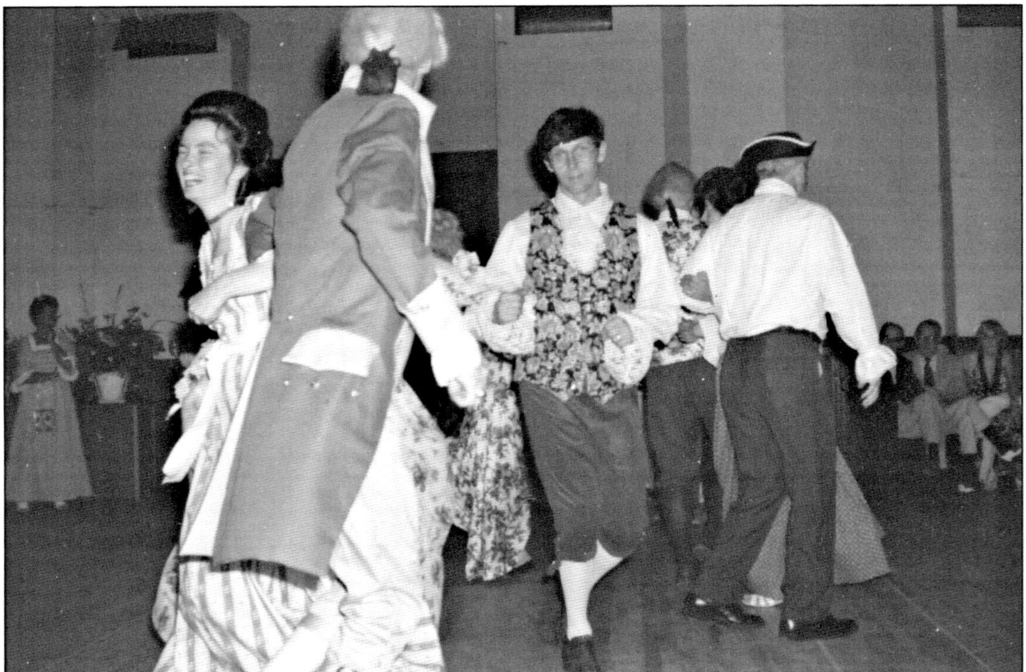

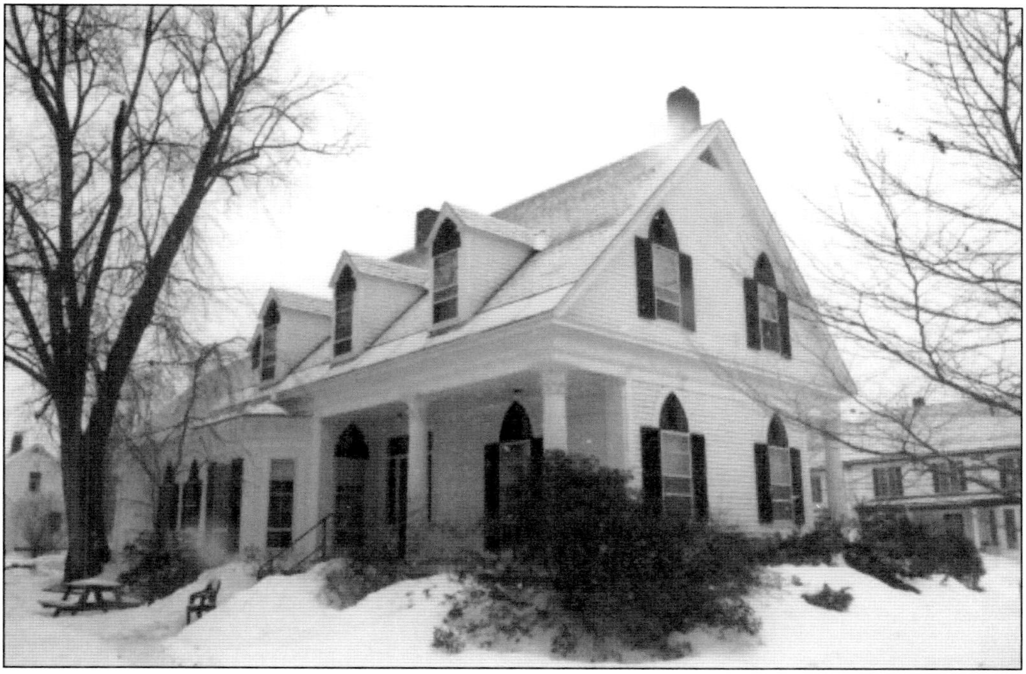

Florentine Films. In 1975, after graduating from Hampshire College in Amherst, Massachusetts, Ken Burns and two college friends founded Florentine Films, initially doing freelance assignments and finishing short documentaries before beginning work in 1977 on *The Brooklyn Bridge*, which won an Academy Award nomination. While editing the film, Burns moved the company to Walpole, eventually acquiring the studio (above) on Elm Street. His documentaries, including *The Civil War*, *Baseball*, *The West*, *Lewis & Clark*, *Jazz*, and *The War* have earned him many prestigious awards, several honorary degrees, and acknowledgement as the premiere documentary filmmaker in the United States, if not the world. At right, Burns reads in his replica of a Monticello garden pavilion he built on his property after filming *Thomas Jefferson*. (Courtesy of Florentine Films.)

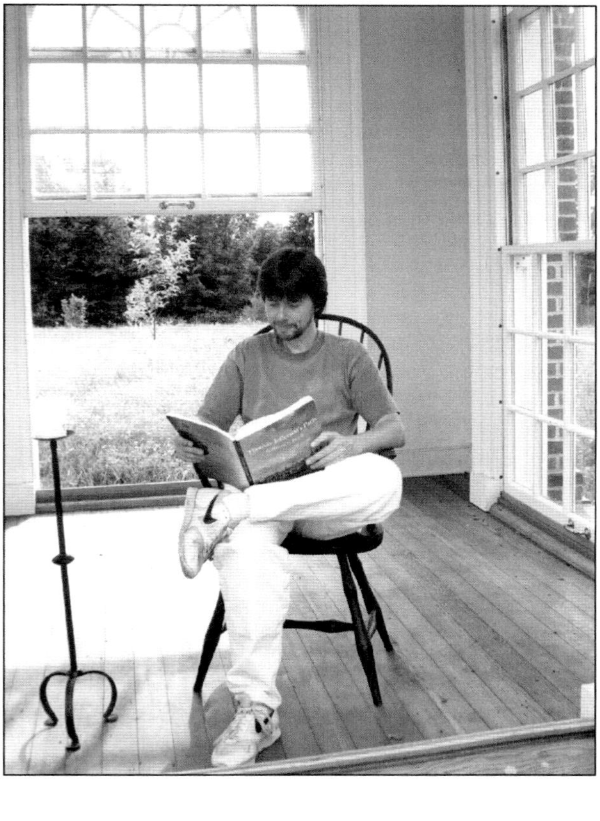

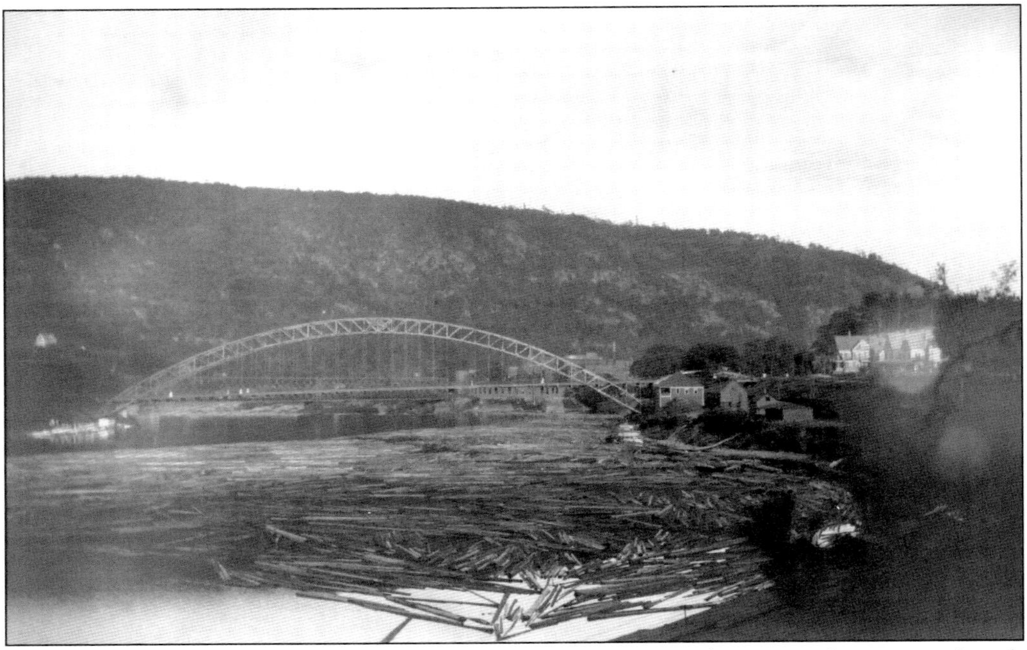

DEMISE OF ARCH BRIDGE. Serving since its completion in 1905 and spanning the river at a length of 540 feet, the beloved arch bridge connecting North Walpole to Bellows Falls, Vermont, was declared unsafe and "closed to all but foot traffic" in September 1971. It soon became known as "the world's largest foot-bridge." Below, the first efforts at demolishing the bridge with explosive charges were made in the fall of 1982. After withstanding several explosive attempts over a number of days, the arch bridge finally was dismantled with a cutting torch and collapsed into the Connecticut River, some say "with a sigh."

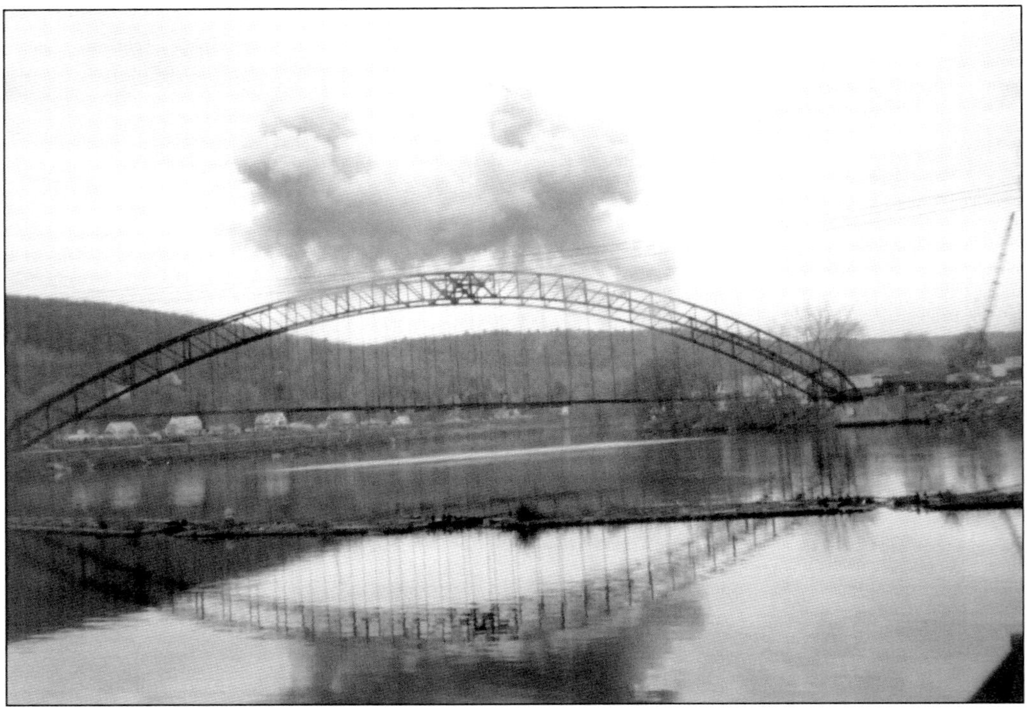

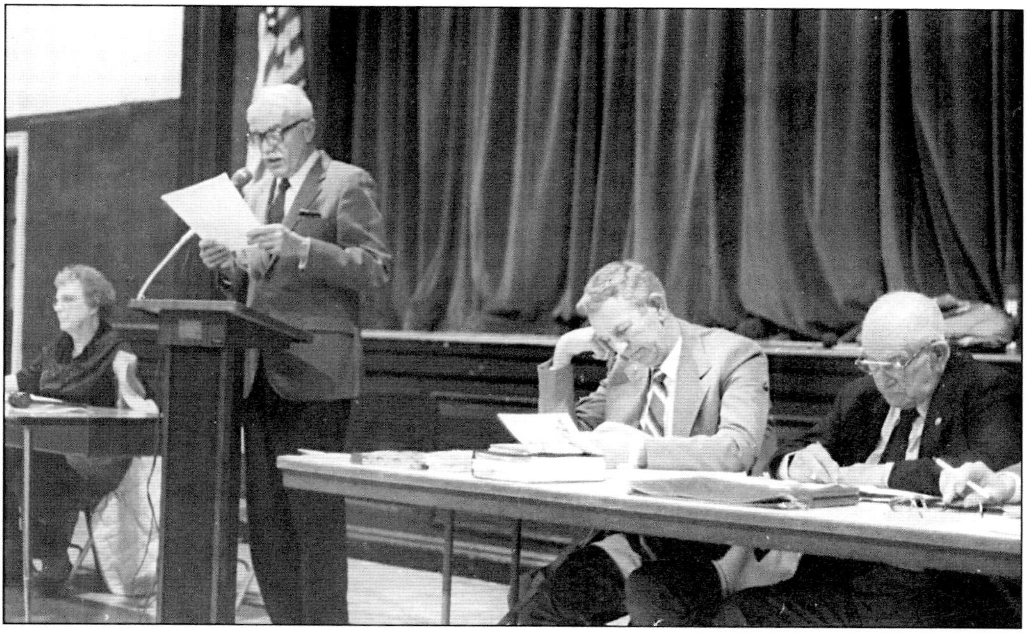

TOWN MEETING. In March of each year, Walpoleans gather for town meeting to decide the issues for the next year. Above, from left to right, Walpole's town clerk Virginia Baldwin, moderator Tucker Burr, and selectmen Paul McGuirk and Louis Ballam attend to the business of the 1983 meeting (the third selectman is not pictured). Ballam served Walpole as selectman for more than 30 years and also served several terms in the state legislature. McGuirk served as selectman from 1980 until 1987; he also was Walpole's postmaster from 1981 until 1992 and then went on to defeat an incumbent for the New Hampshire House from 1993 until 2002. McGuirk especially enjoyed serving the people on a one-to-one basis. Below, townspeople vote in a rare form of direct democracy (self-representation), which exists in few places in the world today—primarily in Swiss cantons and New England towns.

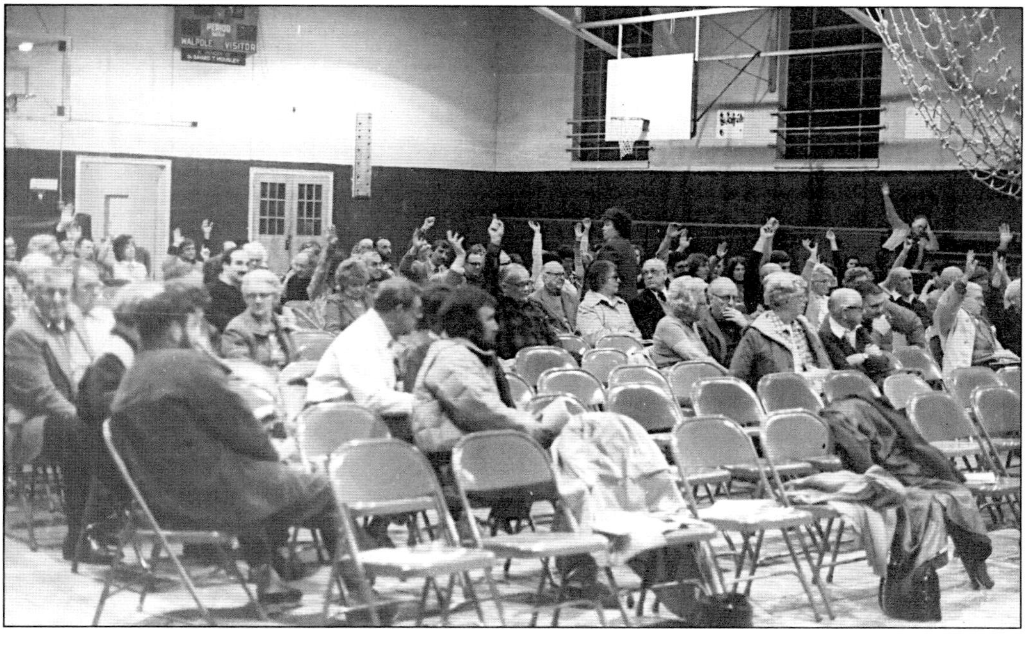

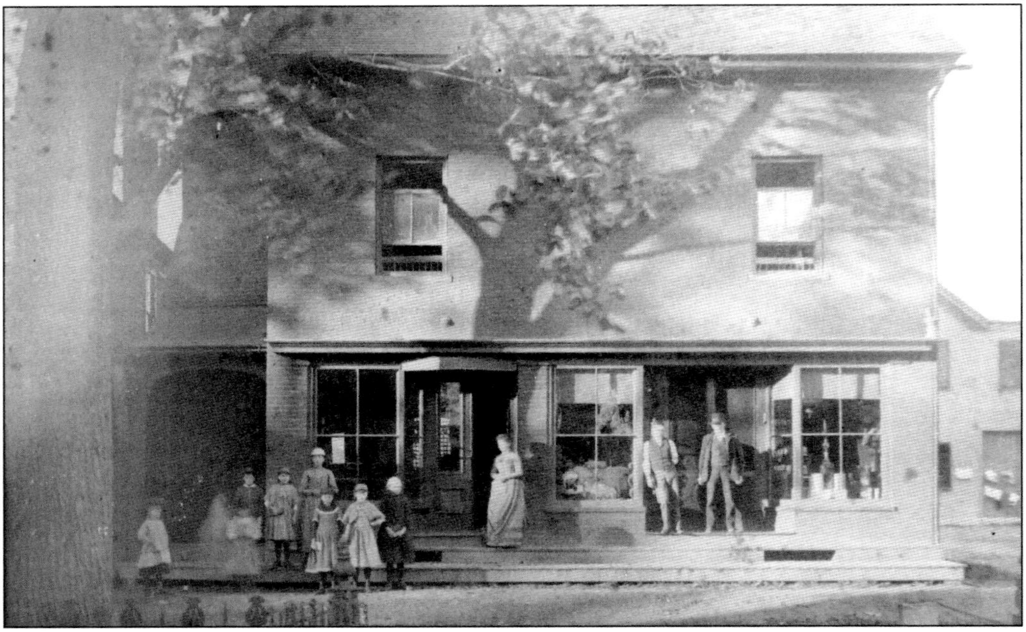

THE VILLAGE STORE. The earliest project undertaken by what was to become the Walpole Foundation was this general store, built about 1842 on Westminster Street; the picture above is from about 1895. Since its construction, the building has been used as A. K. Maynard's boot store and manufactory, a meat market, a furniture store, and, at the dawn of the 20th century, Knowlton's jewelry shop. Then for many years, it was home to Roy Peck's drugstore. By the 1960s, this had become simply the village store, where owner Randall Daniels operated a lunch counter and sold groceries and general merchandise. In 1987, the property was purchased by Les Hubbard for rehabilitation, and the result over time was this conversion (below) to a restaurant (the Walpole Tavern) with living units on the upper floors.

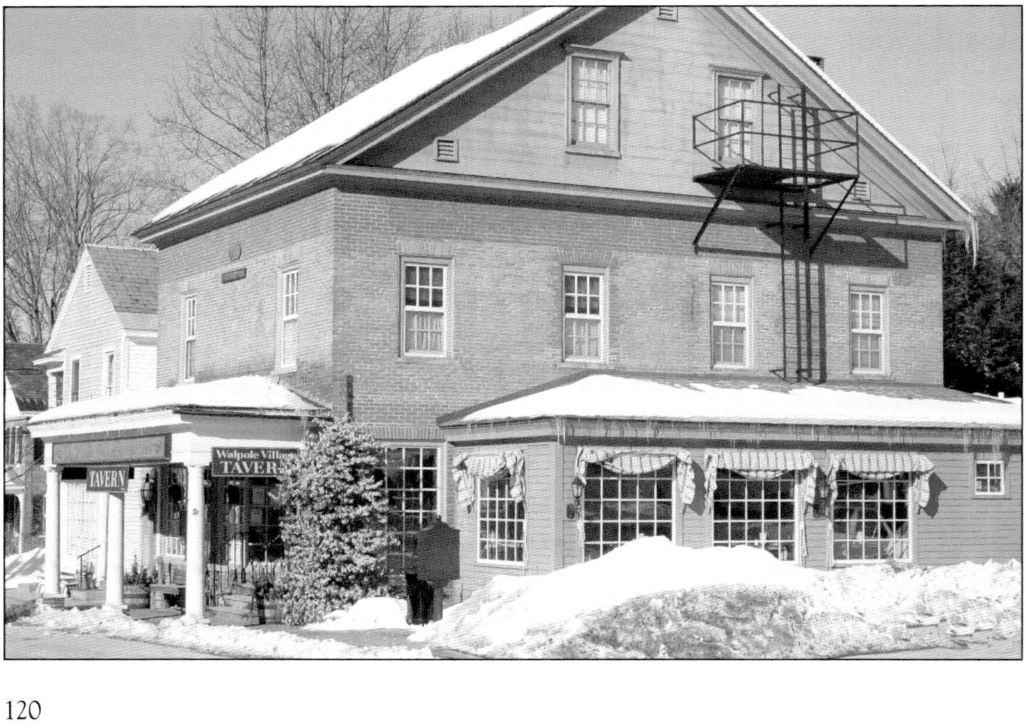

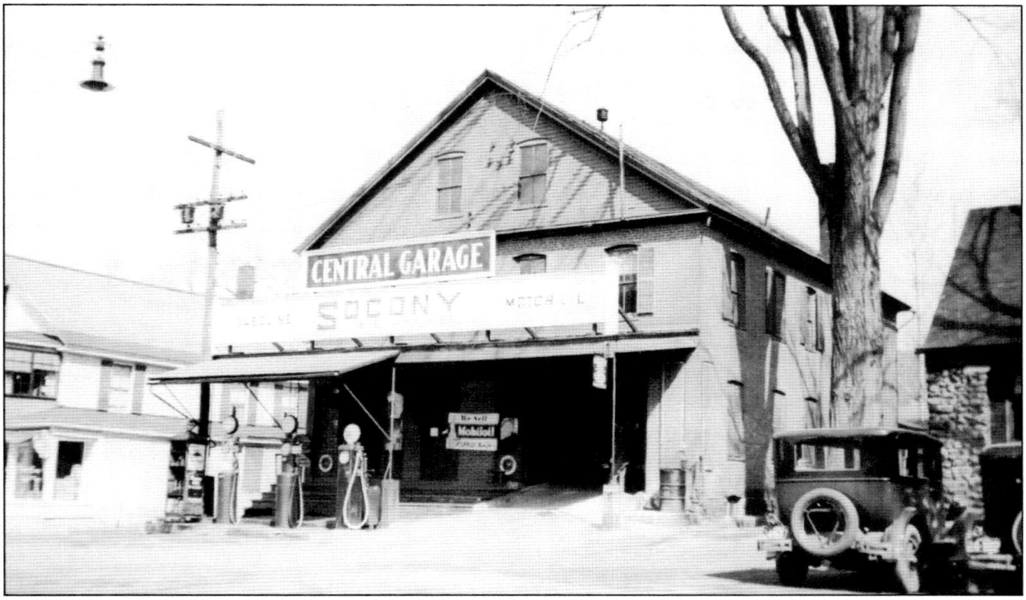

FOUNTAIN SQUARE. The lot just east of the Main Street fountain on the square has seen mercantile business since the earliest days of the community, including as a store of general merchandise, a saddlery and cobbler shop, a tavern, and early in the 20th century, it was a gasoline station, complete with petrol tanks in front, as seen above. This brick building was erected about 1860, as the original building on the site burned in 1859. Renovations to this building were an early project of the Walpole Foundation. Today it offers commercial office space and housing (below).

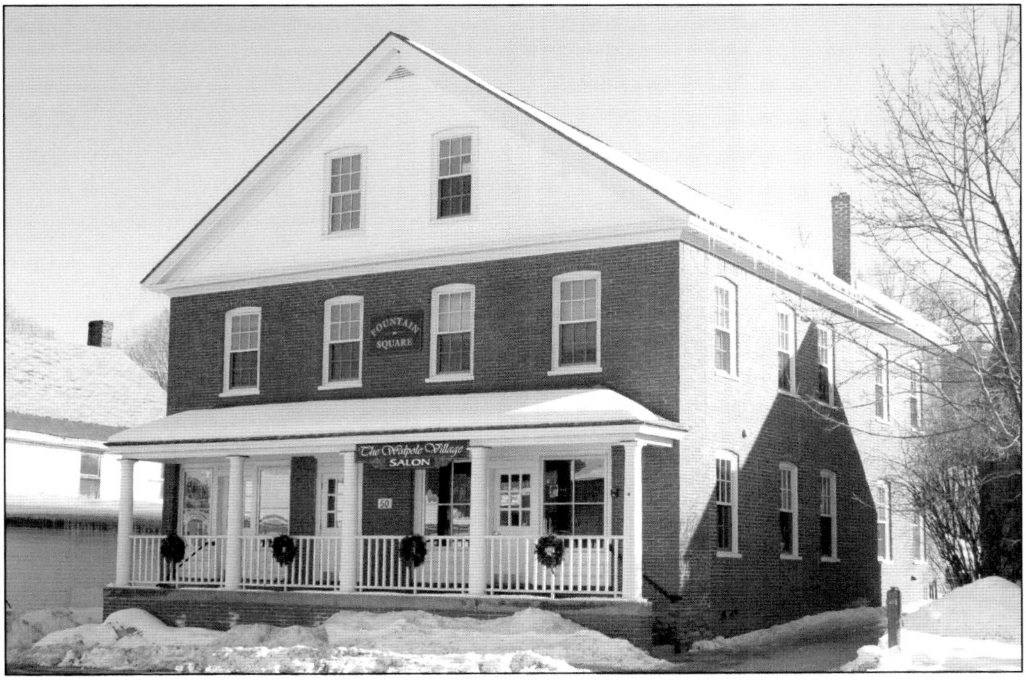

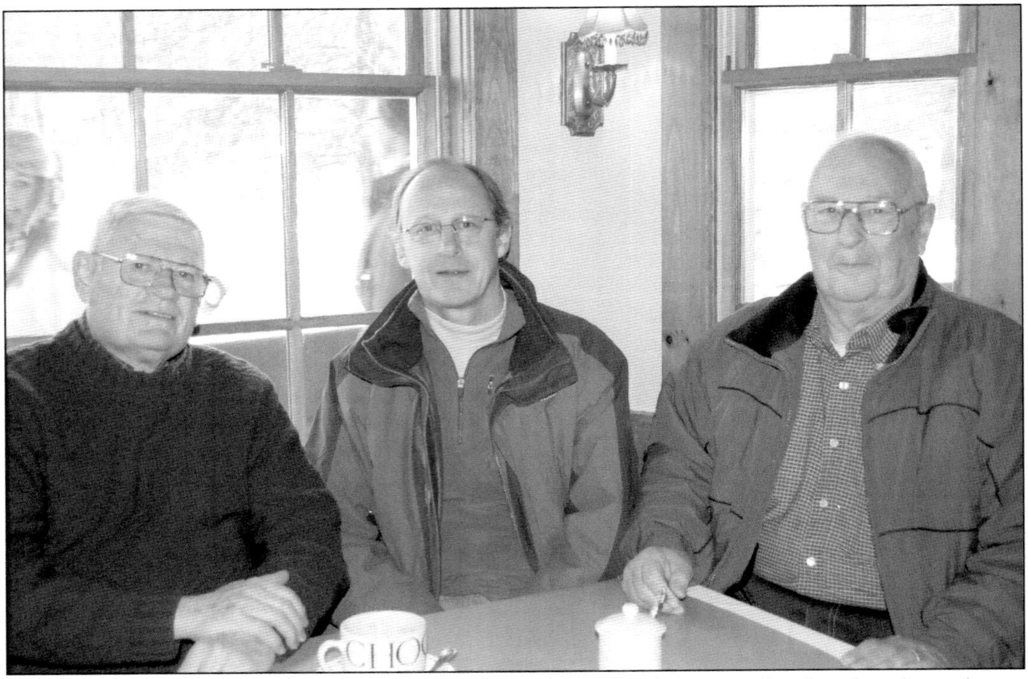

A Community Service Family. Jeffrey and Charles Miller (center and right, above) are shown enjoying a break at Burdick's with Walpole Historical Society Oral History Project leader Bruce Martin. This father/son team has donated over 70 years of community service. Charles has served on the town library committee, school board, and over 30 years as a selectman. Jeff was first elected to the state legislature in 1978 and served until 1989. He has also served Walpole's planning board since 1985, continuing as its chairman. Charles's late wife, Helen, was founder of the Walpole Players, and the theater in town hall is named in her honor. As a legislator, Jeff worked to replace the 1911 Westminster Bridge, which closed in 1985. Replacement, however, was on "no one's list" in Concord. Jeff's amendment to another bill saved the day, and both towns celebrated the new bridge's opening in the spring of 1989 (below).

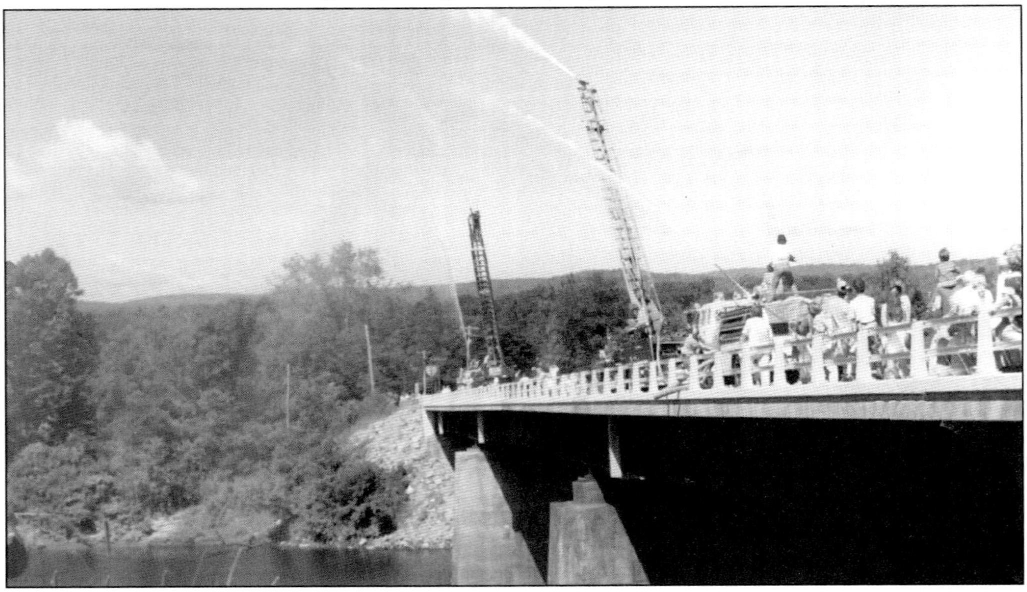

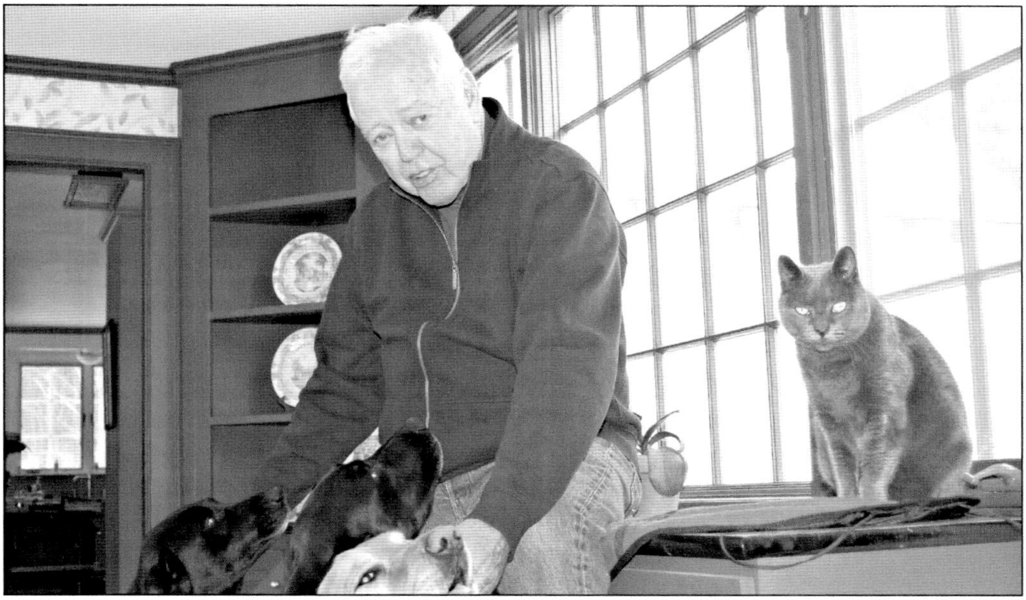

Public Service Personified. John (Jack) Pratt has always served the public. A graduate of Union Theological Seminary and Columbia Law School, his first jobs with the National Council of Churches and Southern California Council of Churches involved civil rights. He came to Walpole in 1992, served as selectman from 1993 to 1998, and entered the New Hampshire House in 1994 where he was House Whip and Judiciary Committee chairman. He is currently a Cheshire County commissioner.

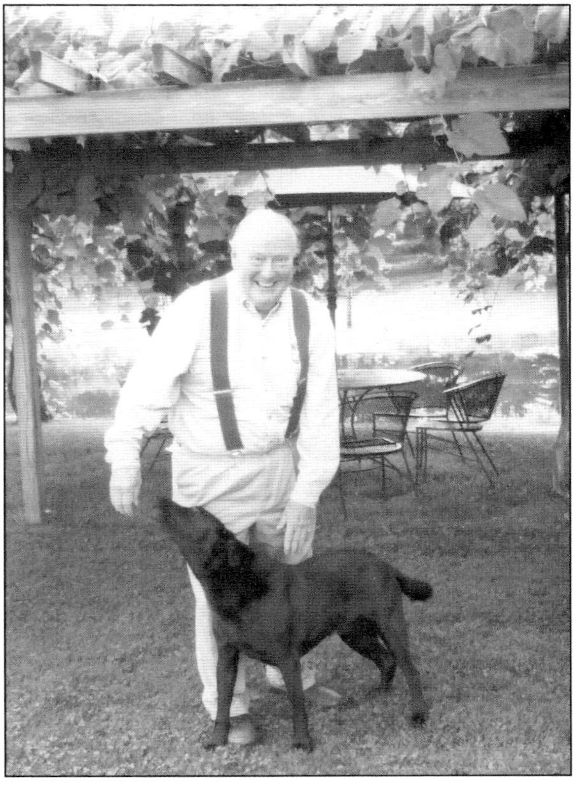

Alyson's Apple Orchard. In 1979, Robert and Susan Jasse acquired large acreage in Walpole. Their vision was not only to grow apples but to also create a center where people could celebrate important occasions. They beautifully landscaped their scenic property and purchased two additional farms. Today the 500-acre orchard is managed using environmentally friendly techniques, and there are four lodging venues, a market stand and playground, and an event center accommodating 250 people. (Courtesy of Alyson's Orchard.)

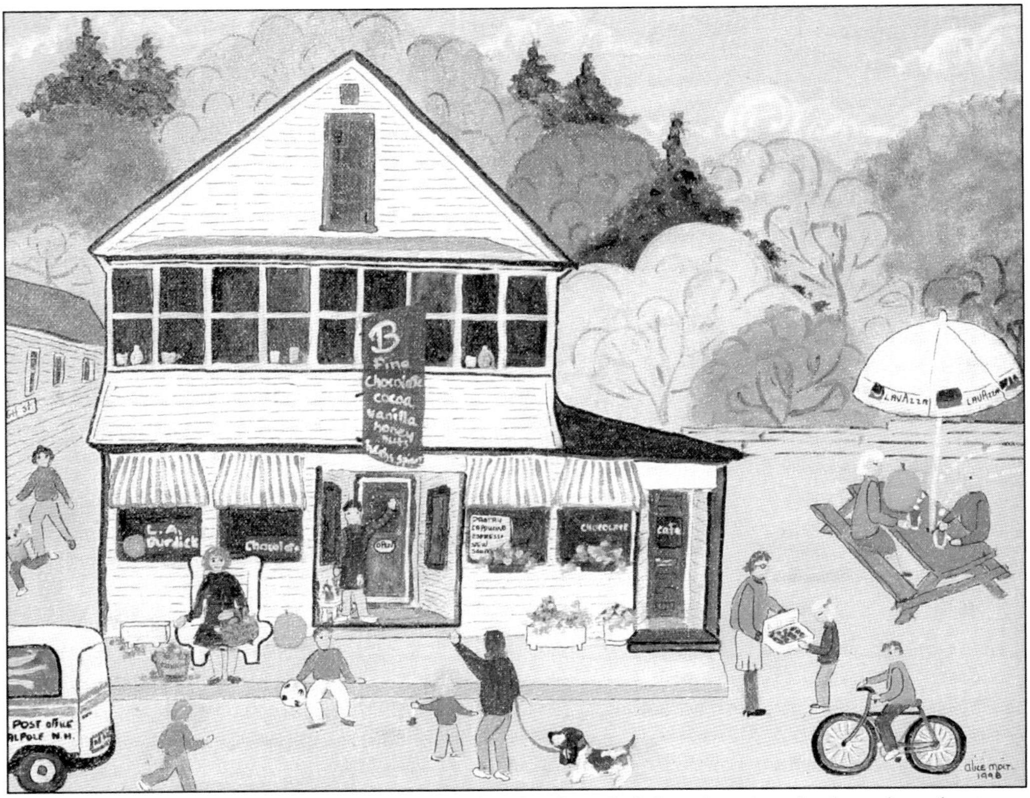

LARRY A. BURDICK. Larry and Paula Burdick, who founded their handmade chocolates business in 1988, moved to Walpole in 1993 to raise their family and focus on restaurant clients. After lines formed outside their workshop, they opened a retail store in 1994 and three years later added a café in an adjacent shop. The shop and café are depicted in the painting (above) by Alice Moir, an area artist. Later, Larry bought the large building (below) in the village center and opened a French bistro, also moving the chocolate shop to that location. The company's award-winning confections are now produced in a state-of-the-art facility installed in a former equipment showroom. He has also opened the Walpole Grocery, supporting local farmers and offering a fine selection of products. (Courtesy of Paula Burdick.)

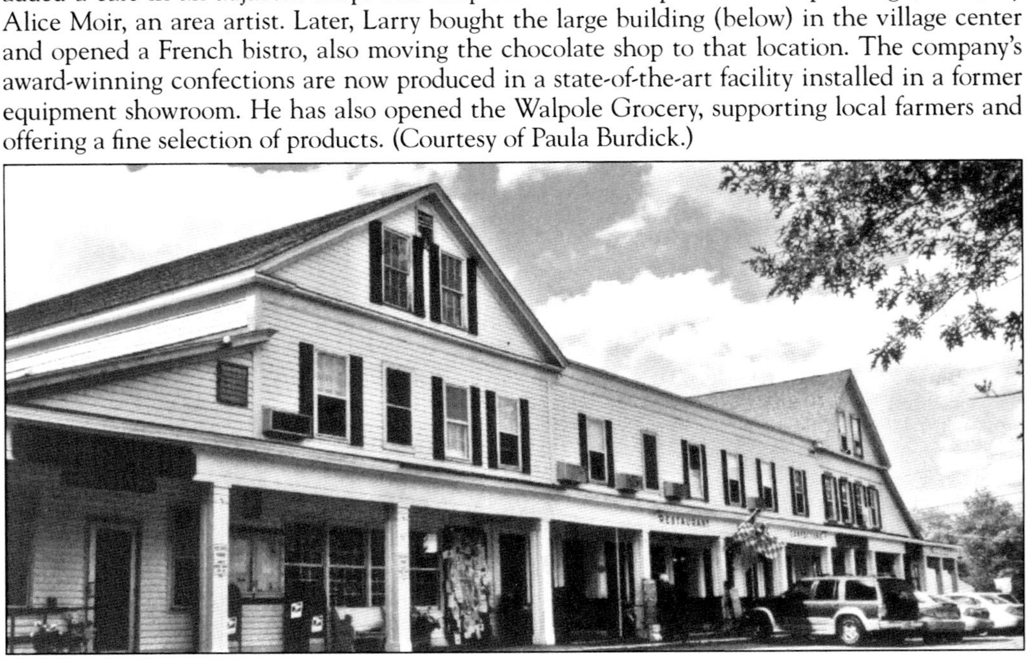

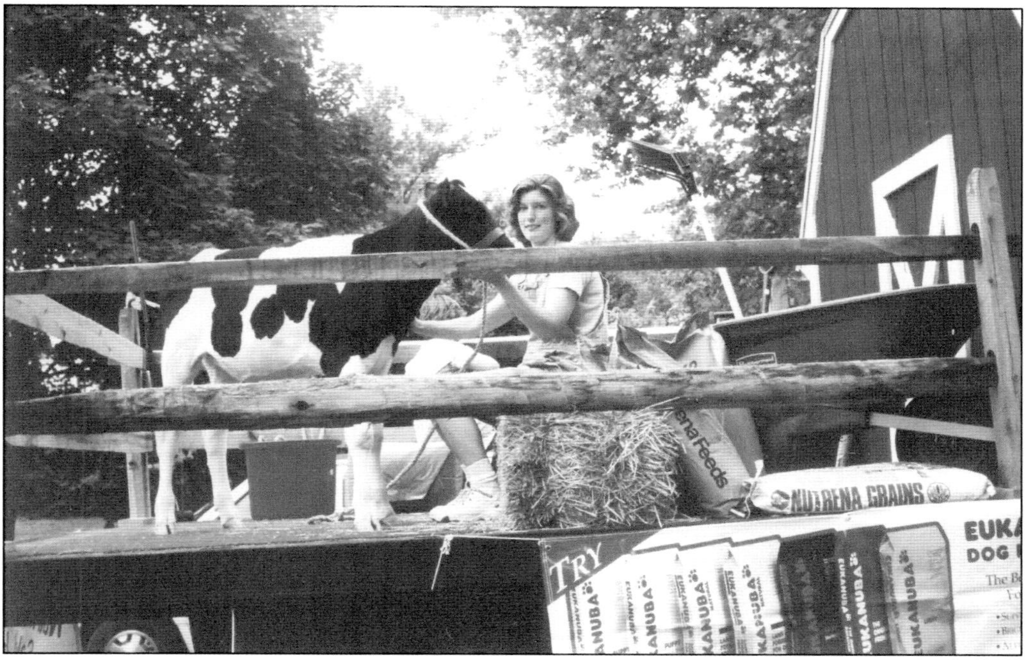

OLD HOME DAYS, 1996. In the tradition that began in 1899, Walpole again paused on a summer weekend for celebration and reflections of the town. Above, Karen McGill Hayman serves as hostess on a float dedicated to Walpole's farming traditions. Below, an unidentified basket weaver demonstrates her craft for workshop participants beneath the front colonnade of the old academy. Walpole Historical Society is a major sponsor of Old Home Day celebrations, currently being held at three-year intervals.

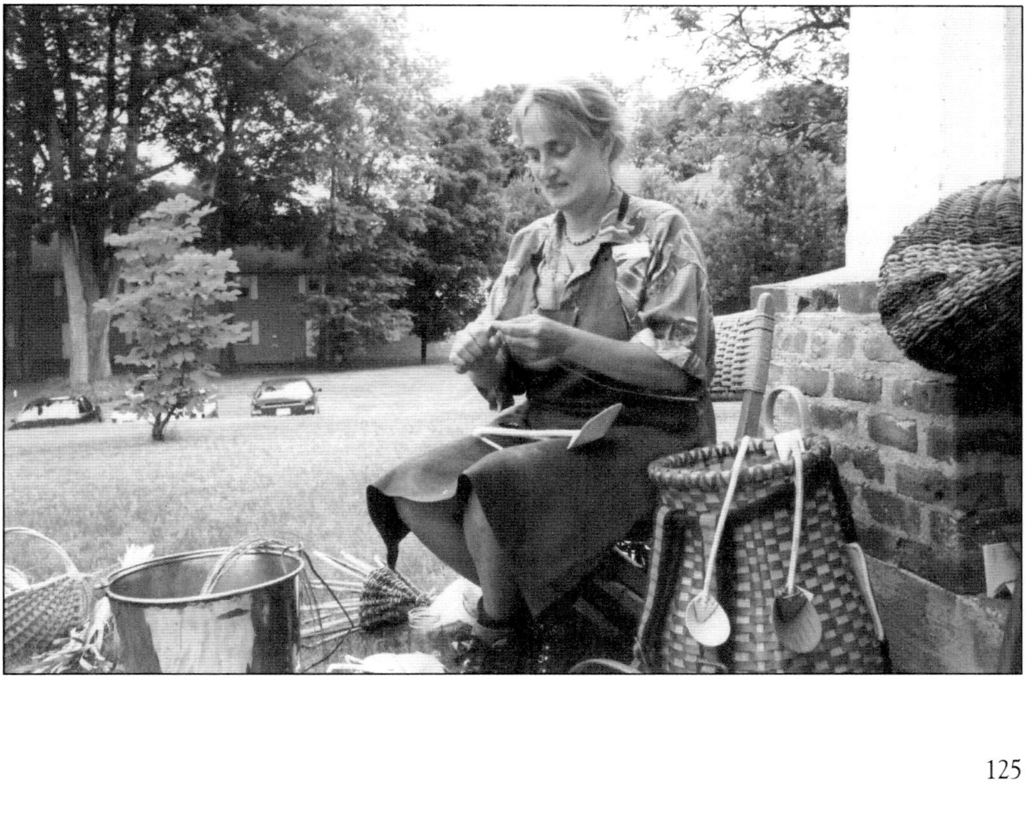

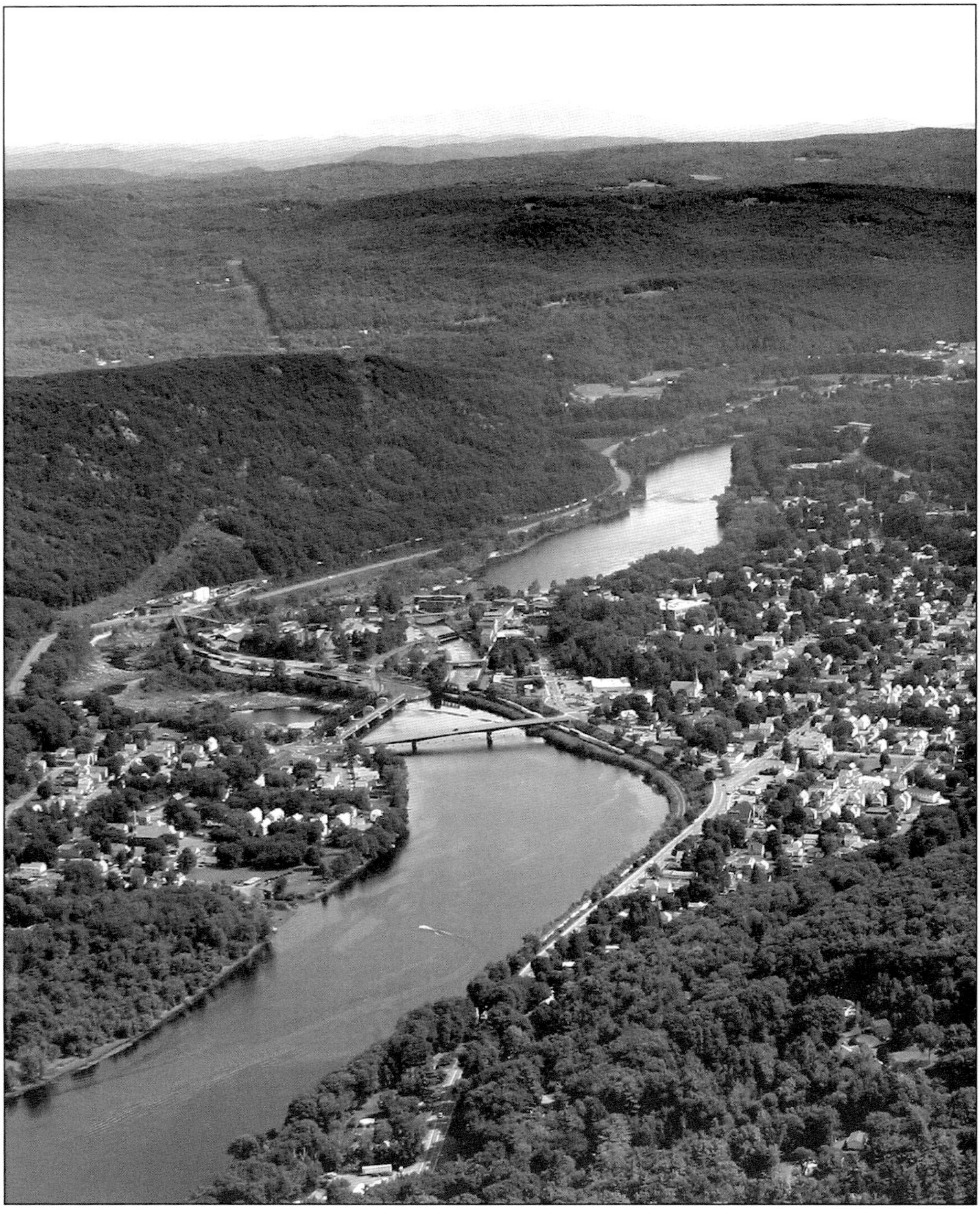

Walpole Valley and Hills. This aerial photograph was taken above the Great Falls (center) of the Connecticut River in North Walpole and provides a sweeping view across the Walpole hills to Mount Monadnock, 25 miles to the southeast. Four of the five bridges that cross the Connecticut River from Walpole are visible, as well as the dam gates running parallel to the railroad bridge (center). Walpole Village is located south of this view off the highway that runs along the river. The village of Bellows Falls, Vermont, is on the right. This American Heritage River has given and taken much across Walpole's history. Since the great floods of 1927 and 1936, the U.S. Army Corps of Engineers has installed a series of flood-control dams upriver and on upper tributary streams, making life on the river more benign. (Courtesy of Len Emery Photography.)

BIBLIOGRAPHY

Aldrich, George. *Walpole As It Was and As It Is.* 1880.

Bellows, Josiah G. *Reminiscences of a Village Life.* Walpole, NH: Walpole Historical Society, 1880.

Bragg, P. Lucile. "History of Susan Bellows (Robeson) House." Walpole, NH: Dr. and Mrs. Lawrence Martin, 1930s.

Calloway, Colin. *The Western Abenakis of Vermont, 1600–1800.* Norman, OK: University of Oklahoma Press, 1990.

Frizzell, Martha McDanolds. *A History of Walpole New Hampshire.* Brattleboro, VT: Vermont Printing Company for Town of Walpole and Walpole Historical Society, 1963.

History of Hubbard Farms, 1921–1996. Walpole, NH: Hubbard Farms, LLC, 1996.

Hurd, D. Hamilton. *History of Cheshire County.* 1886

Paulus, Jeremy, "Kilburn Battled the Indians 236 Years Ago In Walpole," *Walpole Gazette,* August 16, 1991: 1, 13.

Peck, Thomas Bellows. *The Bellows Genealogy.* Keene, NH: Sentinel Printing Company, 1898.

Porter, John. *History & Economics of Dairy Farming in New Hampshire.* Durham, NH: University of New Hampshire Cooperative Extension Service, 2007.

Rising, Dorothy. "Schools of Walpole," Walpole, NH: Walpole Historical Society, *c.* 1950.

Granite Monthly, volume XXXI. Concord, NH: The Granite Monthly Company, 1901: 93.

www.britannia.com

www.civilwar.com

www.johnjhenderson.com